the iconic house

architectural masterworks
since 1900

dominic bradbury

with photographs by richard powers

Thames & Hudson

CONTENTS

Of all the kinds of architecture in the world, it is house and home that we relate to most easily and generously. At heart we know that a house is much more than a machine for living. It has an emotional charge and depth, it is among the most personal expressions of our own characters, and it is a place of refuge and escape as well as day-to-day experience. It might also be a place of work, an art gallery, a nursery, a playhouse, a leisure palace…. It is a building to be shaped according to the way in which we function and wish to order our lives.

No wonder, then, that the idea of the bespoke home, a house tailored exactly to how we want to live, is such a dream and – for many – a hard-won luxury. Rather than sandwiching ourselves into a regulation box, we recognize the value of creating a home perfectly suited to our own way of living, working and playing, with a true sense of cohesion and a custom-made layout – a home that is also, of course, an object of beauty and pleasure.

For the architect, the domestic house has a particular resonance and charge, for many of the reasons above and more, even if it is not a home for the architect him- or herself. A house commission instantly becomes an intensely personal project and forms a unique bond between client and designer, a collaboration that carries over time.

Many of the houses in these pages represent close communion between architect and client, within a particular kind of relationship that is sometimes harmonious and easy, sometimes fraught and demanding. One might think of the troubled bond between Ludwig Mies van der Rohe and Edith Farnsworth, or the up-and-down adventures of Frank Lloyd Wright and Edgar J. Kaufmann, or the positively beguiling role played by Robert Mallet-Stevens's Villa

Noailles in the lives of its parents; add to them the famously tense narrative of the creation of Peter Eisenman's House VI, which stretched the patience of client and architect close to breaking point.

To build a house is truly an adventure and a learning process that carries intense emotional and intellectual power. It requires a sense of daring, even bravery, with all the risks attendant in such a project. It is all the more fascinating for being a story that runs over months and years, often shared with a stranger. In this sense, the architect holds a godlike position, rather like that of a surgeon or doctor, with the power to transform lives for the better, while also seeking to succeed and progress on his or her own terms.

'The residential commission allows one to formulate ideas and develop a set of principles that, one hopes, will inform future work for a long time to come,' architect Richard Meier has written. 'As an expression of architectural ideas they are an essential type. Formally they are likely to offer the most intimate scale at which to work. And symbolically they have always maintained a potent force, both as a vivid representation of lives lived inside their walls and as a powerful influence over the changing course of architecture over centuries.'

For the architect, then, a self-penned home becomes a doubly charged achievement. The architect's own home – and you will find many in this book – inevitably becomes a profoundly important artistic and crafted expression that is much more than simply a home; it is also a manifesto statement. We often talk of the architect's own home as a laboratory of ideas, a test bed, and one that in so many cases has a defining impact upon its creator's career. One thinks of Berthold Lubetkin's Bungalow A, Rudolph Schindler's Los Angeles residence, Philip Johnson's Glass House, Werner Sobek's family home in Stuttgart, and others.

To some extent, the same might be said of that classic parental commission to the architect son or daughter – 'build us a house'. Generally this involves an unusual degree of latitude and indulgence, allowing the architect a rare freedom to explore the themes and ideas that mean most to them within a loose brief and a generous spirit of

understanding that often helps to define the architect's future direction. In this context, we remember houses by Harry Seidler, Robert Venturi, Charles Gwathmey and Richard Rogers.

It comes as no great surprise, then, that the house holds such a distinct and honoured place in our imaginations, and that a home can have more of an influence on the way we think about and perceive architecture than a grand museum or an attention-grabbing super-structure. The iconic houses of the past have a truly magical grip on our collective consciousness, becoming part of the essential language and shorthand of architecture itself.

Houses such as Le Corbusier's Villa Savoye, Frank Lloyd Wright's Fallingwater and Richard Neutra's Kaufmann House are now key markers in our understanding and appreciation of the twentieth-century home. More than this, they are essential to our knowledge of architecture more widely, and of twentieth-century culture and the great artistic movements that it embraces.

1900   VICTOR HORTA (1861–1947)

HOTEL SOLVAY BRUSSELS, BELGIUM

Victor Horta was one of the first architects of his generation to begin actively to question the past and look for a fresh way of doing things without relying on the conventions and traditions of historical precedent. He became one of the greatest impresarios of the Art Nouveau movement. He was also convinced of the need to create totally cohesive buildings that combined architecture with an integrated approach to interiors and furnishing.

His Hotel Tassel of 1893 showed the early possibilities of this approach. With its ornate, organic lines and sculpted beauty, it was arguably the first complete Art Nouveau house.

Many of Horta's clients were from the wealthy Brussels elite, and in 1894 he was commissioned to design a new home for the recently married industrialist's son Armand Solvay, still in his twenties when he first met Horta.

Hotel Solvay's sinuous façade is dominated by two vast balcony-crowned double windows, with the entrance subordinately positioned to one side. Inside, the magnificent staircase splits in two as it ascends to the reception rooms. Horta turned his hand to every detail, including the door bell. This is a house of sophisticated spectacle that truly belonged to the new century.

Such buildings, and the many others assembled in this book, are iconic for many different reasons. They are, above all, experimental and innovative. Indeed, they are often revolutionary, questioning the very precepts of what a house should be and do. Their influence has spread well beyond their original intent and rippled out into the wider world.

Many have been instrumental in establishing a new architectural paradigm, or providing a pivotal reference point for a defined architectural or stylistic movement. All have provided benchmarks in their architects' careers, often becoming the creator's best-known work, as with Staffan Berglund's Villa Spies or Charles Deaton's Sculptured House.

For the most part, such houses are also a highly considered response to a particular site and landscape, as well as to the challenges laid down by a client's particular needs. Overall, they build into an extraordinary map of the shifts, changes and evolutions in recent architecture.

1905 ANTONI GAUDÍ (1852–1926)

VILLA BELLESGUARD BARCELONA, SPAIN

One of Antoni Gaudí's first commissions was for street lamps; his last was the epic (and still unfinished) Sagrada Família Cathedral. In between came a series of extraordinary dreamlike buildings that confirmed Gaudí as one of the most original architects of his day. In particular, his apartment buildings, such as the famous Casa Milà (1910), have become part of the fabric and character of his native Barcelona.

Gaudí's most powerful single-family house is Villa Bellesguard (also known as Casa Figueras). Like so much of his instantly recognizable work, this fused Neo-Gothic and Art Nouveau ideas within one distinctive style.

The building sits on the site of the ruins of a medieval Catalan palace and was commissioned by María Sagués, a merchant's widow. Drawing from nature and history, Gaudí created a typically flamboyant statement based around a cubed form reaching up to a sculpted and crenellated roof line containing the attic level, plus a slim viewing tower.

The structure of the house is brick, but this is only a base for the organic flourishes of interior and exterior. Slate, stone and stone paste were used to coat the building. As a single home, it is one of Gaudí's most concentrated and complete achievements.

JOSEF HOFFMANN (1870–1956)

PALAIS STOCLET BRUSSELS, BELGIUM

A former pupil of Otto Wagner, and a co-founder of the influential Wiener Werkstätte movement dedicated to designing accessible works of craftsmanship, Josef Hoffmann was a Viennese architect whose most famous creation was actually built in Brussels.

The Palais Stoclet was commissioned by the financier and patron of arts Adolphe Stoclet. He and his wife Suzanne were originally intent on building a house in Vienna, where they were then living, but on the death of Stoclet's father they were called back to Brussels and the plan changed. Hoffmann went to work in Belgium, creating a vast mansion that also housed the Stoclets' growing collection of art and artefacts, including startling pieces from Asia and Africa. The Stoclets entrusted Hoffmann with the entirety of the house, and he created a vibrant *Gesamtkunstwerk* – a cohesive artistic vision that included both exteriors and interiors.

From the outside, the house suggests a cubist outline, with a tower rising dramatically to one side, but it is coated in slabs of white Norwegian marble and edged in copper detailing. Inside, no expense was spared either, with the dining room dominated by friezes by Gustav Klimt. Palais Stoclet stands as one of the great pioneer houses of the early twentieth century.

This map is infused with an exoticism that comes of the gradual cross-pollination of ideas and concepts from all around the world, a process that has swiftly gathered pace in our age of mass communication. More rapidly than ever before, ideas become internationally known and can grow into global movements.

From turn-of-the-century Arts and Crafts – exemplified by Baillie Scott's Blackwell or Greene & Greene's Gamble House – right up to the groundbreaking formal experiments of UN Studio, Ushida Findlay, Ken Shuttleworth and others, these famous houses carry us through a rich diversity of architectural expression.

Arts and Crafts placed an emphasis on artisanry and a partial return to pre-industrial-age values of a simpler way of life, rooted in respect for craft and tradition rather than mass production. Yet at the same time – within a transfixing two-way process – Baillie Scott, Edward Prior, Charles Voysey, the Greene brothers and others were very much looking forwards as well as back.

We see the beginnings of a challenge to convention, tradition and the formal way of living exemplified by the Victorian house, with a tentative push towards more flexible and informal living spaces. At the same, Prior, Lutyens and others were creating innovative floor plans laid out in butterfly formation, while at Voewood, in Norfolk, England, Prior also began experimenting with the structural possibilities of concrete.

These early twentieth-century houses are intriguing precursors of the truly revolutionary changes that gathered pace in later years. Most fascinating, in many ways, are those architects whose work in retrospect seems to overlap the great tectonic plates between the continents of past and future, positioned on the very cusp of modernity and Modernism. These were architects such as Adolf Loos, Otto Wagner, Josef Hoffmann and Henri Sauvage, who questioned the Victorian reliance on ornamentation as an indulgence, while pushing for formal and structural innovation.

Thus we see the first appearance of the multifunctional living area – or 'universal space' – and the beginning of radical experimentation with modern materials. By the late 1920s we have architects such as Pierre Chareau and Auguste Perret using glass, concrete and steel as never before, while, as the revolution gathers pace, Schindler and others begin to question and rework the whole way in which we structure and organize the home.

Yet in the early twentieth century we also have the flamboyant experimentation, drama and even excess of Art Nouveau, as exemplified by Victor Horta and Antoni Gaudí, drawing rich inspiration from sinuous natural forms. This gives way to the inter-war glamour and optimism of the Art Deco movement, which – at times – begins to splice with the early exploration of Modernism. The interiors of Seely & Paget's Eltham Palace in London represent the epitome of Jazz Age Deco, while Eileen Gray's pivotal E-1027 house in southern France – while being an icon of early Modernism – is also lifted by Deco influences, with its dynamic outline and terraces reminiscent of the great ocean liners of the 1920s.

1912   **OTTO WAGNER (1841–1918)**

VILLA WAGNER II VIENNA, AUSTRIA

Like Josef Hoffmann, Otto Wagner was active in the Vienna Secession movement – sometimes labelled an Austrian/German version of Art Nouveau – but was also one of the early prophets of Modernism. His work pushed towards a more disciplined architectural language, with less reliance on ornament and a greater emphasis on form, function, materials, clarity and rationality. He stood at the cusp of a new architecture, and buildings such as his Postal Office Savings Bank (1912), with its steel and glass construction, suggest the shape of things to come.

Villa Wagner II – a summer villa for Wagner and his family, surrounded by verdant gardens – reflects the architect's fascination with the possibilities of new materials and methods of construction, employing reinforced concrete, sheet glass, aluminium and glass mosaic. The crisp rectangular form facing the street is punctuated with ordered sequences of windows, while a band of coloured glass tiles contrasts with the white render.

Inside, on the middle level of the three storeys, Wagner designed a prototypical multifunctional space to serve as living and dining room. This key room was an early expression of the move away from the highly formal and traditional floor plan of spaces rigidly delineated according to function.

CARL LARSSON (1853–1919)

LILLA HYTTNÄS/LARSSON HOUSE SUNDBORN, SWEDEN

As an artist, illustrator, designer and writer, Carl Larsson helped, perhaps more than anyone, to define the popular idea of Swedish style. Though he was not an architect, the home he shared with his wife Karin and their many children had an international impact.

Larsson came from a very poor family background and raised himself up through his own talents. His outlook – and that of his wife, who was also an artist and textile designer – was wide-ranging and well informed. When Karin's father gave his daughter and son-in-law a small timber cottage in the village of Sundborn in central Sweden, they radically transformed it with a highly personal version of Swedish Gustavian style, also bringing in elements from other design cultures.

The Larssons were given the cottage in 1888 and it evolved in phases, the couple working closely with local craftsmen to complete major additions in 1890, 1900 and 1912. Arguably, the evolution of the house only ended with Larsson's death in 1919. His watercolours of the house, published in his many books – particularly *A Home* (1899) – carried the Larsson style outwards, and their work remains much praised and imitated, particularly as it was never grand or pretentious but always attainable and romantic.

By the 1930s the Modernist revolution was underway and the architectural tenets that had been applied to the home were being rethought. New materials and advanced engineering helped introduce a wholesale reinvention of the home, as the modern pioneers sought new answers to old questions. The Bauhaus émigrés – Walter Gropius, Ludwig Mies van der Rohe and Marcel Breuer – were massively influential in this process, and famously spread their thinking to Harvard and East Coast USA as they left Germany behind. On the West Coast, too, Richard Neutra, Charles and Ray Eames, and others were establishing a brand of Californian Modernism, with a fresh emphasis on fluid spaces and a close relationship between indoor and outdoor living. Scandinavian Modernism – as exemplified by Alvar Aalto and Arne Jacobsen – offered a warmer, softer approach with a greater reliance on natural materials, closer

to the organic approach of Frank Lloyd Wright in the United States.

Many of these figures were also 'renaissance men', making their work all the more cohesive and rounded. They were writers and theorists, they painted and drew, lectured and taught. Their houses often drew on their talents for designing furniture, lighting and interiors to create a fully integrated work.

In this respect – and many others – the multi-faceted Le Corbusier towered over his contemporaries. His influence on the shape of twentieth-century architecture has been immense, with his approach and philosophy making a huge impact on many figureheads of the time. His Villa Savoye of 1931 was controversial for many reasons, not least because it leaked and became unliveable for the family who commissioned it. But the impact of the house was ultimately epic, crystallizing Le Corbusier's famous Five Points of Architecture, including the free plan, or universal space, and the idea of liberating walls by using supporting pillars – or pilotis – to carry the weight of the house.

Gradually the key components of the Modernist home were established by the movement's pioneers and their iconic buildings – the multifunctional living room, the fluid indoor-outdoor relationship, the curtain wall with its banks of glazing, the raised living space, or reinvented piano nobile. Such ideas were key to a gradual but wholesale change in the way we design and order our homes, based on the desire for a fresh and more informal way of living that promotes a sense of light and space, and vivid connections – where appropriate – to the exterior and to the landscape.

1924   **GERRIT RIETVELD (1888–1964)**

SCHRÖDER HOUSE UTRECHT, NETHERLANDS

Gerrit Rietveld's architectural career was dominated by the spectacular success of his Schröder House – a building that came to define the Dutch avant-garde. Rietveld was commissioned to design the house by Truus Schröder, a young widow who ultimately became his creative collaborator and lover.

The rendered brick-and-timber house constituted a break with tradition in terms of form and structure, but it was also spatially radical, coping imaginatively with restrictive planning codes and Schröder's exacting requirements.

Rietveld encouraged an active engagement with the flexible, adaptable space, creating sliding partitions to open out or separate the whole of the upper floor. His skills as a furniture designer were also expressed in a number of bespoke, integrated designs.

Schröder House stands at the heart of an extraordinary and lasting creative exchange (he eventually moved in and lived out his final years here). It is also the most powerful architectural manifesto statement of De Stijl, the movement in which Rietveld was such a leading light, promoting a fresh modernity based on geometric abstract form. Schröder House, with its use of sculpted primary shapes and colours, made a truly remarkable statement for a Utrecht street corner in 1924.

What seemed revolutionary in the 1930s has now become commonplace, as even period homes are reordered to cater for a more relaxed mode of family living. These ideas have flourished not just because they were innovative, of course, but because they fit with a modern lifestyle, with reassessed notions of comfort, and with a shift in emphasis between 'private' and 'communal' space within the home. Formal separate dining rooms, for instance, have less and less importance compared to one fluid space where we can cook, sit and eat with our families. Servant and maid quarters have given way – for most of us – to compact utility and service areas. Rich sources of light and 'outdoor rooms' have become essential elements, rather than secondary considerations.

As the Modernist sub-term 'International Style' once suggested, the principles and components of Modernism were quickly disseminated and publicized across borders. In the post-war years, especially, the media and architectural press became increasingly important for the

1927 KONSTANTIN MELNIKOV (1890–1974)
MELNIKOV HOUSE MOSCOW, RUSSIA

'Through a supreme sense of balance and a steadfast tension, it tunes itself in order to listen to the pulse of modernity,' said Konstantin Melnikov of his mesmerizing family home and studio. This towering, enigmatic fusion of fortress and grain silo was to become a landmark of intense and resonant power.

It was one of the few private houses to be built in Moscow during the post-revolutionary era, and was a startling statement of a new kind of architecture. Melnikov had found favour with the authorities over the success of his Soviet Pavilion at the Paris World's Fair of 1925, and so was helped to secure the land to build the house

(in later years he was regarded with suspicion by the regime).

The two-storey brick-and-timber building went through a number of design phases until Melnikov fixed upon the idea of two fused cylinders. The front cylinder is dominated by a vast opening window, drawing in light and air and almost doubling as a balcony, while the rear cylinder is peppered with hexagonal windows. The semi-open-plan sleeping rooms contain organic pedestal beds that emerge from the floor. Melnikov House, suffused with avant-garde energy, has become a symbol of twentieth-century Moscow.

1928 LUDWIG WITTGENSTEIN (1889–1951)

WITTGENSTEIN HOUSE VIENNA, AUSTRIA

'You probably imagine,' said Ludwig Wittgenstein, 'that philosophy is complicated enough, but let me tell you, this is nothing compared to the hardship of being a good architect.' During his lifetime, the philosopher involved himself in a number of professions – engineering, gardening, teaching – but none seemed as punishing as architecture, in which his passion for detail left him quite exhausted.

The distinctive three-storey cubist house was commissioned by Wittgenstein's sister, Margarethe 'Gretl' Stonborough-Wittgenstein, who had divorced her affluent chemist husband Jerome Stonborough in 1923. She originally turned to architect Paul Engelmann to design a house for her and her children, but Wittgenstein became increasingly involved in the process, ultimately falling out with Engelmann and taking on the project himself.

Engelmann had been a student of Adolf Loos, who famously declared war on ornamental excess. Wittgenstein went even further, sweeping away Neo-Classical references and banishing curtains, cornicing and other conventional detailing in favour of pure architectural spaces. This led to a somewhat obsessional emphasis on finishes and details. While some have laboured to place the house – now owned and cared for by the Bulgarian Cultural Institute – within a philosophical context, many have simply appreciated its daring experimentalism.

1929 EILEEN GRAY (1878–1976)

E-1027 ROQUEBRUNE-CAP-MARTIN, FRANCE

Though best known as a furniture designer, Eileen Gray was also a well-regarded architect. Among her best-loved buildings stands the house she created for her lover and mentor, Jean Badovici, on the steeply sloping shores of Roquebrune in the French Riviera.

Badovici was an architect-turned-journalist and founder of the French bible of modern architecture, *L'Architecture Vivante*. He encouraged Gray to broaden her work out into architecture, and Gray began to move away from Art Deco influences to embrace Modernism. The name E-1027 is a coded reference to the pair's initials.

Like a sleek white ocean liner, the dynamic house – with its balconies and terraces, and its top-floor living room and main bedrooms – opens up to views across a Mediterranean inlet to Monte Carlo. The interiors were a key part of the project, with Gray specially designing many celebrated pieces, including her E-1027 table.

Le Corbusier was famously transfixed by the house and location, later building his own cabin close by. Badovici also allowed him to paint murals in the house, which infuriated Gray. After many decades of troubled history and decay, the house is now a protected historic monument and widely recognized as one of the great pioneering houses of the Modernist movement.

1932 **JUAN O'GORMAN (1905–1982)**

RIVERA/KAHLO HOUSE & STUDIOS MEXICO CITY, MEXICO

Born to an Irish father and Mexican mother, and steeped in the language and ideas of Le Corbusier, the architect and muralist Juan O'Gorman was a fascinating amalgam. His later work was more immersed in the architectural and cultural history of Mexico, but his most famous project – the house and studios he built for Diego Rivera and Frida Kahlo – owed much to the Parisian buildings of Le Corbusier.

The house and studios – now a museum – represent, arguably, the first arrival of a distinctly European-influenced Modernist style into Mexico, and were certainly controversial additions to the residential neighbourhood.

Two separate structures – one for Rivera and one for Kahlo – are linked by a walkway at roof level. The buildings make the most of Corbusian ideas, such as an open plan and roof gardens, while also being raised up on pilotis, or supporting columns.

Just as fascinating is the way in which the architectural plan – separate working and living spaces, with possibilities for co-mingling – reflected the tempestuous relationship of two of Mexico's greatest artists. The buildings – one painted blue, the other red and white – embody the complex, dramatic 'can't live with you, can't live without you' psychology of their relationship.

1932 **PIERRE CHAREAU (1883–1950)**

MAISON DE VERRE PARIS, FRANCE

The translucent house was an architectural dream for decades before Philip Johnson's Glass House and Ludwig Mies van der Rohe's Farnsworth House of the late 1940s/early '50s. The first to really achieve this dream was architect and furniture designer Pierre Chareau.

Chareau's L-shaped, three-storey Maison de Verre was the result of close friendship and close collaboration. It was commissioned by Chareau's long-time acquaintances Dr Jean Dalsace and his wife, who wanted a new home and consulting rooms to replace an eighteenth-century townhouse in the heart of Paris. However, the tenant on the upper floor would not move, so Chareau could only work on the bottom section. He used the remnants of the original stone as a frame for his new, steel-supported Maison de Verre.

The famous glass-brick façade allows light to pour into the house, and turns it into a shimmering lightbox at night. The consulting rooms are on the ground floor, but the house is dominated by a dramatic double-height living room. Chareau worked with Dutch architect Bernard Bijvoet and craftsman Louis Dalbet on the many bespoke, fitted features. Completed after many years – a symbol of inter-war optimism – this is Chareau's only surviving building.

1941 CURZIO MALAPARTE (1898–1957)

CASA MALAPARTE PUNTA MASSULLO, CAPRI, ITALY

Casa Malaparte is a vibrant statement building
that assumes great dramatic power by virtue of
its response to an extraordinary setting. Perched
on a rocky promontory, with the ocean to three
sides, the house appears like an isolated fortress,
with its terracotta outline standing out against the
grey of the rugged surrounding stone. A set of
steps reaches up and opens out to a roof terrace,
suggesting a ziggurat-style ascent towards an
abstract viewing platform facing the sea and the
Gulf of Salerno. It is one of the most powerful
images of the early Modernist movement.

The house was built by the flamboyant and
controversial novelist, dramatist, journalist and
political activist Curzio Malaparte. Initially he
commissioned Adalberto Libera, a leading Italian
Modern movement architect. However, architect
and client soon fell out and Malaparte continued
work on the development of the house himself,
overseeing its construction by local craftsmen
and creating 'a self-portrait cut in stone'.

The two-storey house is moulded to the site's
topography, like a sculpted object. Bedrooms and
service spaces sit at ground-floor level, while the
upper storey contains the two master bedrooms
and a large stone-flagged living room, with windows
opening to the panoramic views at either side.
The room at the far and most exposed end is
Malaparte's study, overlooking the open ocean.

The building conjures up the romantic image of
the writer living and working in isolation, surrounded
by nature. In the late 1990s, the house – which
featured in Jean-Luc Godard's film *Contempt* – was
restored by the foundation established to care for
the exposed building.

1947 RICHARD BUCKMINSTER FULLER (1895–1983)

WICHITA HOUSE KANSAS, USA

Architect, engineer, inventor, writer and philosopher
Richard Buckminster Fuller was a man well ahead
of his time, and is today cited as a key influence
by a wide range of designers, planners and
environmentalists. He achieved his greatest impact
with his patented geodesic dome, which was a star
of the Montreal Expo of 1967, but it is his work in
prefabricated modular architecture – groundbreaking
in approach, and a key marker in the evolution of
the concept of a factory-produced home suited to
mass production – that continues to obsess
disciples today.

His Dymaxion ('Dynamic Maximum Tension')
House of 1929 was a lightweight steel-and-
aluminium all-in-one home, owing much to marine
architecture, caravans and the car industry. After the
war – during which Fuller designed mass-produced
structures and shelters for military use – he returned
to the Dymaxion concept and refined it with the help
of the Beech Aircraft Company.

The fully functioning prototype, with a circular
aerodynamic design and living spaces arranged
around a central service core, was dubbed the
Wichita House. Orders came in but delays in
finalizing production meant the project's bankers
withdrew support. Today the prototype is housed
in the Henry Ford Museum, Michigan – a monument
to a visionary designer who truly wanted to change
the world and the way we live.

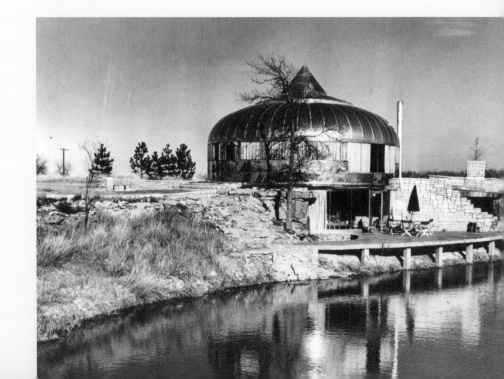

presentation of an architect's ideas and persona. John Entenza's *Arts & Architecture* magazine played a key part in establishing the Case Study programme of groundbreaking Californian homes, while photographers such as Julius Shulman and Ezra Stoller helped translate the vision of the architect into accessible and evocative images for widespread consumption, providing vibrant sources of inspiration to a broad audience.

But the concept of International Style also suggested a reduced importance for contextualism and regionalism, which were – ultimately – to prove so important to the Modernist movement as a whole. Modernism drew on the intense and diverse power of regional expression around the world, and embraced the work of architects who, while fascinated by modernity, had a particular respect for the rich sources of inspiration to be found in their own cultures and landscapes. One thinks particularly of Luis Barragán, who so mesmerizingly fused vernacular flavours and spellbinding colours from his native Mexico with the all-pervading influence of Modernism, or Geoffrey Bawa, who in Sri Lanka successfully melded an open range of references into something particularly Asian, where sustainability and an openness to landscape were key.

The work of contemporary architects such as Glenn Murcutt, Ricardo Legorreta, Herzog & de Meuron, Kengo Kuma, Rem Koolhaas, Shigeru Ban and others reminds us what a global business architecture has now become, and how we draw on influences from all over the world in making our homes, as well as constructing the built environment around us. These are architects who use their own backgrounds and cultures, yet work across borders and in many very different territories. Increasingly, we enjoy the idea of a house that is, ideally, contextual in its response to a specific site and location, yet also draws on a multitude of international themes and could well be designed by an architect from halfway around the world.

1962 **PAUL RUDOLPH (1918–1997)**

MILAM RESIDENCE PONTE VEDRA, JACKSONVILLE, FLORIDA, USA

A graduate of Harvard, where he was taught by Walter Gropius, Paul Rudolph established himself in Florida in the late 1940s. The last of his so-called 'Florida Houses' is the ambitious and accomplished Milam Residence.

The house was commissioned by the lawyer Arthur Milam and his family, to be positioned on a dune site overlooking the Atlantic. Up until that point, Rudolph had been convinced that a façade should reflect the building behind it, but with the Milam House he began to move in a new direction.

The sculpted, cubist *brise soleil* is largely independent of the rest of the two-storey concrete block structure. While helping to deflect the high sun, it also lends the building a sense of monumentality in contrast to the modest scale of the actual house.

Inside, a typical spatial and volumetric complexity is apparent. The interior was conceived as a number of living platforms at different levels, including a sunken conversation pit created in the living-room floor.

Rudolph's interest in the monumental can be seen in later projects, such as his Yale Art and Architecture Building. Arthur Milam remained an admirer and commissioned Rudolph to design additions to the house in the 1970s.

1968 MATTI SUURONEN (b. 1933)

FUTURO HOUSE VARIOUS LOCATIONS

Like Richard Buckminster Fuller's Dymaxion/ Wichita House, Finnish architect Matti Suuronen's Futuro House was a landmark design in the evolution of the modular, prefabricated, factory-produced home. Like Dymaxion, Futuro drew upon other industries, such as car manufacture and aero engineering, while also drawing heavily upon space-age, sci-fi imagery. Its flying saucer shape was inspired by the dome of a grain silo that Suuronen had once designed, but its dynamic shape suggested the golden idea of mobility.

The prototype evolved from a lightweight ski cabin that Suuronen was asked to design, and could be delivered to site by lorry or helicopter. The adjustable steel supporting legs also allowed the reinforced plastic structure to be easily positioned, even on rough terrain.

The early days of Futuro seemed to justify the optimism of the concept and the age. This 'dwelling of the future' generated widespread international interest, and Futuros were also used as observation posts by the Swedish air force, as offices, clubhouses, even a bank. However, the price was always an issue and, with the oil crisis of the early 1970s and a rise in the cost of plastics, production was halted. It is now a cult icon that remains an inspirational design.

1969 STAFFAN BERGLUND (b. 1936)

VILLA SPIES TORÖ, SWEDEN

If a single house can be said to define an architect's career, then Villa Spies (also known as Villa Fjolle) defines Staffan Berglund's. This dramatic building is pushed into a rocky site on the small island of Torö, looking out over the sea and archipelago not far from Stockholm. Like the work of Charles Deaton and Matti Suuronen, it is emblematic of 1960s futuristic architecture at its most flamboyant and imaginative.

The client was businessman Simon Spies, who made his fortune in the travel industry and launched a design competition for a vacation house that could be reproduced to order. Berglund won with his design for a plastic-capped pleasure dome. The vacation home idea stalled, but Spies liked the concept so much that he commissioned Berglund to design his own family's weekend retreat.

Unlike the single-storey house envisaged for the competition, Villa Spies consists of two storeys. The lower level is made of concrete, but the fibreglass-roofed upper storey has glass walls and is dominated by a large open-plan kitchen, dining and living area opening out to terraces, the circular swimming pool and sea views. This hedonistic and playful retreat is packed with innovative home technology, including a retractable dining table that appears from the floor at the touch of a button. It was much publicized in the early 1970s but has seldom been photographed since.

1978 CARLO SCARPA (1906–1978)

VILLA OTTOLENGHI BARDOLINO, VERONA, ITALY

Villa Ottolenghi was one of Carlo Scarpa's last commissions – along with the Brion-Vega Cemetery at San Vito d'Altivole, where he is buried – but this sensitively conceived house reveals an architect and designer at the height of his creative powers. Though completed posthumously by his colleagues, it retains a cohesive and original design.

The house was commissioned by lawyer Carolo Ottolenghi for his son. Planning restrictions on the sloping site, near Lake Garda, permitted only a single-storey building. Scarpa turned this to his advantage with a highly imaginative solution that pushed the house into the landscape so that it almost disappears into the verdant hillside. With creepers entangled over the reinforced concrete, the façade facing the lake is virtually invisible.

To the rear a sunken walkway helps to bring in light, while recalling the labyrinthine passages of Ottolenghi's – and Scarpa's – native Venice. Inside, the fluid, complex and open plan of the main living spaces is arranged around nine supporting columns made of stone and concrete bands. The roof doubles as a paved terrace. Villa Ottolenghi, with its organic approach and emphasis on craftsmanship, detailing and materials, holds echoes of Frank Lloyd Wright – an acknowledged influence – while cementing the reputation of a master architect.

It is, of course, fascinating to delve into the many connections, bloodlines and patterns that one can pick out while exploring the different houses in this book, and the way in which seemingly diverse buildings and architects may link in to one another. Certain themes have become increasingly important, such as sustainability and environmental awareness – as seen, for example, in the work of Richard Neutra, Pierre Koenig and Werner Sobek. Prefabrication and the idea of the modular home is another recurrent theme, as seen in the work of Richard Buckminster Fuller, Jean Prouvé and Richard Horden. Looking through these pages, other connections become apparent as one moves through time, taking in diverse iconic buildings from around the world and across the decades.

1991   **MATHIAS KLOTZ (b. 1965)**

CASA KLOTZ PLAYA GRANDE, TONGOY, CHILE

Mathias Klotz has quickly established himself as one of the most original architectural voices in Latin America. One of his most respected and – in a sense – romantic houses was the simple beach house that he created for himself at Tongoy.

Here, on an expanse of open dunes, Klotz designed a rectangular box floating just above the ground, supported by modest pilotis. The back of the house is largely blank, but the façade facing the Pacific is dominated by a central double-height window reaching almost to the flat roof line. The upper level of the two-storey structure is punctured to either side of this window by two square openings framing

sheltered, elevated terraces. To the front of the house, a deck projects out towards the ocean.

Inside, the central double-height living room dominates, with ancillary spaces to either side, downstairs and up. Finishes are simple, reflecting the beach-house aesthetic, with the exterior planking coated in a thin whitewash.

This early work embodies a new form of regional Modernism, and the particularly Chilean ideal of crisp architecture in an eyecatching natural context. Klotz's later buildings have become increasingly sophisticated, but they retain an emphasis on pure geometry and clean lines, coupled with a deep understanding of site.

Assembling this list of extraordinary houses was, in itself, an intriguing task. The aim was to create a balanced compilation of iconic houses that represent a rich geographical, chronological, thematic and stylistic spread. To this end we decided to limit any architect to one entry alone, while placing the emphasis on – for the most part – new-build, one-off houses.

Working within these criteria, many key houses suggested themselves, but others may not seem quite such obvious choices. Our list is partly objective and partly subjective, as your own would be. But there is no doubting the richness of the mix and the importance of seeing so many of these buildings as they are now, with – for the majority of entries – inspirational new photography by Richard Powers. In many cases, these pictures present original images of familiar buildings, and invite us to revisit and reassess them within the framework of a fresh perspective.

1993   USHIDA FINDLAY

TRUSS WALL HOUSE TOKYO, JAPAN

During the 1980s and '90s, Japanese architect Eisaku Ushida (b. 1954) and Scottish architect Kathryn Findlay (b. 1953) – both former associates of Arata Isozaki – stepped away from the prevailing architectural trend towards hard geometrical Minimalism and embarked on a very different journey. Their buildings were organic, fluid, sculpted forms that presaged the twenty-first-century fascination with dynamism, plasticity and radical geometry.

Two Tokyo houses in particular grabbed wide attention – the Soft and Hairy House of 1994, and its predecessor, the Truss Wall House. Both are innovative courtyard houses, standing out in contrast to their bland suburban surroundings.

The Truss Wall House, sitting alongside the street and passing railway line, is an abstract white building with the appearance of a convoluted shell. It wraps around a central court and is crowned by a roof terrace.

The form of the house was made possible by a patented truss wall construction system, using a combination of malleable reinforcing bars, wire mesh and poured concrete. The surfaces were then coated in a smooth layer of mortar, creating the impression of a single carved object, with much attention being paid to finishes and texture. After a series of such radical, experimental buildings, Kathryn Findlay relocated the practice to the UK.

When looking back over the book, two things will no doubt strike the reader again and again. One is the great courage and imagination of both the architects and clients who created these houses, many of which were so radical and daring in their day, so unusual and so avant-garde, conceived in – for the most part – a climate of conservatism. The opportunities to build our own home may now be more available than ever, the bespoke home more attainable, but that does not diminish the effort or commitment involved.

The other wonder is the intoxicating breadth of ideas, inspiration and original thought contained in these buildings – a glorious treasure trove of architectural thinking, carrying well over a lifetime. As we look around us in any town or city today, we cannot help but see too much mediocrity threaded through our built environment, especially the bland housing estates that multiply year on year. Looking back over more than a hundred years of innovation, of beauty, of imagination, at this wonderful resource of iconic houses, must surely inspire us to ask – if nothing else – for something more than mediocrity, especially from the places in which we live. For some, this book might just help, in some small way, to inspire thoughts and dreams for the iconic homes of the future.

1995   **KENGO KUMA (b. 1954)**

WATER/GLASS HOUSE ATAMI, SHIZUOKA, JAPAN

Kengo Kuma has talked of his ambition to create a new kind of architecture, shifting emphasis from the outward appearance of buildings to the way in which they interact with and frame the natural world. Reassessing ideas of transparency, craftsmanship, materiality and environmental sensitivity, he talks of the 'erasure' of architecture.

His ideas are explored to a radical and sublime extreme in the Water/Glass House, which overlooks the Pacific – influenced by the work of Bruno Taut, who had built a house nearby. Kuma's intention was to dissolve the divisions between the building and its ocean views as far as possible, creating an open viewing platform. The three-storey building functions as both a residence and a small hotel, with an entrance via a walkway at mid-level.

Most famous are the glass pavilions at the uppermost level, sitting within shallow infinity pools that reach out to the ocean. These 'floating' rooms transform the sense of interior and exterior. 'Architecture is not a form; it is relativity with nature,' says Kuma. 'Through the project of Water/Glass I learned how you could inherit the tradition of Japanese architecture within a modern context and technology and combine them together.'

1900

BLACKWELL BOWNESS-ON-WINDERMERE, CUMBRIA, ENGLAND

The romantic Cumbrian landscape has an illustrious pedigree when it comes to Arts and Crafts. Writer and philosopher John Ruskin, a founding father of the movement, made his home at Brantwood on Lake Coniston, and Arts and Crafts architect Charles Voysey designed two houses around Lake Windermere. Here, too, on a hillside spot overlooking the lake, Voysey's contemporary Mackay Hugh Baillie Scott built a remarkable house at the turn of the century.

Blackwell was commissioned as a family holiday home by Manchester brewery owner and philanthropist Sir Edward Holt, also a key figure in the development of lakeland reservoirs which supplied clean water to the city of Manchester. Railway access to the Lakes had made Windermere a fashionable resort for the wealthy of Manchester and Liverpool, and a series of large homes had sprung up along its shores.

Baillie Scott had become a much sought-after architect, capturing the attention of distinguished clients such as Ernst Ludwig, the Grand Duke of Hesse, who asked the designer to create the interiors of his house in Darmstadt in 1897. Baillie Scott was also an able publicist, publishing his work in magazines such as *The Studio*. Blackwell offered him the opportunity to create a house on a large scale, in an enticing location, and with the freedom of expression that comes with designing a holiday retreat rather than a principal home.

Instead of positioning the façade of the L-shaped house so that it faced the lake to the west, Baillie Scott oriented it to the south, in order to make the most of natural sunlight: lake views were preserved for key rooms. While a service and servants' wing is positioned to one side, the best of the house is taken up largely by three rooms on the ground floor.

Chief among these rooms is the main hall – the familiar throwback to the medieval great hall seen in many Arts and Crafts houses of the period – in this case, complete with a dramatic fireplace topped by a minstrels' gallery. A dining room stands to one side, also a masculine space of oak and stone, but lifted by a bespoke hessian wall-covering in a floral pattern. The greatest surprise is the white drawing room at the far end of the house, overlooking the lake. A poetic and calming space of white plasterwork and refined detailing, with an exquisite fireplace enlivened by rich blue tilework for contrast, it is a true haven, complete with a window seat and a framed view of Windermere and Coniston fells.

While the inglenooks, galleries and great fireplaces refer back to a fabled golden age of craft, this is also a house which – with its central heating, electric light, fluid layout and deeply sophisticated aesthetic – was at the same time very contemporary.

As in the greatest Arts and Crafts houses, the quality of detailing and artistry throughout is striking. The repeated decorative motifs – in the carving, plasterwork, stencils and even the ornate guttering – are tied into the natural world: peacocks, foliage, roses, acorns and berries. 'In the decoration of the house no excuse can be urged for the failure to achieve beauty,' Baillie Scott once wrote. 'If it has no beauty it is useless and less than useless.' Blackwell suggests the depth of Baillie Scott's mastery of the holistic view of architecture and interiors as one cohesive, crafted entity.

The house is also tied to its site by the use of local stone and slate. The gardens are by Thomas Mawson, a landscape designer who lived locally but had a national reputation.

Blackwell was included by Hermann Muthesius in his 1904 book *Das Englische Haus*, in which he described Baillie Scott as a 'northern poet'. The Holts would have heartily agreed with this assessment, and the house continues to delight to this day. Recently restored and now open to the public, it is emblematic of a still-inspiring culture of care, attention to detail and exceptional skill.

Positioned at the brow of a hill, the house has a masculine feel, but the light, tranquil drawing room offers a distinct contrast. Its inglenook fireplace, set amid ornate white plasterwork, becomes a carefully conceived room within a room.

Biography

MACKAY HUGH BAILLIE SCOTT (1865–1945)
Born in Kent to a farming family of Scottish descent, Baillie Scott studied agriculture before moving into architecture. He was apprenticed to Charles Davis, Bath's City Architect, and then moved to the Isle of Man to set up his practice in 1889, followed by a move to Bedfordshire. By the 1890s, Baillie Scott's work was in great demand both in England and on the Continent, supplemented by a range of his own furniture designs. Large-scale commissions were mixed with more modest suburban designs, all within a refined Arts and Crafts style.

Key Buildings

Red House Douglas, Isle of Man, 1893
Majestic Hotel Onchan, Isle of Man, 1893
White House Helensburgh, Scotland, 1900
48 Storey's Way Cambridge, England, 1913
Waldbühl Uzwil, Switzerland, 1914

Highly crafted but unpainted woodwork dominates the great hall – or 'living hall' as Baillie Scott put it – and the adjoining dining room, decorated with hessian wall hangings.

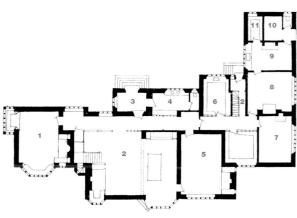

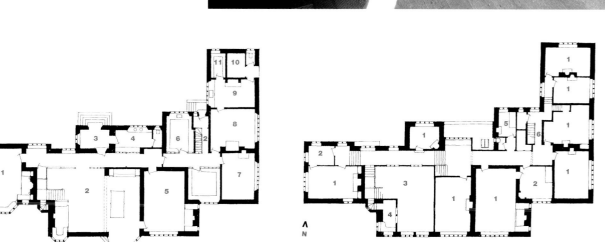

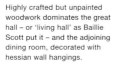

ground floor

1 drawing room
2 hall
3 porch
4 cloakroom
5 dining room
6 pantry
7 servants' hall
8 kitchen
9 scullery
10 coal store
11 larder

first floor

1 bedroom
2 dressing room
3 upper part of hall
4 gallery
5 bathroom
6 linen closet

EDWIN LUTYENS

GODDARDS   ABINGER COMMON, SURREY, ENGLAND

Goddards was born of a unique and unusual set of circumstances. It was not originally commissioned as a conventional country-house residence at all, but – in a remarkably generous philanthropic gesture on the part of its patrons – as a country retreat for 'disadvantaged' women. This was, in itself, a storybook proposition, and one that was interpreted by Edwin Lutyens within a typically romantic and deeply English version of the Arts and Crafts tradition.

The building was commissioned by Sir Frederick Mirrielees, a wealthy entrepreneur, and his wife Margaret, a shipping-line heiress. With a country home of their own nearby, they bought a 7-acre (2.8 hectare) estate and decided to set up a 'Home of Rest for Ladies of Small Means'.

Lutyens was introduced to his new clients by renowned landscape designer Gertrude Jekyll, a friend, collaborator and – for a time – a mentor. Lutyens had designed Jekyll's own Surrey

home, Munstead Wood, a few years earlier, and would often spend his weekends there.

The particularly individual context of the new project led to a house that was both grand and simple at the same time. In its scale, the building was clearly ambitious, but the nature of its use led to the supremacy of an almost Shaker-like simplicity within, rather than the atmosphere of luxurious splendour usually associated with Lutyens's great country houses. Ultimately, this interior simplicity – even after the house was adapted for single-family use – well suited a house so in tune with the Arts and Crafts aesthetic and the ideal of a crafted, medieval-inspired, rural home, with a return to the 'pure' values of a pre-industrial age.

To suit its use as a retreat, Lutyens designed a double-winged building in a butterfly formation. The two wings were joined by a large and open common room at the centre, modelled

on a medieval hall, with a large fireplace at one end and exposed timber beams, and servants' quarters above. The wings held a total of six bedrooms on the upper level, with a kitchen and dining area below to one side, and to the other a ground floor dominated by a large skittle alley, which was crowned by dramatic brick arches pushing out into the orchard to the rear.

Goddards provided sanctuary to many women before the Home of Rest was moved and the Mirrielees asked Lutyens to convert the house into a weekend home for their son and daughter-in-law. In 1910 the house was updated and spaces enlarged, but Lutyens kept to the constraints of his original structure and the innate simplicity of the house survived.

Just a few years after Goddards, the architect – increasingly in demand – made a break from Arts and Crafts and began working in a more imposing Neo-Classical style. But

With its red tiles, timber frame, lime-washed walls and locally made brick, Goddards makes use of local materials and vernacular traditions. Inside, the original furnishing mixed antiques and new pieces by the Art Workers' Guild.

Goddards was groundbreaking in its butterfly pattern, with its wings opening out to sun and landscape – a pattern that was to find great favour in Edwardian England and was also seen in, for instance, Edward Prior's Voewood/ Home Place (see pp. 44–47). The geometric purity, the essential rigour and emphasis on a combination of function and crafted simplicity all presage the evolution of architecture into a modern age.

It is this intriguing combination of old and new – within a house that has a foot in both past and future – which makes Goddards so fresh and powerful. The house is now maintained by the Lutyens Trust and the Landmark Trust, but acclaim remains with the architect who, with masterful imagination, subtly designed a building that seemed as though it belonged completely and naturally to its site, landscape and county.

Biography

EDWIN LUTYENS (1869–1944)
Born in London, Lutyens studied architecture at South Kensington School of Art. He set up his own practice in 1889, after an apprenticeship with country-house architects Ernest George & Peto. His work varied between Arts and Crafts buildings and grand Neo-Classical structures, influenced by Norman Shaw, William Morris and Philip Webb. Within England he was best known for a series of highly influential country houses, as well as for being the architect of the Cenotaph memorial. However, he also, famously, took his career to a new level in planning imperial New Delhi and some of the city's most striking buildings.

Key Buildings

Munstead Wood Munstead, Godalming, Surrey, England, 1896
Orchards Munstead, Godalming, Surrey, England, 1899
Deanery Gardens Sonning, Berkshire, England, 1902
Castle Drogo Drewsteignton, Devon, England, 1930
Viceroy's House/Rashtrapati Bhavan New Delhi, India, 1931

ground floor

1 common room
2 dining room
3 kitchen
4 w.c.
5 storeroom
6 office
7 scullery
8 larder
9 cloakroom
10 skittle alley
11 library

first floor

1 bedroom
2 dressing room
3 bathroom
4 servant's room
5 storeroom

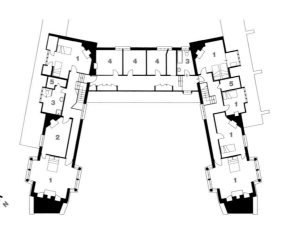

The restrained and sometimes utilitarian interiors let the craftsmanship shine through. In the skittle alley, brick arches help to define a functional yet quietly beautiful space. In the rear garden court, created by the butterfly formation of the house, a typical Lutyens and Jekyll water feature – here, a well pond – is the focal point.

The Villa Majorelle – one of the glories of the Art Nouveau period – was more than a meeting of minds between architect and client. It was a unique collaboration, blending architecture, interior design and decoration in a now-famous combination, and uniting two very distinct talents. The result was a true spectacle – a sensuous drama filled with flamboyant, organic curves and sculpted forms.

The house was commissioned by Louis Majorelle, one of the great Art Nouveau furniture designers. In 1879 he and his brother had taken over the family furniture firm, based in Nancy. In 1885 he had married the daughter of a local theatre owner, Jeanne Kretz, whose initials gave rise to the other name for their family home – Villa Jika.

Majorelle was inspired by natural forms and by working with exotic timbers, but he later expanded his woodworking studios to add a metalwork atelier. He also opened shops that sold his work in many major French cities. As co-founder of the École de Nancy, an affiliation of local craftsmen and designers, he acquired an international reputation, and gradually Nancy became a centre for Art Nouveau design.

With the construction of the metalwork atelier, Majorelle had already established himself as something of an architectural patron, as well as collaborator: the atelier design was by local architect Lucien Weissenburger, on land gifted by Majorelle's mother-in-law. The gift was generous enough to provide in addition a site opposite the factory, where the Majorelles decided to build their family home. They turned to Henri Sauvage, whom Majorelle had known for some years, to design the building, in conjunction with Weissenburger. It was Sauvage's first architectural commission. Villa Majorelle, then, became a team building – uniting voices from Nancy and Paris – but the ultimate effect was one of total cohesion, united by the devices and desires of Art Nouveau.

Sauvage, who later collaborated with the Majorelle family on a series of buildings and pavilions, designed the towering structure with almost church-like volumes and large windows, especially on the upper levels, which bathed the rooms in light. Here, at the top of the house, Majorelle and Sauvage created a large studio with views out across the street and to the factory.

Majorelle himself, of course, designed much of the furniture and woodwork for the house, including the staircases and high balconies. He also designed much of the ironwork, from railings to the entrance canopy to the ornate guttering. Stained glasswork, meanwhile, was commissioned from Jacques Gruber, while the eyecatching fireplace in the dining room – a focal point that appears to have grown out of the parquet floor itself – is by Alexandre Bigot.

Majorelle's fortunes began to fade later in his life, after a disastrous fire at the factory and after the chaos of the First World War, but Villa Majorelle has been preserved as a majestic expression of the Art Nouveau style. In the 1990s it was classed as a Historic Monument and a restoration programme followed, initiated by the town of Nancy.

Often, when one looks at a collaborative process, the joins and conflicts can be seen. At Villa Majorelle, the *mélange* is totally seamless and beautifully expressive. The building became a showcase for Majorelle, for Sauvage, for Nancy, for Art Nouveau itself, as well as being the centrepiece of an ongoing creative relationship.

Biographies

LOUIS MAJORELLE (1859–1926)
A designer and decorator, Majorelle was one of the great Art Nouveau exponents. Born into a family of furniture designers in Nancy, he studied first in Nancy and then at the École des Beaux-Arts in Paris. He returned to his hometown on the untimely death of his father to take over the family company. His son was Jacques Majorelle, the painter and creator of the Majorelle Gardens in Marrakech.

HENRI SAUVAGE (1873–1932)
The son of a wallpaper entrepreneur, Sauvage studied at the École des Beaux-Arts in Paris, where he first met Louis Majorelle's brother. He initially ran his own wallpaper company. From 1898 he worked as an architectural designer in the Art Nouveau style, in collaboration with Charles Sarazin, and established himself as an architect, designer and artist.

Key Buildings

Villa Océana Biarritz, France, 1903
Villa Leuba/Villa Natacha Biarritz, France, 1908
Grand Hotel Les Terrasses Tréport, France, 1909

The first truly Art Nouveau building in Nancy, the three-storey residence is an exuberant statement, with something of a fairy-tale quality, reinforced by the organic qualities of the window frames, balconies and ironwork, recalling bending boughs and plant-like tendrils enveloping and embellishing the stonework like some extraordinary architectural ivy.

1902

VILLA MAJORELLE

The fluid, sculpted forms of
fireplaces, stairways and
doorways draw the eye and
invite one from room to room.

ground floor

1 entrance
2 hall
3 kitchen
4 office
5 dining room
6 sitting room
7 terrace

first floor

1 bedroom
2 closet
3 bathroom
4 w.c.
5 boudoir
6 terrace

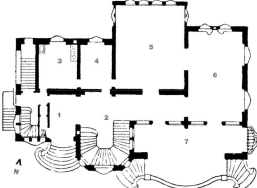

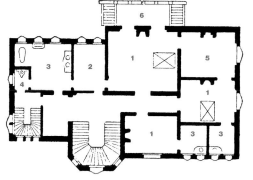

Hill House is a place of powerful convergence. It is a building that sits at the turn not only of two centuries, but also of two different eras, embodying the shift from a Victorian outlook, with its reliance upon Neo-Classicism and Historicism, to a more progressive and modern approach to domestic life and its architecture. At the same time, it effectively splices the influences of Art Nouveau, Arts and Crafts and the imposing, baronial-style Scottish architectural tradition into a cohesive, forward-looking building. Beyond this, Hill House is one of the greatest achievements of a truly original thinker – an architect, designer and artist whose unique personal style has become instantly recognizable and as distinctive, in its own way, as that of Gaudí or Barragán.

The story of convergence is written on the very outline of the building. The rendered sandstone lends a sculptural quality to the composition, blending the spiralling staircase tower and lofty chimneys with the decidedly modern and innovative sweep of a half-cylinder main staircase, like a submarine conning tower but with large vertical windows. Few buildings feel so explicitly on the cusp of the old and new.

Inside, the home is decidedly poetic. The proportions of the rooms and their layout have an experimental feel, enhanced by the quality of the local light. The decoration and detailing are highly accomplished and original. The vision for the house is total. Mackintosh – together with his wife, Margaret Macdonald-Mackintosh – was involved in every aspect of the interior, from light fittings to fitted furniture to bespoke

fireplaces and the pewter fire tongs that hung alongside them, right down to the distinctive 'Hill House' long-backed chair.

The house was commissioned by Walter W. Blackie, of the Glasgow publishing company Blackie & Son, and his wife Anna. In 1902 the family decided to move from Dunblane to Helensburgh, about 25 miles west of Glasgow. Blackie bought a plot of land, formerly a potato field, and Mackintosh was suggested as the architect. 'I told him that ... I rather fancied grey rough cast for the walls, and slate for the roof; and that any architectural effect sought should be secured by the massing of the parts rather than by adventitious ornament,' wrote Blackie.[1]

The key living areas – drawing room, library and dining room – make the most of the views of the Clyde, while drawing in light from the generous and unbaronial windows. The romantic space of the drawing room contrasts with the more masculine counterpoints of the library and dining room. In particular, the large drawing-room window seat offers a seductive viewing spot in a feminine environment enlivened by wall stencils and specially designed fabrics.

At the same time this is a highly practical home. Like Voysey, Prior and others of the period, Mackintosh was a designer of pragmatism as well as beauty, creating strong service spaces and accommodating family needs, including adding a nursery for a new Blackie arrival even as building was underway.

There is a great sense of romance to Mackintosh's work, especially at Hill House, but this is always tempered with restraint and a real sense of understanding for the day-to-day demands and desires of domestic life. It seems extraordinary to us now that – along with Windyhill in Kilmacolm – Hill House was one of only two major residential commissions carried out by Mackintosh, and that his architectural career faltered after the completion of the second phase of the Glasgow School of Art.

While he may have felt unappreciated or misunderstood during his lifetime, his work inspired great interest and gained a significant following at home and abroad. Now, of course, his voice is recognized as pivotal in the great shift towards a new kind of architecture, and as inspiring and evocative in its own right, with 'Mackintosh style' still very much in demand.

1 Quoted in James Macaulay, *Charles Rennie Mackintosh: Hill House*, Phaidon, 1994.

Biography

CHARLES RENNIE MACKINTOSH (1868–1928)

Born in Glasgow, where his father was a police force clerk, Mackintosh spent his most productive years in the city. He forged a unique style which combined Arts and Crafts influences – especially Voysey and Baillie Scott – with Art Nouveau, Scottish vernacular and a progressive modernity. Much of his work in Glasgow was with architects Honeyman & Keppie, where he became a partner. He left Glasgow in 1914 for Suffolk, London and France, developing furniture designs and painting watercolours.

Key Buildings

Windyhill Kilmacolm, Scotland, 1901
Willow Tea Rooms Sauchiehall Street, Glasgow, Scotland, 1904
Scotland Street School Glasgow, Scotland, 1906
Glasgow School of Art Glasgow, Scotland, 1899/1909

ground floor

1 entrance
2 library
3 living/music room
4 dining room
5 cloakroom
6 hall
7 pantry
8 storeroom
9 kitchen
10 laundry room
11 wash house

first floor

1 bedroom
2 bathroom
3 nursery
4 dressing room
5 pantry
6 storeroom
7 upper part of hall

attic

1 bedroom
2 bathroom
3 box room
4 schoolroom

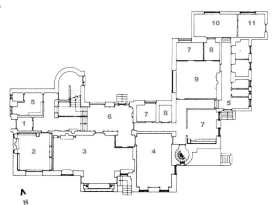

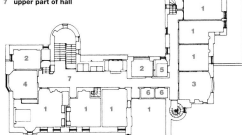

1903

HILL HOUSE

The many bespoke pieces in the house include the clock in the entrance hallway, the lamps cradling the gas lighting and the long-backed chairs. Only rarely did the Blackies move away from Mackintosh's cohesive approach, as in the wood-panelled dining room, where they introduced their own furniture.

EDWARD PRIOR

VOEWOOD/HOME PLACE HOLT, NORFOLK, ENGLAND

Voewood is a house intimately rooted to its setting and site. Its architect, Edward Prior, was always interested in exploring local materials and vernacular references, but he was also interested in practicality and economy. By excavating the flint, sand and gravel used in the construction of the building, dramatic sunken gardens were formed at the front of the house. Voewood, then, was born of the earth, with an organic quality heightened by the fluid form of the house and the way it ties itself to the landscape, gardens and complementary outbuildings.

Prior – while modest about the role of the architect, and passionate about supporting the talents of builders and craftsmen – was a pioneering figure within the Arts and Crafts movement. Keen to promote quality and workmanship, and inspired by Norman Shaw, Philip Webb, William Morris and John Ruskin, he was a progressive, experimental architect fascinated by the possibilities of new materials and structural solutions.

Voewood, for all its beautifully detailed and organic appearance, is one of the first reinforced concrete structures in Britain. The sand and gravel quarried from the gardens were also used to help make the concrete that was turned on site into foundations, structural beams and floors. The edifice was then faced with a sculpted mix of the local flint, brick, Sandringham brown stone and slim terracotta tiles from Cambridgeshire that were often woven together in herringbone patterns, window surrounds or spiralling chimney stacks.

The formation of the house was radical, too, with Prior being one of the early advocates of the Edwardian butterfly pattern, or X-shaped formation. It was a form explored at Prior's earlier house, The Barn, in Devon during the 1890s, and it later became fashionable among Arts and Crafts architects.

Voewood – rechristened Home Place for part of its life – was commissioned by the Reverend Percy Lloyd and his wife. It was felt that the fresh, breeze-blown air of north Norfolk might be beneficial to Mrs Lloyd, who suffered from poor health.

The plan of Voewood is certainly highly creative and innovative. A double-height great hall – so beloved of the Arts and Crafts movement – is positioned right at the heart of the building, with the main entrance to the west. Laid out over four floors in total, the house is highly crafted but it is hardworking, too, with simple beauty to be found even in the pantries, larders and stores to the rear.

Surprisingly, Mrs Lloyd was not taken by the building, which – together with St Andrew's Church at Roker – is now seen as Prior's highest achievement. The family soon rented out the house and later it was put to institutional use as a boys' school, a cottage hospital and a retirement home, with part of the estate passing to a neighbouring hospital complex.

In recent years, however, the house has been lovingly restored by rare-book dealer Simon Finch, who has carefully removed the fire doors and care home amenities, and has restored Voewood – at last – into a family home, with restricted public access for weddings, events and tours. The gardens, attics and semi-subterranean garden rooms have also come back into usage, reminding us of the breadth of Prior's vision and his extraordinary artist's eye for texture and detail.

Biography

EDWARD PRIOR (1857–1932)

Educated at Harrow and Cambridge, where he was a prize-winning athlete, Prior went to work for mentor Norman Shaw in 1874. Six years later he established his own practice. As well as being a practising architect, he was a scholar and theorist, writing key accounts of Gothic art and architecture. He was also co-founder of the Art Workers' Guild. In later years he became the Slade Professor of Art at Cambridge and founded the Cambridge School of Architecture.

Key Buildings

Henry Martyn Hall Cambridge, England, 1887
Bothenhampton Church Bothenhampton, Dorset, England, 1889
The Barn Exmouth, Devon, England, 1896
Cambridge Medical Schools Cambridge, England, 1904
St Andrew's Church Roker, Sunderland, England, 1906

The craftsmanship and ingenuity of the house are obvious at every turn. Even the triangular zones formed at the joins of the wings to the body of Voewood's butterfly plan are utilized as squared-off spiralling staircases, twisting upwards.

The house was designed to maximize connections not only to the gardens, including the walled garden to the east, but also to the two integral verandas, or 'cloisters', leading onto the large terrace overlooking the sunken gardens. The butterfly pattern creates opportunities to bring a wealth of natural light deep into the building, often with windows to either side of key rooms. Voewood's upstairs landing (below left) features internal windows that look down into the great hall, like an updated version of a minstrel's gallery.

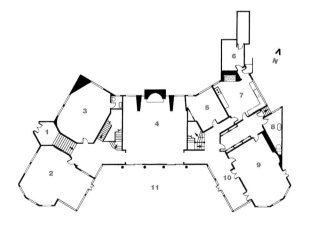

ground floor

1 entrance
2 music room
3 games room
4 hall
5 snug
6 pantry
7 kitchen
8 w.c.
9 dining room
10 mosaic room
11 terrace

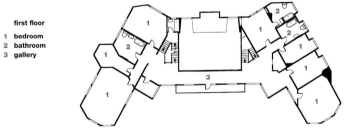

first floor

1 bedroom
2 bathroom
3 gallery

1905

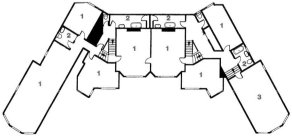

second floor

1 bedroom
2 bathroom/w.c.
3 recreation room

In Arts and Crafts architecture there is a constant and intriguing contradiction between references to the past and pushes for innovation. With Charles Voysey, especially, the idea of a return to pre-Victorian craftsmanship and quality joined with a progressive outlook to form a coherent philosophy applied to a series of highly influential and much admired houses.

These are new-century buildings that are carefully imagined and crafted, with great attention to detail and context, while incorporating a beautifully conceived and evolving portfolio of design ideas and motifs. At the same time one sees the shoots of modernity in Voysey's extraordinary use of natural light, the fluid nature of his floor plans and, on occasion, his hesitant acceptance of technology as long as it did not lead to compromise in workmanship or aesthetics. There is also a sophisticated view of domestic life: servants' quarters and service spaces are integral to the home rather than an afterthought.

While Voysey's houses are buildings of great beauty, they also have a restraint and simplicity that can seem at odds with the complex wallpaper patterns for which he was also well known, and which some commentators see as highly influential in the emergence of Art Nouveau.

Voysey's houses are famously hardworking. Every aspect of functionality – from door locks and storage to guttering and ventilation flues – has been considered and then interpreted in effective, simple and highly crafted solutions, using honest, natural materials.

All of this is displayed to great effect at The Homestead, one of Voysey's most accomplished and cohesive country houses. The architect/designer was given free rein to consider every detail of domestic space, and to shape a home for his client, Sydney Claridge Turner. Voysey formed a warm friendship with Turner, a bachelor and manager of a London insurance company, who asked for a weekend retreat and entertaining space by the sea at Frinton within walking distance of the golf club.

The site is a corner plot within streets of substantial turn-of-the-century houses (The Homestead was one of the earliest buildings on its street). The service elements – kitchen, pantry and smaller bedrooms above – follow the slope of the site, with the heart of the building at the highest point alongside Second Avenue.

Much of the ground-floor living space is taken up by one sizeable, open-plan living room, or parlour, with light coming in from either side and a porthole window looking seaward.

To one side sits a large inglenook fireplace, with details including modest bird-motif tiles incorporated into the surround. To the other side is a large recess that denotes the veranda pushing into the outline of the house, offering a sheltered viewing point over the gardens.

The ingenuity and thoughtfulness of the design are impressive. Much of the furnishing is built-in and bespoke, with generous amounts of storage provided throughout and the potential of every spare foot maximized. The octagonal, partially wood-panelled dining room, for instance, incorporates large cupboards for china, cutlery, glassware and more.

Along with The Orchard, Voysey's own house, The Homestead is one of the most complete and thorough expressions of the architect's craft. It underlines his deeply intelligent approach to problem-solving and invention, allied to a discerning eye for craftsmanship and artistry, yet applied with a careful restraint that helps makes the house so fresh, spacious, generous and ultimately rich.

Part of the site slopes gently downwards, so Voysey created a slightly twisted L-shaped plan, with the building lines running parallel to the intersecting roadways beyond, while cradling a private garden to the rear. Voysey motifs enrich the house throughout, from the heart-shaped letter box at the entrance to bespoke wooden latches and locks for every internal timber door.

Biography

CHARLES F. A. VOYSEY (1857–1941)
A Puritan reverend's son, born in Yorkshire, Voysey was educated by his father and by private tutors before being articled to architect J. P. Seddon in 1873. He then worked with George Devey's office before founding his own practice in 1882, later becoming a friend and neighbour of fellow Arts and Crafts practitioner Edward Prior. Voysey made a great impact with a series of country houses and cottages, while also designing wallpapers, textiles and furniture, proving himself a pre-eminent pattern-maker as well as architect.

Key Buildings

Perrycroft Colwall, Herefordshire, England, 1894
Norney Shackleford, Surrey, England, 1897
Broadleys Windermere, Cumbria, England, 1898
The Orchard Chorleywood, Hertfordshire, England, 1899
Moor Crag Windermere, Cumbria, England, 1899

The rooms are airy and well lit. Even the inglenook fireplace in the parlour features two small windows, which stop the recess from becoming forbidding. Voysey's trademark ventilation flues are designed with a combination pattern of birds and trees.

ground floor

1 entrance porch
2 hall
3 dining room
4 parlour
5 veranda
6 cloakroom
7 w.c.
8 pantry
9 kitchen
10 storeroom
11 larder
12 scullery
13 coal and wood store

first floor

1 bedroom
2 dressing room
3 bathroom
4 w.c.
5 sitting room/study

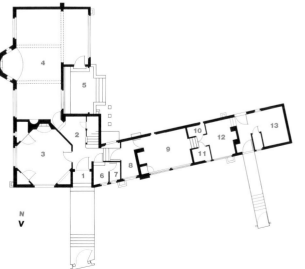

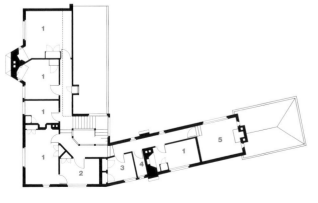

1908

Craftsmanship and detailing were all-important to Charles and Henry Greene and to the Gamble House. Both architects and clients shared common aims of creating a house that was allied to the landscape but also expertly crafted, with exquisite finishing. The result was a uniquely cohesive building, where no corner was forgotten and where the emphasis on the bespoke was extended to furniture, lighting and the rugs upon the floors.

In many ways, like William Morris and John Ruskin before them, the Greenes were advocates of an Arts and Crafts approach that on the one hand emphasized the quality and beauty of craft and original invention, and on the other harboured a suspicion of industrialization and mass production. The Gamble House, with its blend of Arts and Crafts, Swiss chalet and Japanese influences, could be seen as harking back to an age of pre-industrial artisanship.

But the house is more complex than this, and is in fact a very forward-looking building. The Greenes, naturally, found beauty and inspiration in the past, but they were consciously seeking to invent a distinctly twentieth-century style of American architecture, one that connected to nature and elevated the beauty of natural materials but also endeavoured to embrace modernity and modern domesticity, from electric lighting and intercom systems to hygienic state-of-the-art kitchens.

'Let us begin all over again,' Charles Greene once said. 'We have got to have bricks and stone and wood and plaster: common, homely, cheap materials, every one of them. Leave them as they are … why disguise them? The noblest work of art is to make these common things beautiful.'[1]

This philosophy is played out on a large and highly accomplished scale at the three-storey, 8,100 square foot (750 sq m) Gamble House. This timber-framed, redwood-clad building is perhaps the leading example of the tailored American Arts and Crafts home. Along with the Greenes' own designs, it features the workmanship of the Peter Hall Manufacturing Company, who made much of the furniture, stained glasswork by Emil Lange, and occasional pieces by fellow Arts and Crafts pioneer Gustav Stickley.

For the enlightened clients – David Gamble, whose father founded the Procter & Gamble pharmaceutical company, and his wife Mary – Pasadena presented a possibility for building a highly individual winter retreat. The area is known as Little Switzerland for its once-clean air, historically reputed to have healthful benefits, and the Gambles wanted to make the most of this, even buying neighbouring land and planting orange trees to disguise the smell of a nearby pig farm.

Their sophisticated timber house makes the most of natural cross-ventilation and overhanging eaves to mitigate the heat, while also integrating a series of terraces – with sleeping porches above – that overlook the Arroyo Seco canyon.

Inside, natural daylight is filtered through internal windows and supplemented by electric lighting, which in the early 1900s was still regarded with some suspicion for its supposed ill effects upon health. While the house constantly connects outwardly with the landscape, internal privacy is maximized by means of a layout that carefully compartmentalizes the building at the same time as offering flexibility.

David and Mary Gamble's heirs, Cecil and Louise Gamble, considered selling the house in the 1940s but overheard a potential buyer talk of painting the house white as soon as the deal was done. Fearing the whitewash, some years later they donated the house to the City of Pasadena and the University of Southern California, and it became a National Historic Landmark. It has remained much as it was in the days of the Greenes and the Gambles – still the ultimate meeting of minds and very much the holistic, ergonomic and crafted American dream home.

1 Quoted in Linda G. Arntzenius, *The Gamble House*, University of Southern California School of Architecture, 2000.

The overhang of the roof line shelters the house from heat, while also protecting a series of raised verandas, or sleeping porches, which complement the principal bedrooms on the second of the three levels. The discreet uppermost level was designed as a billiard room.

Biographies

CHARLES GREENE (1868–1957) & HENRY GREENE (1870–1954)

The Greenes grew up in St Louis, Missouri, and attended architectural school in Boston. Charles was more interested in the arts while Henry focused on engineering, giving them a complementary range of expertise. Having followed their parents to Pasadena, they founded Greene & Greene in 1894. Their primarily domestic architecture, centred in California, fused Arts and Crafts philosophy with mainly Japanese and Spanish colonial influences.

Key Buildings

Cuthbertson House Pasadena, California, USA, 1902
Charles Greene House Pasadena, California, USA, 1902
Blacker House Pasadena, California, USA, 1907
Pratt House Ojai, California, USA, 1909
Thorsen House Berkeley, California, USA, 1909

Within the building a dozen different kinds of wood have been used for their varying tones and qualities, always with rounded, softened edges. Joints are usually exposed, revealing the skill that underpins the house's construction, and personalized motifs are constantly repeated and revisited.

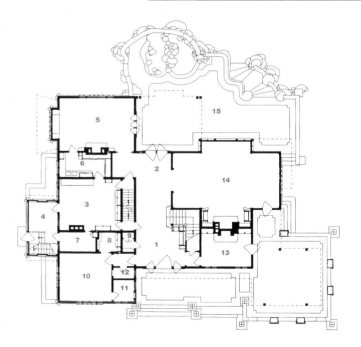

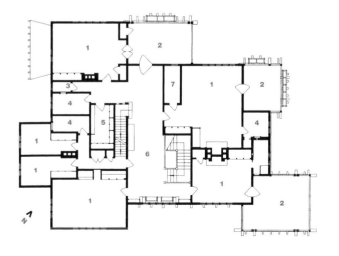

far left: ground floor

1 front entry hall
2 rear entry hall
3 kitchen
4 porch
5 dining room
6 butler's pantry
7 cold room
8 closet
9 cloakroom
10 guest room
11 bathroom
12 w.c.
13 den
14 living room
15 terrace

left: first floor

1 bedroom
2 sleeping porch
3 w.c.
4 bathroom
5 linen closet
6 hall
7 closet

1908

THE GAMBLE HOUSE

Many years before the arrival in America of Walter Gropius, Ludwig Mies van der Rohe and Marcel Breuer, Rudolph Schindler launched an architectural revolution on the West Coast. Arguably, the house he designed for himself on North Kings Road in Los Angeles was the first truly modern house in America, breaking with all tradition and laying out new principles of architecture and design. Even by today's standards, some of its principal elements – such as the outdoor sleeping platforms, or 'baskets', on the roof of the building – seem radical. The Schindler House turned tradition on its head and created the framework for a new paradigm.

In the autumn of 1921, after a period working for Frank Lloyd Wright and supervising the construction of Wright's Barnsdall/Hollyhock House in Los Angeles, Schindler decided to launch his own practice and create his own house. He and his wife, Pauline, were close friends with Clyde Chace, an engineer, and his wife Marian. Together the four of them decided to build a low-cost house on a generous plot of land, using concrete, glass, timber and innovative 'tilt slab' construction techniques.

'The basic idea was to give each person his own room – instead of the usual distribution,' wrote Schindler, 'and to do most of the cooking right on the table, making it more a social "campfire" affair, than the disagreeable burden to one member of the family.'[1]

Essentially, the house was designed as a single-storey building with three spokes radiating around a pivotal fireplace. In the original floor plan, each of the four residents was granted their own studio, combining to create a larger apartment for each couple. The third spoke contained the communal kitchen and utility area, with a guest room and garaging. As Schindler wrote: 'The rooms are large studio rooms, with concrete walls on three sides, the front (glass) open to the outdoors – a real California scheme.'[2]

The building was extraordinary – both socially and architecturally. It gave each individual their own private living space, zoned according to the arrangement of the furniture, but it also provided areas where all four inhabitants could come together. Breaking with convention, the house was, in a sense, all about liberation, engineering individual freedom, social interaction by choice and connections to the natural world.

The Schindler House is remarkable for its fluid nature. Key rooms spill out onto patios and porches, with each 'apartment' oriented to opposite sides of the landscaped garden, itself designed as a series of outdoor rooms. This idea is extended further by two sleeping 'baskets' up on the roof, protected only by canvas covers.

The arrival of children and other practical concerns meant that the Chaces left the house in 1924. They were replaced in 1925 by Schindler's friend and – for a time – working partner, Richard Neutra. Eventually the house became home to the Schindlers alone.

While the property drew a constant stream of visitors and friends, the importance and impact of Schindler's achievement took some time to be widely recognized. With influences ranging from Frank Lloyd Wright, Japan and a camping trip the Schindlers had taken in Yosemite Park, the house was a truly pioneering building, its lightness of touch and execution unknown in the architectural scene of the time. As such, it was a key influence on later generations of Californian Modernist houses, including the Case Study programme and beyond, becoming an early prototype for a new kind of American home.

1 Quoted in Kathryn Smith, *Schindler House*, Harry N. Abrams, 2001.
2 Ibid.

Biography

RUDOLPH M. SCHINDLER (1887–1953)

Born in Vienna, Schindler studied under Otto Wagner and Adolf Loos before moving to America in 1914. He went to work with Frank Lloyd Wright in Chicago before founding his own practice in Los Angeles in 1922, collaborating for a period with Richard Neutra. Schindler's work concentrated principally on family houses and apartment buildings suited to the Californian climate, being open to the landscape, spatially innovative and distinctively modern.

Key Buildings

Lovell Beach House Newport Beach, Los Angeles, California, USA, 1926
Wolfe House Catalina Island, California, USA, 1929
Pearl M. Mackey Apartments Los Angeles, California, USA, 1939
Bethlehem Baptist Church Los Angeles, California, USA, 1944

main floor:
1 hall
2 Rudolph Schindler's quarters
3 patio
4 Pauline Schindler's quarters
5 guest room
6 kitchen
7 Marian Chace's quarters
8 Clyde Chace's quarters
9 garage

1922

SCHINDLER HOUSE

AUGUSTE PERRET

STUDIO-RESIDENCE FOR CHANA ORLOFF PARIS, FRANCE

'He plays a role,' said Le Corbusier of his mentor, Auguste Perret. '"*Je fais du béton armé* [I build with concrete]." He proclaims it to every visitor to his studio.... That resounded throughout his office like a flag in the wind or a salvo of a cannon.'[1]

Perret was one of the great architectural experimentalists of his age. Like Frank Lloyd Wright in America, Perret worked on the cusp of two very different ages, guiding architecture and design from one realm to the next, and busily laying the foundations for the Modernist movement and a new architecture. These foundations were laid in concrete, of course, as Perret sought to take this raw, messy and prosaic material and transform it into something poetic and refined, almost literally paving the way for a liberation of form, while still guided – in many respects – by classical principles.

Perret tested his methods and his engineering on many industrial buildings, particularly in the years following the First World War. But soon he was applying his ideas to public institutions, ecclesiastical buildings and private homes. In particular, he found himself designing an avant-garde series of studio-residences for some of the artists and intellectuals with whom he often associated in Paris. These included the painters Georges Braque and Cassandre, and also the sculptor Chana Orloff.

Orloff was a much respected Jewish figurative artist. She was born in the Ukraine but her family fled the pogroms of the region when she was eighteen and moved to Palestine (Orloff was to maintain links with Israel throughout her life, often returning there to work and exhibit). In 1910 she moved to Paris and began to establish herself as a sculptor, becoming friends with painters such as Modigliani and Soutine. Her subjects included Picasso, Matisse and architects Pierre Chareau and Auguste Perret.

Orloff's husband Ary Justman, a poet, died in an influenza epidemic only a few years after their marriage, leaving her to bring up their son alone. Nevertheless, by the 1920s her reputation was secure and she was exhibiting in France and abroad. By this time, the idea of a bespoke studio-residence had become fashionable, and Orloff commissioned a building from Perret. It was to be constructed

in the area west of Parc Montsouris, in the 14th arrondissement – a locale that attracted many artists, including Braque.

The concrete-framed building that Perret designed – with a uniform, cubist façade that some have compared to the outline of a face – was modest in size, at around 670 square feet (62 sq m). It was built on three levels. The ground floor, with large, practical entrance doorways, fed into a spacious double-height gallery, with a mezzanine level looking down into it, illuminated by large banks of glass. At the top of the house, on the third level, there is an apartment with a living room to the front, top-lit by a large skylight, and two bedrooms to the rear.

The concrete frame, with its semi-industrial aesthetic, helped liberate the internal spaces to provide the large expanses required for gallery and studio. It is a simple backdrop of a kind that has now become familiar from contemporary galleries and studios, but at the time it was somewhat revolutionary, especially when coupled with the building's distinctly Modernist, abstract façade.

For Orloff, the studio and gallery were not always a safe haven. When the Germans invaded Paris during the Second World War, she had to flee to Switzerland. She returned to find her studio damaged and many of her works destroyed. The dreadful experience provided some inspiration for post-war works, examining the theme of the returning exile, and thereafter her studio-residence provided a constant base as she moved between France and Israel until her death in 1968.

1 Quoted by Karla Britton in *Auguste Perret*, Phaidon, 2001.

Biography

AUGUSTE PERRET (1874–1954)

The son of a builder, Perret was born at Ixelles in Belgium. In 1881 his family moved to Paris. Perret studied at the École des Beaux-Arts under Julien Guadet. With his brothers Gustave and Claude, he formed a practice in 1905, known as Perret Frères. Perret was one of the early pioneers of the sophisticated use of reinforced concrete and was an eminent forebear of the Modernist movement, although also influenced by Neo-Classicism. Le Corbusier worked in Perret's atelier as an apprentice from 1908 to 1909.

Key Buildings

Rue Franklin Apartment Building Paris, France, 1904
Church of Notre-Dame Raincy, France, 1923
Studio-Residence for Georges Braque Paris, France, 1929
Museé des Travaux Publiques Paris, France, 1948
Church of St Joseph (and reconstruction works) Le Havre, France, 1956

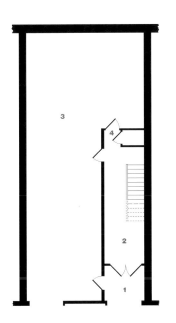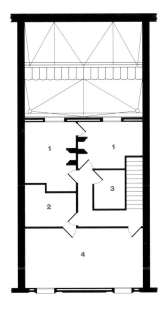

far left: ground floor

1 entrance
2 workshop
3 studio
4 w.c.

left: upper level

1 bedroom
2 kitchen
3 bathroom
4 loft/gallery

ELIEL SAARINEN

SAARINEN HOUSE CRANBROOK, BLOOMFIELD HILLS, MICHIGAN, USA

The contribution of Eliel Saarinen to architecture and design was broad and threefold. As an architect and furniture designer, he created a series of powerful and innovative buildings and interiors in his native Finland before moving to the States in the 1920s. As a mentor and partner, he worked with his son, Eero Saarinen, who was to become one of the great Modernist pioneers of American mid-century design. Thirdly, he was a great educator, helping to set up the Cranbrook Academy of Art – inspired by the example of the Bauhaus School – as a multidisciplinary centre of American design excellence (Florence Knoll, Harry Bertoia, and Charles and Ray Eames were among its alumni).

As chief architect of the Cranbrook Educational Community and head of the Department of Architecture and Urban Design, Saarinen also designed two high schools, a science institute and a museum of art under the patronage of philanthropist and newspaper publisher George G. Booth, whose son Saarinen had taught. It was at Cranbrook that Saarinen also created for himself and his family an extraordinary home.

Like Greene & Greene's Gamble House (see pp. 52–55) or Mackintosh's Hill House (see pp. 40–43), the Saarinen House was a cohesive and complete architectural and design vision – a *Gesamtkunstwerk*. The house forms part of the 315-acre (127 hectare) Cranbrook campus, and was designed to be intimately connected to the working life of the academy, where Saarinen's wife, Loja, a textile designer, also founded and ran the Department of Weaving and Textile Design.

The building was a fusion of Arts and Crafts and Art Deco influences, while also blending Eliel Saarinen's talents with Loja's textile designs, and even work by the young Eero in parts of the house. The exteriors of the two-storey, U-shaped, red-brick building fall very much within the Arts and Crafts tradition, with the two rear wings protecting a courtyard created as an outdoor room. Yet inside, the interiors are decidedly Deco of the most adventurous kind.

Key living spaces are to the front of the house, with the generous living room providing the main entertaining space off the front hallway. To the rear, one wing of the house is devoted to a covered porch. The other houses a long, vaulted studio – a multifunctional space

The Arts and Crafts outline of the Cranbrook house is softened by the creepers and greenery that have wrapped around it. The projecting studio and covered porch at the back help to frame a courtyard enclave, which many principal rooms rely on for light and a calming aspect.

that served as a working area for both Eliel and Loja Saarinen, but could also be cleared for receptions and parties when more space was required than the living room allowed.

The Saarinens asked 20-year-old Eero to design much of the furniture in the upstairs master bedroom. The adjoining bathroom is a streamlined hymn to hygiene and Deco styling.

In many ways, the house was the spiritual centrepoint of Cranbrook, and it was home to the Saarinens until the early 1950s, when it became the quarters of a sequence of subsequent Cranbrook Academy presidents. In the early 1990s the building was fully restored and opened to visitors.

The Saarinen House successfully embodies a fusion of not just Arts and Crafts and Deco themes, but also Finnish traditionalism and a highly innovative approach to spatial and structural order. As such, it is a clear precursor of the Modern movement to come, as well as an exemplar for the young Eero Saarinen. Now shrouded in a green envelope of creepers and planting, the Saarinen House shows itself to have been a truly harmonious family affair.

Biography

ELIEL SAARINEN (1873–1950)

Born in Finland, Saarinen studied fine art and architecture. In the early years of the twentieth century, he worked with Herman Gesellius and Armas Lindgren, designing a series of major works in and around Helsinki, including the railway station. He also worked in furniture design. In 1923 he emigrated to the United States, where he was joined by his wife and two children. He helped to establish the Cranbrook Academy of Art, of which he became president in 1932. In later years he collaborated with his son Eero Saarinen and designed a series of church buildings.

Key Buildings

Finnish Pavilion, World's Fair Paris, France, 1900
Pohjola Insurance Building Helsinki, Finland, 1901
Hvitträsk Kirkkonummi, Finland, 1902
Helsinki Central Railway Station Helsinki, Finland, 1909
National Museum of Finland Helsinki, Finland, 1910

ground floor
1 living room
2 dining room
3 pantry
4 kitchen
5 porch
6 studio

1930

SAARINEN HOUSE

A long rug by Loja Saarinen leads to the living-room fireplace. All the wooden furniture in the room was designed by Eliel Saarinen and made by Swedish cabinet-maker Tor Berglund on site at Cranbrook using walnut, ebony and rosewood. The adjoining book room provides a more intimate retreat, while the alcove at the end of the flexible studio forms a secondary sitting room. At the centre of the house is the octagonal dining room, a highly crafted wood-panelled space.

1931

It is hard to overstate the importance of Le Corbusier for twentieth-century architecture. For many he was the greatest architectural figure of the age, who reshaped our whole sense of form and space. He is credited with redefining architecture and articulating the Modern movement in both buildings and words, but he is also attacked for Modernism's occasional excesses in its most brutalist phases. He is, above all, the one Modernist architect that the world knows and recognizes, even if it does not always love him.

Villa Savoye, too, holds a privileged position within the Modernist canon and is richly familiar. It was the culmination of a series of Parisian villas developed by Le Corbusier in the 1920s, many in association with his cousin Pierre Jeanneret. Savoye was the ultimate expression of the 'purist' villa and embodied Le Corbusier's 'five points of a new architecture', with its supporting pilotis, roof garden, open plan, horizontal strip windows and free façade (several of these points were made possible by the use of a reinforced concrete structure that liberated the house from the need for supporting walls).

The intensely dynamic plan made use of a spiral staircase and sweeping internal access ramps. The imaginative circulation patterns, the contrasts of open and enclosed space, the dissolution of boundaries between outdoors and in, all create a rich sense of 'promenade', with a wealth of discoveries to be made as one moves through the building.

The house was commissioned by Pierre and Emilie Savoye, who lived in Paris and wanted a country home for weekends and holidays.

'This villa was constructed in the greatest simplicity,' wrote Le Corbusier, 'for clients who were quite without preconceptions, either old or new.'[1] Madame Savoye was, however, explicit in setting out a brief for the house that involved all the latest technology as well as the service and guest spaces needed for entertaining.

Le Corbusier described the house as a 'box in the air'. The pilotis structure raises the main living spaces into the crisp cube of the upper level, maximizing views of the landscape. The ramp that leads up through the house, complementing the staircase, continues from the first-floor roof garden to a modest upper level holding a solarium, partially shaded by those funnel-like curving walls.

Unfortunately, the house leaked and suffered from persistent damp, among a series of problems that soured architect/client relations. There was even talk of a lawsuit before the war interrupted everything and the house was abandoned. It sustained some damage in the war years and was threatened with demolition, but in 1964 it was listed as a historic monument.

Villa Savoye is, of course, so much more than a machine for living in. It is a highly sculpted artwork and an ergonomic, functional home. It is also a prototypical sacred space dedicated to a new way of living. 'One concern has been uppermost in my mind,' wrote Le Corbusier towards the end of his life. 'To make the family sacred, to make a temple of the family home.'[2]

1 Quoted in Jacques Sbriglio, *Le Corbusier: The Villa Savoye*, Birkhäuser, 2008.
2 From Le Corbusier, 'Mise au Point', in Jean Jenger, *Le Corbusier: Architect of a New Age*, Thames & Hudson, 1996.

Biography

LE CORBUSIER (CHARLES-ÉDOUARD JEANNERET-GRIS) (1887–1965)
Architect, artist, sculptor, furniture designer, writer and theorist, Le Corbusier was born in Switzerland and studied at the École d'Art in La Chaux-de-Fonds before going to Paris in 1908, where he worked with Auguste Perret. In 1912 he established his own practice in Switzerland and designed the Maison Blanche for his parents. He later relocated to Paris and adopted his *nom de plume*, derived from his great-grandfather, Lecorbésier ('raven'). Numerous projects of all kinds took him across the world, but he preferred to retreat to his simple cabin and studio in Roquebrune-Cap-Martin, where he died while swimming in the bay.

Key Buildings

Villa La Roche-Jeanneret Paris, France, 1925
Unité d'Habitation Marseilles, France, 1952
Chapel of Notre Dame du Haut Ronchamp, France, 1955
Dominican Monastery of Sainte Marie de la Tourette Eveux-sur-Abresle, France, 1960
Palace of Assembly Chandigarh, India, 1962

Villa Savoye – with its bold crisp outline, uniform slim pillars, banks of horizontal glazing and what appear to be giant funnels emerging from the roof line – is often considered the masterpiece of machine-age modernity.

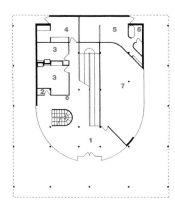

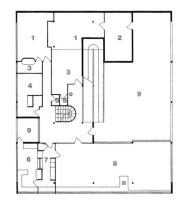

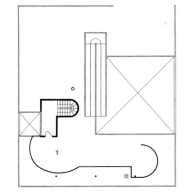

ground floor

1 entrance hall
2 w.c.
3 maid's room
4 laundry room
5 chauffeur's room
6 bathroom
7 garage

first floor

1 bedroom
2 boudoir
3 bathroom
4 guest room
5 w.c.
6 kitchen
7 pantry
8 salon
9 terrace

second floor

1 sun terrace

The 'purist' building contains integrated furniture and design work. The sculpted bathing area in the master bathroom has a fixed and tiled couch whose shape echoes Le Corbusier and Charlotte Perriand's famous recliner, designed around the same time.

1931

In the late 1920s Arne Jacobsen was looking to the future. Having – like Alvar Aalto – grown up in Finland, immersed in Scandinavian Neo-Classicism as well as the vernacular style, he ultimately realized that he needed to break with the past and develop a new kind of style. By the mid-1920s, he was travelling to Paris and Berlin, drawing in the influence of Le Corbusier, Walter Gropius and Ludwig Mies van der Rohe, and starting to move away from the more traditional leanings of his earliest work.

In 1929 he built the first of a series of houses for himself – a crisp, flat-roofed building at Charlottenlund. This was followed by an exercise in futurism, the 'House of the Future' – a circular building, complete with rooftop heli-pad, designed in collaboration with Fleming Lassen for an exhibition in Copenhagen. This house was one of the first Jacobsen projects in which he had had the opportunity to design a building from top to bottom, including interiors and furnishings. It was not only a highly experimental prototype, but also attention-grabbing. Its success led to a series of new commissions for the young architect.

Chief among these commissions was the Rothenborg House at Klampenborg, a small coastal community some miles to the north of Copenhagen, overlooking the sound separating Denmark from Sweden. The lawyer Max Rothenborg and his wife asked Jacobsen for a large villa, embracing the vision of a new type of Scandinavian modernity.

Here Jacobsen was to explore the idea of the *Gesamtkunstwerk*, the complete work of art. Mostly associated with the Arts and Crafts movement and with designers such as Greene & Greene, the concept of formulating a harmonious building in which nearly every detail was architect-designed greatly appealed to Jacobsen. With the Rothenborg House, as with later buildings, he turned his talents to furniture, lighting and other elements within a totally cohesive, self-informing project.

For the building itself, Jacobsen designed a complex structure, shifting between single- and double-storey sections within a broadly U-shaped plan. The house opens up to the gardens at the front and incorporates a series of terraces – both on raised ground level and up on the roof – which give it a strong sense of connection with the landscape. At the same time the surrounding woodland provides a green backdrop to the distinctive white building. To the rear, the house is more discreet and private: the U-shape is formed by garaging to one side and a two-storey section to the other, together forming a type of cradle around the entrance area and driveway.

The Rothenborg House was the most important building of Jacobsen's early years. It allowed him the creative freedom to explore the future within a highly sophisticated and considered design. It also allowed him to develop ideas about the relationship between structure and surroundings – house, interiors and landscape – that would lead to other commissions and would be taken further in later projects.

The house, having been somewhat altered over the years, was recently sensitively restored. It now encapsulates a vibrant push towards a new Modernist aesthetic – a combination of beautifully sculpted lines and functional precision – and it marks Jacobsen out as one of the movement's most accomplished figures: a pioneer of Scandinavian design, whose furniture still brings a 'contemporary' touch to the twenty-first-century home.

ARNE JACOBSEN (1902–1971)

A multi-faceted and multi-talented designer, Jacobsen preferred to take a holistic approach to projects, creating harmonious interiors, textiles and furniture for many of his architectural projects. He trained as a stonemason and then studied in Copenhagen, where he worked with Paul Holsøe before founding his own practice. His organic, sensitive version of Scandinavian Modernism has proved perennially popular, especially his iconic furniture designs.

Key Buildings

Bellavista Housing Project Klampenborg, Denmark, 1934

Søholm Housing I & II Klampenborg, Denmark, 1951/55

Royal SAS Hotel & Air Terminal Vesterbro, Copenhagen, Denmark, 1960

St Catherine's College Oxford, England, 1966

Danish National Bank Copenhagen, Denmark, 1971

The fluid, interconnecting, principal living spaces are housed in a single storey that opens out onto the secluded terrace and gardens. Services and bedrooms are in the double-height section of the building. Recent restoration works have respected the integrity of the house while updating fittings and furniture in a contemporary style.

A backdrop of green woodland perfectly offsets the crisp white sculpted exterior. The roof deck and terraces – complete with outdoor fireplace – create an easy, natural relationship between indoor and out. The main entrance is in the more enclosed area of the building, partly enfolded by two sections of the house to one side and the garage to the other.

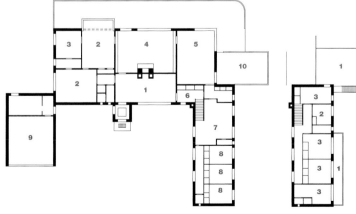

far left: ground floor

1 hall
2 bedroom
3 bathroom
4 living room
5 dining room
6 closet
7 kitchen
8 servant's room
9 garage
10 winter garden

raised ground level

1 balcony/terrace
2 bathroom
3 living area

left: basement

1 fuel storage
2 cellar
3 wine cellar
4 pantry
5 larder
6 laundry room
7 laundry drying room

1933

ROBERT MALLET-STEVENS

VILLA NOAILLES HYÈRES, PROVENCE, FRANCE

The villa that transformed the career of Robert Mallet-Stevens was a grand stroke of fortune for a young architect who had built little and was best known for his film sets. The Vicomte and Vicomtesse de Noailles' first choice of architect was Ludwig Mies van der Rohe, who declared himself too busy. The Noailles also considered Le Corbusier. 'We then asked the opinion of Mr Metman, director of the Musée des Arts Décoratifs and an old friend of both our families…' wrote the Vicomte. 'He did not hesitate, saying that when the museum had given exhibitions of modern architecture, the only one who seemed to him to have any taste or imagination was Mallet-Stevens.'[1]

In the beginning, the commission for a holiday villa in the south of France seemed relatively modest – a five-bedroomed home to be built on a parcel of land gifted by the Vicomte's mother. But the Villa Noailles became a legendary project, which ultimately lasted a decade, as the house was extended again and again to create a compound of around sixty rooms.

The Noailles were fascinating clients, standing at the forefront of the French avant-garde and counting among their circle a host of painters, sculptors and film-makers, who often stayed at the estate for months on end (Man Ray even made a film there, *Les Mystères du Château du Dé*).

The villa occupied a hillside spot, dominated by the ruins of an old château. Mallet-Stevens designed a pebble-dashed, Deco-influenced villa around the ruins, with a series of terraces and balconies facing south. But the initial construction was barely complete before the Noailles requested additional bedrooms, followed by other phases which added a swimming pool, gym and squash court, radically enlarging the complex.

The Vicomte said of Mallet-Stevens: 'We liked each other. He drew up plans which we approved of. To be quite frank, I found he had imaginative qualities but a little too much taste for the unexpected.'[2] Mallet-Stevens's 'Cubist château' proved career-defining and placed him at the heart of a richly creative hub. After the villa's inception in 1923, other commissions followed, including a luxury house for the couturier Paul Poiret.

The villa was requisitioned during the war and suffered some damage. Recently it has undergone restoration and is now a centre for the arts. It remains a glowing example of 1920s Deco architecture and a monument to the extraordinary lives of its creators.

1 Quoted in Dominique Deshoulières et al (eds), *Rob Mallet-Stevens: Architecte*, Archives d'Architecture Moderne, 1981.
2 Ibid.

Biography

ROBERT MALLET-STEVENS (1886–1945)

Born in Paris, Mallet-Stevens came from a family of
wealthy art collectors. He studied at the École Spéciale
d'Architecture in Paris and initially worked in film-set
design and interior design before expanding into
architecture. Influenced by the Art Deco style and
working chiefly in reinforced concrete, he made his
mark on Paris with five houses at Rue Mallet-Stevens.
His reputation was somewhat undermined by his own
request that all his archives be destroyed upon his
death, but he is now recognized as one of France's
most influential twentieth-century architects.

Key Buildings

Villa Paul Poiret Mézy-sur-Seine, France, 1924
Rue Mallet-Stevens Paris, France, 1927
Villa Cavrois Croix, France, 1932
Maison Barillet Paris, France, 1932
Passy Fire Station Paris, France, 1935

1   entrance
2   glass roof
3   second dining room
4   first dining room
5   reading room
6   hall
7   pink salon
8   vicomte's bedroom
9   vicomtesse's bedroom
10 guest room
11 gymnasium
12 swimming pool
13 *galerie d'actualité*
14 squash court
15 *sautoir*
16 vaulted rooms
17 cubist garden

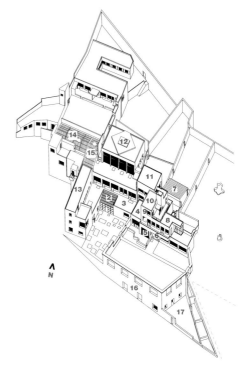

N

1933

VILLA NOAILLES

The Noailles were keen to establish their villa as a kind of laboratory of art and design. Working closely with Mallet-Stevens, they commissioned Cubist-inspired gardens from Gabriel Guévrékian, as well as an open-air room and furniture from Pierre Chareau, sculptures from Giacometti and Henri Laurens, and stained-glass windows from Joël and Jan Martel.

Berthold Lubetkin was always fascinated by the potential of architecture to change people's lives. Like fellow émigrés such as Serge Chermayeff and Erich Mendelsohn, he arrived in Britain in the 1930s with a wealth of rich experience behind him and a breadth of influences and education. He believed that Modernist buildings could foster wellbeing and improve health and social cohesion; at the same time he was obsessed with the structural possibilities offered by a new wave of architectural engineering. His views were reinforced by time spent working with Auguste Perret in Paris and by his discovery of the work of Le Corbusier.

For all Lubetkin's housing projects – including the luxurious Highpoint developments in London's Highgate, where he secured a penthouse for himself – it is his impact on zoos that really captured the public imagination. With engineer Ove Arup, who collaborated on many projects with Lubetkin and his Tecton practice, Lubetkin famously designed the much-loved Penguin Pool at London Zoo, with its wonderfully fluid, sinuous, concrete walkways.

Lubetkin went on to design, among other buildings, zoo structures at Whipsnade and Dudley, as though testing out ideas and themes that would later be applied on a far larger scale. His zoo buildings were highly popular and brought his work to a wide audience. These projects also afforded him a degree of artistic freedom that would be so curtailed in the post-war years, when the bureaucracy and small-minded conservatism that surrounded many of his later commissions forced him into retreat.

While working at Whipsnade, Lubetkin began developing a bungalow, or 'dacha', for himself and his family, just on the edge of the zoo estate. As with his Highpoint penthouse, Lubetkin could use this modest weekend retreat, and the sense of freedom it embodied, to develop his ideas without compromise. 'When one is one's own client,' he pointed out, 'one can sing one's own song.'[1]

On a dramatic hilltop site, he carved out a small plateau and positioned the house – also known as 'Hillfield' – to make the most of the countryside views over the valley below. The main living room overlooks this landscape, as does a small veranda, cantilevered outwards from the front façade. A linear T-shaped plan, with bedrooms positioned to the rear, is subverted by a curving arm which envelops the entrance area and creates a sun trap, also softening the overall outline of the building. Rather like the spiral staircases at Highpoint and elsewhere, these moulded counterpoints to the strict linear geometry of the overall design suggest Lubetkin's early passion for sculpture.

Lubetkin also experimented at the bungalow with a number of innovations that were developed further in later work. In particular, there was the shadow gap – that slight sense of separation between house and ground that gives the impression of a floating wall, and thus a light, floating structure. There was also the idea of the tapering corridor, here leading to the bedrooms, creating a wedge-shaped pattern with natural closure rather than a dead-end wall. In addition, colour was used to great effect in the original building, in the form of bolts of red and blue.

Lubetkin built another bungalow nearby – 'Bungalow B', or 'Holly Frindle' – for Ida Mann. Essentially a more compact variant on the original house, it suggested the potential for reproducing a simply but elegantly conceived Modernist dacha of modest scale. Recent restoration work by Mike Davies and Rogers Stirk Harbour has resuscitated both houses.

Lubetkin did not use his bungalow for long, passing it on to a friend. But his modest country home packed many strong ideas into a small building. Sadly, it has taken time for it to be appreciated, and adulation came too late for the architect, only now regarded as one of the masters of English Modernism.

1 Quoted in Malcolm Reading and Peter Coe, *Lubetkin and Tecton*, Triangle Architectural Publishing, 1992.

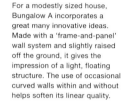

For a modestly sized house, Bungalow A incorporates a great many innovative ideas. Made with a 'frame-and-panel' wall system and slightly raised off the ground, it gives the impression of a light, floating structure. The use of occasional curved walls within and without helps soften its linear quality.

Biography

BERTHOLD LUBETKIN (1901–1990)

Born in Georgia, Lubetkin studied at an art school in Moscow just after the Russian Revolution. He continued his studies in Berlin and then in Paris. In 1931 he moved to London and a year later co-founded Tecton. His series of zoo buildings were followed by the Highpoint buildings. Post-war work in social housing projects followed, but Lubetkin became bitterly disillusioned by British conservatism and retreated from architecture.

Key Buildings

Penguin Pool, London Zoo Regent's Park, London, England, 1934
Highpoint I/Highpoint II Highgate, London, England, 1935/38
Dudley Zoo Dudley, West Midlands, England, 1937
Finsbury Health Centre Finsbury, London, England, 1938

The hilltop site was landscaped before construction of the house to create a platform. The veranda becomes a central feature – complete with outdoor fireplace – from which to appreciate the commanding views. The strength of the exterior spaces and the relationship between indoor and out is perhaps more reminiscent of Californian Modernism than of 1930s English architecture.

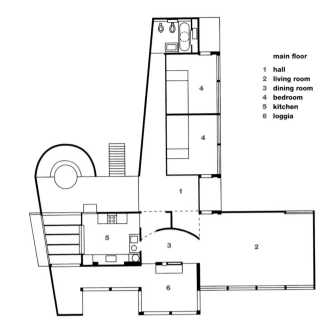

main floor

1. hall
2. living room
3. dining room
4. bedroom
5. kitchen
6. loggia

Eltham Palace is a flamboyant, opulent house for the most flamboyant and opulent of clients. Here, Sir Stephen and Virginia Courtauld created a combination of old and new, plus something in between, with interiors threaded through with luxurious Art Deco detailing and the very latest in home technology. It is one of the most impressive Deco statements in London and fascinates with its extraordinary narrative.

Stephen Courtauld drew his fortune from the family textile business, but his own business and personal interests were highly varied. These included the Ealing Film Studios, orchid breeding and adventure travel. He sponsored the British Arctic Expedition, was awarded the Military Cross in the First World War and was part of an expedition that successfully ascended the Innominata ridge of Mont Blanc.

Courtauld had a distinctly reserved persona, but his wife was outgoing and highly sophisticated (she even had a snake tattoo). The daughter of Italo-Hungarian parents, with a failed marriage to an Italian aristocrat behind her, she was very aware of the latest fashions and styles. Together, the Courtaulds were a high-society couple, and in the 1930s they commissioned an exceptional building to suit their privileged lifestyle.

From the reign of Edward II to Charles I, Eltham Palace had been a royal household. Henry VIII grew up here, and originally the site was larger than Hampton Court. After the Civil War, however, the palace gradually fell into ruin, and the Great Hall was used as a barn during the estate's sojourn as a farm. By the time the Courtaulds acquired the site in 1933, the Great Hall was the only key building left – one that was to be restored and converted into a dramatic music room serving the new palace.

The Courtaulds commissioned John Seely and Paul Paget to design a lavish new house around the existing site, using the Great Hall as the tip of one arm of a U-shaped building, with a vast entrance area at the meeting of the two wings. Seeking to integrate the existing hall, Seely & Paget designed the exteriors in a 'Wrenaissance' style, partly inspired by Sir Christopher Wren's work at Hampton Court but distinctly 'contemporary' in its pattern and plan. Inside, the new house was undoubtedly cutting-edge, with its sleek, sophisticated lines and clean, unfettered beauty. It is a striking combination, this juxtaposition of Edward IV's fifteenth-century Great Hall, the imposing hybrid exteriors and the ocean-liner modernity of the lavish spaces within.

The interiors were the result of a collaboration between the architects, clients and interior designers, and made for a truly palatial twentieth-century home, with every convenience from centrally piped music to internal telephones to underfloor heating and an integrated vacuum cleaning system with sockets throughout.

The stunning entrance hall, topped with a glass dome, was the work of Swedish designer Rolf Engströmer, who commissioned Jerk Werkmäster to create the marquetry in the maple panels. Other key spaces were the work of society decorator Peter Malacrida, who designed the dining room and Virginia's bedroom and bathroom.

With lacquered doors by Narini, rugs by Marion Dorn, and much in the way of integrated Deco features and furniture, preserving the simple, sweeping lines of the interiors, the house is a hymn to sophisticated luxury. Even the Courtaulds' pet lemur, Mah-Jongg, was housed in splendour within a bespoke heated cage complete with jungle murals.

Surrounded by 19 acres (over 7.5 hectares) of landscaped, moated gardens, Eltham Palace is a mesmerizing reinvention of a historic site. A powerful hybrid, it draws its authority not so much from without as from within, crowned by the swirling entrance hall that conjures up a defining image of the Deco style and – with its spirit of pre-war optimism – the exuberant shift into a sumptuous but modern way of living.

The 'Wrenaissance' style of Eltham Palace's exterior is unusual, but does little to suggest the dramatic modernity within. The pieces of furniture in the extraordinary entrance hall are reproductions of the original, bespoke designs by Rolf Engströmer.

Biographies

JOHN SEELY (1900–1963) & PAUL PAGET (1901–1985)
Seely and Paget met at Trinity College, Cambridge, and formed a practice in 1926. Seely later became Lord Mottistone, and the pair's society connections helped source their early commissions. Later, they specialized in ecclesiastical architecture, particularly reconstructing war-damaged London churches. Paget ultimately became chief surveyor at St Paul's Cathedral.

Key Buildings

Chapel of the Venerable Bede Durham, County Durham, England, 1939
St Mary's Church Islington, London, England, 1955
The Grand Priory Church of the Order of St John
Clerkenwell, London, England, 1958
All Hallows-by-the-Tower, St Andrew's Church
Holborn, London, England, 1961

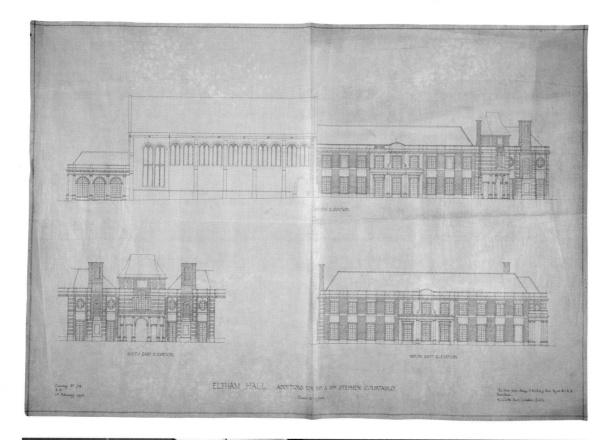

Bespoke marquetry panels by Jerk Werkmäster stand either side of the front door, bathed in light from the overhead cupola and the elongated glass window above the doorway. Many other bespoke elements carry the theme of refined Deco luxury through the house, including the stunning bedroom and bathroom by Peter Malacrida and the lacquered doors by Narini.

GIUSEPPE TERRAGNI

VILLA BIANCA SEVESO, LOMBARDY, ITALY

Giuseppe Terragni's career was tragically short, but rich in content. His working life lasted only sixteen years, even this being interrupted by the war, before being cut down by it. Much has been made of his associations with Mussolini's regime and the naïvety with which he chose to link himself, through his architectural work, with the fascist state. But much has also been made of his brilliance and originality, particularly in his residential work, and recently his reputation has been through a period of reassessment that has sought to take a broad and apolitical view of the achievements that placed him at the forefront of the Italian Modernist movement.

Much of Terragni's work was centred on Milan and on Como, where he based his practice. Between these two cities lies the small town of Seveso – the Terragni family's homeland and the place where he built a house for his cousin, Angelo Terragni. The Villa Bianca was named not for its colour, as the stucco of the house was originally painted a pale pink, but for Angelo Terragni's beloved lost daughter.

The house shares certain characteristics with Terragni's Casa del Floricoltore, a house built around the same time for florist Amedeo Bianchi in nearby Rebbio. Raised on pilotis, this design took the idea of the flat-roofed Modernist rectangle and pulled it and cut into the form, with entrance ramps added and a raised porch looking out over the landscape. Some of these ideas were explored further at Villa Bianca, although the overall impression is one of greater solidity and mass within a simpler and more pleasing composition and outline.

In some ways, this is a house of two very different faces. To the front, Terragni created a long, raised terrace leading to a central entrance hall; the dining room to one side pushes out from the main outline of the house, framed by a light external banded structure with the outline of a large portico. To the rear, Terragni experimented with a ramp entrance, as at Casa del Floricoltore, but here leading up to the raised ground floor and the central hall.

The upper level holds the three bedrooms and a semi-enclosed terrace sitting within the outline of the house, which functions as an indoor/outdoor room and viewing platform, and also holds steps leading up to a big roof garden with a partial sun-shade canopy that cantilevers out at points from the main body of the house.

The more one looks at the outline and formation of Villa Bianca, the more one recognizes the dexterity of its compositional arrangements. This concrete and brick structure is much more than a Modernist box, bringing, as it does, a wealth of ideas to the notion of the family home.

At Villa Bianca one sees several of the devices that appear in many contemporary Neo-Modernist European homes – the long, horizontal window bands, the floating canopy and especially the raised indoor/outdoor veranda contained within the outline of the building. Looking at such homes, one cannot help but note a debt to Terragni and the vibrant quality of his Italian houses.

Biography

GIUSEPPE TERRAGNI (1904–1943)

Born into a family of builders, Terragni studied architecture at the Milan Polytechnic and was a founding member of the 'Gruppo 7' – a group of Italian Rationalist architects. In 1927 he formed a practice in Como with his brother Attilio, an engineer. He became associated with the totalitarian architecture of Mussolini's fascist movement before being called to the army. Having served on the Russian front, he returned home and died at his fiancée's house in Como.

Key Buildings

Novocomum Apartment Buildings Como, Italy, 1929
Casa del Fascio/Casa del Popolo Como, Italy, 1936
Casa del Floricoltore/Casa Amedeo Bianchi Rebbio, Italy, 1937
Antonio Sant'Elia Nursery School Como, Italy, 1937
Casa del Fascio/Casa del Popolo Lissone, Italy, 1939

ground floor

1 terrace
2 hall
3 dining room
4 living room
5 ramp
6 utility room
7 kitchen

first floor

1 bedroom
2 bathroom
3 study
4 terrace

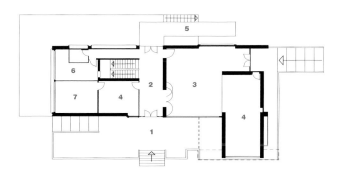

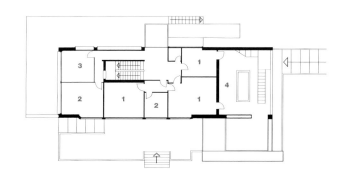

1938

SERGE CHERMAYEFF

BENTLEY WOOD HALLAND, EAST SUSSEX, ENGLAND

The house at Bentley Wood forms an important and dramatic chapter within an extraordinary and cinematic life story. Serge Chermayeff – designer, architect, painter, writer – was a true 'renaissance man' in many respects. Blessed with prodigious creativity and powers of original thought, he found himself moving across continents and from one profession to another. Bentley Wood was a highly significant and deeply personal project for him, but it almost finished him and ultimately helped to propel his life in yet another new direction.

Chermayeff's vision for Bentley Wood was startlingly sophisticated and – within the English context, at least – way ahead of its time. It was an experimental project; a testing ground for Chermayeff's Modernist-inspired ambitions. With its jarrah timber frame and red cedar cladding, together with its emphasis on linking inside and out, it seems more the kind of house one associates with post-war California than with the soft, rolling landscape of Sussex.

Chermayeff bought a generous slice of land totalling just over 80 acres (over 32 hectares) in the mid-1930s, around the highpoint of his intensely creative partnership with Erich Mendelsohn, crowned by the great success of their De La Warr Pavilion in Bexhill. Here at Bentley Wood, Chermayeff wanted to create a country retreat for himself and his family, with plans that were originally somewhat larger than the six-bedroomed house that was finally built.

The first planning application and appeal were refused, but a revised scheme was approved in 1937, by which time Chermayeff

had spent some time at Bentley Wood, reconsidering the site and working on some initial landscaping. Timber was always going to be the material, and arguably the choice had some suitably vernacular flavour, but the execution was to be powerfully innovative.

The two-storey house shows great sensitivity to site and landscape, with the relationship between the building and the surroundings intimately considered. The large living room on the ground floor, with space on the plan for a grand piano, leads out to a large terrace via sliding glass doors, which enable a seamless transition between inside and out. Chermayeff also worked with landscape designer Christopher Tunnard to create an integrated approach to the gardens (the design once led the eye to a carefully positioned and specially commissioned Henry Moore sculpture, now at the Tate). Upstairs, a row of bedrooms accesses a long balcony, with views out across the South Downs.

Garaging and service spaces to the rear of the main house create an L-shaped plan, cradling the driveway and entrance. Inside, the house was deeply refined and luxurious – 'a Rolls Royce of a house', as one commentator put it. Piped music and concealed heating were among the amenities, along with push-button bell pushes and switchboard systems in the bedrooms, bespoke drinks cabinets and other integrated designs. Artworks included pieces by John Piper, Ben Nicholson and Pablo Picasso.

The sophistication of both architecture and interiors makes this Chermayeff's most striking, original and influential solo project. Yet it was one that also contributed to a financial implosion which saw Chermayeff selling the house just a year after its completion and setting sail for the United States, to begin a new life as a teacher.

This was a shocking ending to a brief but brilliant architectural career in England, supplemented by later work as an academic and commentator. Bentley Wood continued to attract attention for its rigour, discipline, vitality and great sensitivity, presenting the soft, sensual face of Modernism allied to a gracious and luxurious way of living. While Chermayeff may not be as much of a household name today as the Californian post-war pioneers, his work at Bentley Wood was just as groundbreaking and extraordinary, while his life story made for pure Hollywood.

SERGE CHERMAYEFF (1900–1996)
Born in Chechnya, Chermayeff was educated in England and embarked on early careers as a dancer and journalist. He co-directed the Modern Design Studio of furniture company Waring & Gillow before moving into interior design, stage design and then architecture. From 1933 to 1936 Chermayeff worked in partnership with Erich Mendelsohn, with the De La Warr Pavilion in East Sussex chief among their projects. In 1940 Chermayeff emigrated to the United States and began a new and distinguished career as a teacher and writer, while also pursuing his work as a painter.

Key Buildings

Shann House Rugby, Warwickshire, England, 1934
De La Warr Pavilion (with Erich Mendelsohn) Bexhill-on-Sea, East Sussex, England, 1935
64 Old Church Street (with Erich Mendelsohn) Chelsea, London, England, 1935
Gilbey Offices Camden, London, England, 1937
ICI Dyestuffs Offices Blackley, Manchester, England, 1938

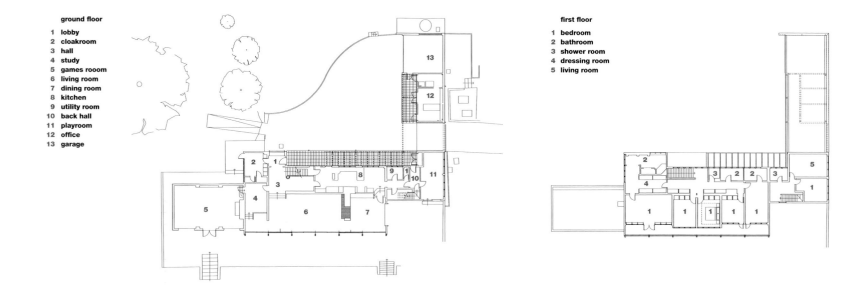

ground floor

1 lobby
2 cloakroom
3 hall
4 study
5 games rooom
6 living room
7 dining room
8 kitchen
9 utility room
10 back hall
11 playroom
12 office
13 garage

first floor

1 bedroom
2 bathroom
3 shower room
4 dressing room
5 living room

The relationship between
interiors, gardens and setting
is carefully considered and fluid,
with terraces, balconies and
glazing promoting a sense of
connection to the verdant rural
landscape.

WALTER GROPIUS

GROPIUS HOUSE LINCOLN, MASSACHUSETTS, USA

The term 'International Style' caused Walter Gropius some irritation. Its intimation of the defeat of local context and regional vernacular was at odds with the Modernist master's own sensitivity to landscape, surroundings and history. While Gropius's house in Lincoln is widely held up as one of the great exemplars of International Style – and of Modernism itself – it is also a highly contextual building, designed specifically for its site and very different from, for instance, the houses he built for himself and the other Bauhaus masters in Germany in the 1920s.

Gropius House successfully exemplifies the key Bauhaus and Modernist principles, whereby design and beauty follow on from function and practicality, and intelligent engineering and industrial materials allow freedom of floor plan, fluidity and openness to landscape, as well as a calming, minimal aesthetic. At the same time, however, Gropius was adamant that this was to be an American building, a New England building, bound into its position and culture, complete with fly-screened terrace, timber frame, white clapboard walls and brick chimney.

'When I built my first house in the USA,' he wrote, 'I made it a point to absorb into my own conception those features of the New England architectural tradition that I still found alive and adequate. The fusion of the regional spirit with a contemporary approach to design produced a house that I would never have built in Europe with its entirely different climatic, technical and psychological background.'[1]

Gropius had arrived in America in 1937, after three post-Bauhaus years in England. He became director of the Department of Architecture at Harvard University, working alongside his Bauhaus partner Marcel Breuer for a number of years, both in teaching and practice. Philanthropic landowner Mrs James Storrow gave him a small budget and a beautiful 4-acre (1.6 hectare) site near Walden Pond, about half an hour from the Harvard campus.

For the construction of his two-storey house, Gropius picked a position on top of a modest hill, in the middle of an orchard. He took careful account not only of the site, framing glorious views across woodland landscape, but also of the wishes of his wife and adopted daughter (he had in 1920 divorced his first wife Alma Mahler, widow of Gustav). While drawing in vernacular flavours, the house was distinctively modern and avant-garde, with its flat roof, cubic form and angular entrance canopy. Inside, the ground-floor layout was fluid: the living room and dining room were largely open-plan, and a study was separated off to one side by a wall of glass bricks. Enough space was squeezed into the 2,300 square foot (213 sq m) building for maid's quarters to the other side of the stairwell.

Upstairs, Gropius provided three bedrooms and a dressing room. He also devoted part of the floor plan to a large roof deck, with views out across the countryside. Thoughtfully, he added a separate spiral staircase so that his daughter and her friends could easily access this 'tree house' from outside and use it independently of the main building.

Gropius House, and the house that Marcel Breuer built for himself next door, were incubators for design ideas suited to the New England setting. They led to a number of house commissions in the years that followed, before the two giants of design parted company.

For Gropius and his family it was a tailored and beloved home. As his daughter, Ati Gropius Johansen, later wrote: 'No problem during the design process was ignored or simply given over to a stale or inefficient solution. No opportunity to appreciate beauty, whether natural or man-made, was ever missed.

'To many of my friends, when I was growing up, this house was … a curiosity. They loved to visit our unusual house which was so different from theirs. I remember a woman who once asked my mother, "Mrs Gropius, don't you find it terribly exhausting to always live so far ahead of your time?"'[2]

1 Walter Gropius, 'Scope of Total Architecture', 1956.
2 Ati Gropius Johansen, writing in *Historic New England Magazine*, Fall 2003.

While drawing upon Modernist principles, this innovative house ties itself to the region and setting by using a timber frame coated in timber cladding, painted white. Traditional aspects are reinvented or reinterpreted, such as the dramatic covered entrance and the integrated, partially covered roof terrace, also accessible via the outer spiral staircase.

Biography

WALTER GROPIUS (1883–1969)

Founder of the Bauhaus and author of some of the key buildings of the Modernist canon, Gropius was one of the most influential and widely respected architects of the twentieth century. Born in Berlin, he initially worked with Peter Behrens before co-founding his own practice and later becoming director of the Bauhaus School. He left Germany for Britain in 1934 and then moved to the States. In 1945 he founded The Architects' Collaborative (TAC) practice, responsible for the Pan Am building and others.

Key Buildings

Fagus Factory Alfeld an der Leine, Germany, 1925
Bauhaus Building Dessau, Germany, 1926
Houses for the Bauhaus Masters Dessau, Germany, 1926
Graduate Center, Harvard University Cambridge, Massachusetts, USA, 1950
Pan Am/MetLife Building New York, New York, USA, 1963

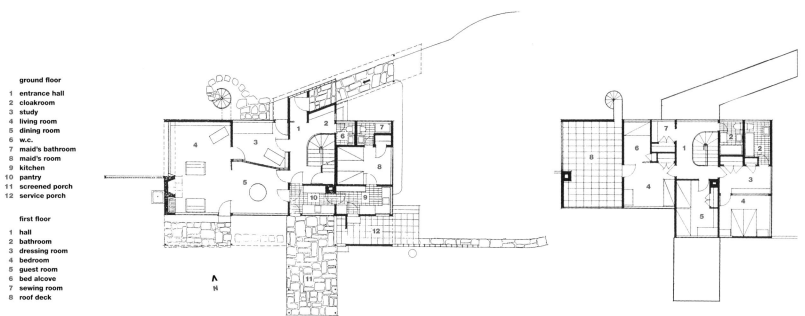

ground floor

1 entrance hall
2 cloakroom
3 study
4 living room
5 dining room
6 w.c.
7 maid's bathroom
8 maid's room
9 kitchen
10 pantry
11 screened porch
12 service porch

first floor

1 hall
2 bathroom
3 dressing room
4 bedroom
5 guest room
6 bed alcove
7 sewing room
8 roof deck

Situated at the heart of historic and elegant Hampstead village, 66 Frognal is a reminder of how controversial – as well as pioneering – Modernist architecture could be in England. Nikolaus Pevsner called the house 'a minor masterpiece', while politician Sir Robert Tasker labelled it 'one of the greatest pieces of vandalism ever perpetuated [*sic*] in London'.

Its architect was Colin Lucas. His future partners at Connell, Ward & Lucas – Amyas Connell and Basil Ward – had experience of a conservative backlash from press and public even with their first design, High and Over, one of the first European-influenced Modernist country houses in England. But this was truly a case of the shock of the new and, by the time Lucas joined the architectural practice, there seemed to be a familiar pattern of outraged reaction to groundbreaking work.

With 66 Frognal, Lucas walked right into the firing line, along with his client, solicitor Geoffrey Walford. Lucas had long been fascinated by the possibilities of concrete construction and, with his Noah's House project in Buckinghamshire, had created one of the first fully concrete buildings in the UK. Walford was drawn to Connell, Ward & Lucas for their innovative work with form, structure and mass, but also for their understanding of reinforced concrete, which he believed would give him the fluid, flexible living spaces and long, unbroken windows that were of such importance to him.

Work began on the drawings for a three-storey family house for Walford, his wife Ursula and her four children before a site was secured, but the plans remained largely unchanged once the corner plot in Hampstead had been found. Essentially, the house presents its private face – a cubist composition of rectangular slabs and strip windows – to the street, while dramatically opening itself up to the rear garden. Here, at the back, the house is enlivened not only by vast windows, especially to the living room, but by a series of terraces and balconies, which – rather like Eileen Gray's E-1027 (see p. 17) – suggest the stacked decks of an ocean liner.

The planning battle to get this avant-garde house approved was fraught and aroused an increasingly bitter public debate (among the chief objectors was local architect Reginald Blomfield, who owned a Neo-Classical villa nearby). The plans went to the London County Council and the case then went before the High

Court. Walford represented himself, and ultimately won full permission for his house.

'I can only regret', he wrote, 'that this building should offend the susceptibilities of some people and be beyond the comprehension of others. To me it has proved to be an experience of intense interest and delight.'[1]

Later additions to the cutting-edge design included a swimming pool at ground-floor level and extra living space on the top floor, incorporating what had been the roof terrace. Recent restoration works by Avanti Architects have further updated the house, while respecting as far as possible Lucas's original designs.

66 Frognal was a hard-fought, hard-won house, conceived in a climate of English conservatism, which can still be a frustrating force. Only recently, many of the same arguments were revisited in an application to demolish Greenside, another of Lucas's buildings. Yet in pushing on with Frognal, the architect and his client not only created a pioneering London building but significantly advanced the cause of British Modernism.

1 Writing in the *Journal of the Royal Institute of British Architects*, reproduced in Dennis Sharp and Sally Rendel, *Connell, Ward & Lucas: Modern Movement Architects in England 1929–1939*, Frances Lincoln, 2008.

COLIN LUCAS (1906–1984)

Lucas came from an avant-garde family, his mother a composer and his father an inventor and entrepreneur. He studied at Cambridge and then worked as an architect-builder experimenting with concrete construction. He joined forces with a practice already established by New Zealanders Amyas Connell and Basil Ward in 1934. The practice was short-lived, lasting only five years, but was highly influential. With a series of innovative houses, the trio established a powerful variant on International Style. Lucas later joined the London County Council Architect's Department.

Key Buildings

CONNELL, WARD & LUCAS

High and Over Amersham, Buckinghamshire, England, 1931

New Farm/The White House Haslemere, Surrey, England, 1933

Noah's House Bourne End, Buckinghamshire, England, 1934

The Concrete House Westbury-on-Trym, Bristol, England, 1935

Greenside/Bracken Virginia Water, Surrey, England, 1936

The building is raised up on pilotis, which provided covered garaging space below. The ground-floor level originally contained just the entrance hall and a playroom, although later a swimming pool was added. The main living accommodation is on the second level, with service spaces facing the street and the large living room and master bedroom looking out into the garden to the rear.

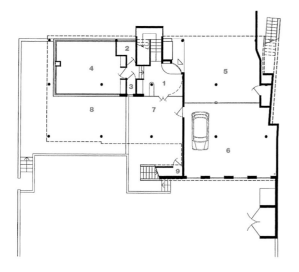

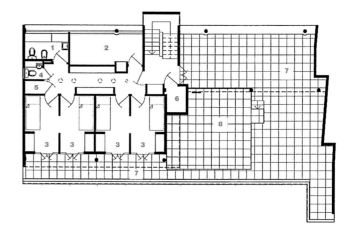

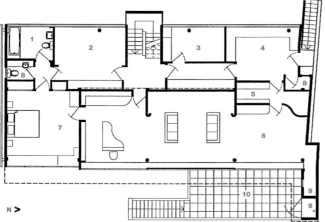

N >

above left: ground floor

1 hall
2 shower room/w.c.
3 cloakroom
4 playroom
5 carport
6 garage
7 upper terrace
8 lower terrace
9 storeroom

left: first floor

1 bathroom
2 dressing room
3 maid's room
4 kitchen
5 pantry
6 living room
7 bedroom
8 w.c.
9 storeroom
10 terrace

above: second floor

1 bathroom
2 bedsit room
3 bedroom
4 w.c.
5 shower room
6 plant
7 terrace
8 raised terrace

The third storey originally held four modest children's bedrooms, which could be rearranged via sliding partition walls. The large roof terrace alongside was partially eroded by the later addition of extra living space. The balconies and occasional porthole windows at the rear are reminiscent of the stacked decks of ocean liners.

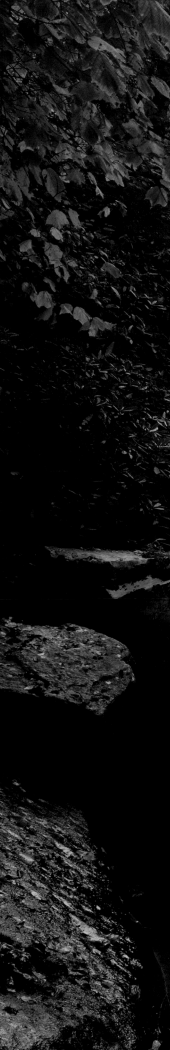

1939

FRANK LLOYD WRIGHT

FALLINGWATER   BEAR RUN, PENNSYLVANIA, USA

In an increasingly environmentally conscious age, the intellectual and aesthetic grandeur of Fallingwater, tied to its intrinsic sensitivity to nature and landscape, assumes even greater importance than ever. Along with Le Corbusier's Villa Savoye (see pp. 64–69), Fallingwater is surely one of the most influential houses of the twentieth century, and arguably the best loved and most widely applauded. While Corbusier can be a divisive figure, Wright and Fallingwater draw in almost universal praise.

'When organic architecture is properly carried out, no landscape is ever outraged by it but is always developed by it,' said Wright. 'The good building makes the landscape more beautiful than it was before the building was built.' At Fallingwater, Wright's romantic attentiveness to site and landscape – and his ideas of an organic, holistic architecture – reached new heights.

The commission for Fallingwater came when Wright was well into his sixties and already an architectural statesman, with plenty enough autobiographical drama to fill a Hollywood film script. But Fallingwater became an exquisite drama of its own, and a high point of Wright's third and final phase.

This building was to be lent extraordinary power by the surrounding landscape, with the house cantilevered out over the stream that gives Bear Run its name. Here, in the Appalachian mountains, the cosmopolitan and well-travelled Pittsburgh department store owner Edgar J. Kaufmann had a holiday cabin; the family loved to swim and play in the stream and its waterfalls, leading down to the Youghiogheny River. Kaufmann's son became an architectural student of Wright's, through the Taliesen Fellowship scheme, and introduced his father to Wright's work.

'He loved the site where the house was built and liked to listen to the waterfall,' said Wright. 'So that was the prime motive in the design. I think you can hear the waterfall when you look at the design. At least it's there and he lives intimately with the thing he loved.'[1]

Wright designed a three-storey building amid the woods, with a series of moulded concrete terraces – plus a section of the living room – pushing out towards and over the stream below. Vertical elements are formed of locally quarried stone, while the rocks of the site itself at times push into the building,

reinforcing the intimate sense of connection between the artificial and the natural worlds.

The ground floor holds a large, open-plan living room and dining area, flagged with stone, leading directly out to terraces to east and west, with the waters of the stream flowing below. The floor above holds three bedrooms and further terracing, with the third and final storey devoted to a study and gallery at the summit of the house. A separate guest lodge and carport were built a short distance away.

Kaufmann's own concerns about the viability of the siting and the structural athletics with the relatively new and untested reinforced concrete led to strains between architect and client and the use of further steelwork that arguably compromised the structure with extra weight, rather than enhancing it. This compounded structural problems that required considerable repair works (these were carried out in 2002 by the Western Pennsylvania Conservancy, to whom Kaufmann's son had donated the property in 1963). But both architect and client were very much in accord with the principles of blending the house into the site, and Wright successfully integrated into the design additional features that had been requested by Kaufmann, such as the plunge pool by the stream.

There is no doubting the overwhelming success of this organic approach, nor the way in which the banks of glazing, the positioning of the house and the use of the many terraces help to create a platform for appreciating the sounds and seasons of the setting.

Fallingwater, in many respects, represents a highly refined riposte to the idea of the Neo-Classical country house that Wright found so offensive in its bold imposition on the landscape. Here, by contrast, Wright created a building that works with nature and respects it absolutely, offering an enduring source of inspiration to advocates of a sustainable, sensitive architecture which also embraces beauty, character, texture, craft, sophistication and daring.

1 Quoted in Patrick J. Meehan (ed.), *The Master Architect: Conversations with Frank Lloyd Wright*, Wiley, 1984.

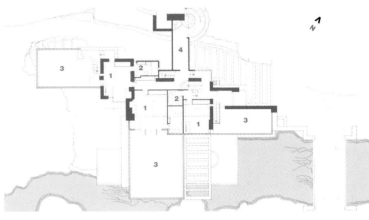

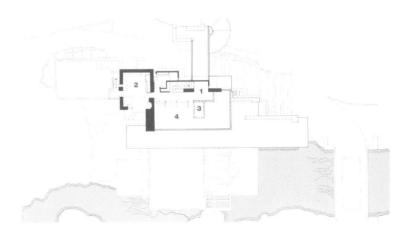

top: ground floor	centre: first floor	above: second floor
1 entrance	1 bedroom	1 bed area
2 cloakroom	2 bathroom	2 study
3 dining area	3 terrace	3 planter
4 main room	4 bridge	4 terrace
5 staff room		
6 kitchen		
7 terrace		
8 fountain pool		
9 plunge pool		
10 bridge		

ALVAR AALTO

VILLA MAIREA NOORMARKKU, FINLAND

In the case of Villa Mairea, an unusually close and productive relationship between a pioneering architect and enlightened clients led to an extraordinary building. The summer house that Alvar Aalto designed for friends and patrons Maire and Harry Gullichsen was an experimental building embodying Aalto's love of both modernity and nature. The villa combines a rich range of influences – Modernist, American and Finnish vernacular, Japanese, and a nod to Frank Lloyd Wright's Fallingwater (see pp. 100–105) – within an organic work of art. It is one of Aalto's most inspirational buildings, presenting a warmer, softer version of Modernism allied to natural materials and a woodland setting, while also marking his move away from the limits of functionalism.

By the time the Gullichsens commissioned Villa Mairea, architect and clients had already known one another for a number of years. Maire, the daughter of Finnish industrialist Valter Ahlström, had a love of painting and collected modern art; her husband was head of the Ahlström timber and paper company, having taken it over after the death of Maire's father. Both husband and wife held progressive views and a passion not just for art but also for social reform. They had already become patrons of Aalto with commissions for a number of Ahlström projects, but they were also his business partners, having co-founded with Nils-Gustav Hahl the furniture company Artek, which distributed many of Aalto's designs.

In the late 1930s, the Gullichsens asked Aalto to design a summer villa at Noormarkku, sited on the rural Ahlström estate. The house was to be a luxury home for a new, forward-thinking generation. The Gullichsens offered Aalto creative freedom but in fact they collaborated closely, discussing every detail as the villa evolved and making significant changes to the designs even while the house was under construction.

As with so many of Aalto's projects, the attention to detail is intense. He specially designed many elements, ranging from door handles to tea trolley (this went on to become one of Artek's most famous designs). His wife, Aino Marsio-Aalto, also assisted in the design of sections of the interior, including the kitchen.

Set atop a modest hill and surrounded by pine forest, Villa Mairea is like a sophisticated tree house in the woods. It is a two-storey, L-shaped structure, but its floor plan does not do justice to the wealth of spatial ingenuity within the house and the way that the linear quality of the building's essential outline is softened and moulded at every turn by curving walls, sinuous supporting columns and plentiful elemental materials – timber, brick, stone, concrete, steel and glass.

While the house was radical, it was also specifically tailored to the Gullichsens' needs, integrating Maire's love of art and Harry's desire for a library where he could hold business meetings. The sliding windows and adaptable partitions also made the house flexible. Its sculpted aspect is further accentuated by the kidney-shaped pool cradled within the courtyard, partially formed by the shape of the house.

'All the evidence indicates that they egged each other on to ever more ambitious ideas as the work progressed,' their son, Kristian Gullichsen, has written. 'The final result clearly reflects the architect's reading of his clients' personalities.'[1]

Ultimately, Villa Mairea has become one of the twentieth century's most famous houses, highly in tune with current thinking on the integration of architecture and natural environment. It is a house which reminds us all that the Modernist home can be a place of great beauty, pleasure, comfort and sensuality, as well as an ode to function and geometry.

1 Writing in Juhani Pallasmaa (ed.), *Alvar Aalto: Villa Mairea 1938–39*, Alvar Aalto Foundation, 1998.

Biography

ALVAR AALTO (1898–1976)

Aalto grew up in a rural part of Finland, valuing the beauty of the natural world around him. He studied in Helsinki and established his own practice in 1923, marrying architect Aino Marsio the following year. Initially influenced by Neo-Classicism, Aalto was increasingly drawn to Modernism and developed his own unique style, drawing upon his love of nature, natural materials and an ergonomic, humanist approach to architecture. Famously, his talents as a designer were applied to furniture and many other areas, as well as to architecture.

Key Buildings

Paimio Tuberculosis Sanitorium Paimio, Finland, 1933
Viipuri Library Viipuri, Finland, 1935
Experimental House Muuratsalo Island, Finland, 1953
National Pensions Institute Helsinki, Finland, 1956
Church of the Three Crosses Vuoksenniska, Finland, 1958

ground floor

1 main entrance
2 entrance hall
3 w.c.
4 cloakroom
5 library
6 music room
7 winter garden
8 living room
9 dining room
10 office
11 kitchen
12 staff room
13 sauna
14 dressing room
15 swimming pool

first floor

1 studio
2 upper hall with fireplace
3 bedroom
4 children's hall/playroom
5 guest room
6 terrace

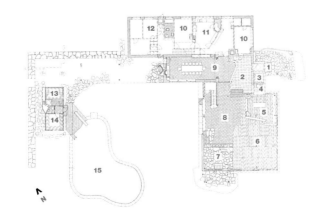

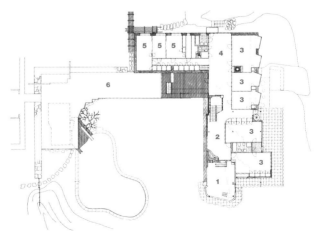

RICHARD NEUTRA

KAUFMANN HOUSE PALM SPRINGS, CALIFORNIA, USA

It was Richard Neutra, together with his friend and colleague Rudolph Schindler, who pioneered the idea of intimately connecting the modern Californian home to the natural world. For Neutra, buildings were not simply architectural spaces but also places of wellbeing that could make a great impact on our physical and psychological states. He moved well beyond practical ergonomics in creating structures that were beautiful, carefully integrated both inside and out, and tailored to his clients' needs.

Ultimately, the development of this key relationship between interior and exterior has become one of the great lessons handed down by the Californian Modernists, especially Neutra. Such fluidity is seen in many seminal Neutra houses, including the Lovell Health House of 1929, the first steel-framed, single-family house in America, and the Miller House in Palm Springs. But its most famous expression is surely to be seen at the Kaufmann House.

Here, the flexibility of the design masterfully erodes the barriers between indoor and outdoor living, allowing for natural cross-ventilation and easy through-flow to garden and pool. Seamlessly combining Neutra's appreciation of Japanese architecture, the box-like adobe pueblos of the desert, and International Style, the Kaufmann House is a compound of pavilions in pinwheel formation, connected by spider-leg breezeways and slim intersections.

Within the main living room the glass wall retracts completely, in revolutionary fashion, allowing direct access to the terrace and pool. Neutra effectively skirts restrictions on second storeys by creating a semi-enclosed roof terrace, christened the 'gloriette', with a protective screen of aluminium louvres to protect the space from the sun. The gloriette, complete with fireplace and dumb waiter, becomes a secondary living room, with extraordinary views of the rugged landscape and the towering San Jacinto mountains.

The 3,200 square foot (300 sq m) house was commissioned by the department store magnate Edgar J. Kaufmann, who had asked Frank Lloyd Wright to build Fallingwater for him a decade before (see pp. 100–105). To be located on a site next door to Albert Frey's Raymond Loewy House, this new home was intended as a winter retreat, to be used only in the month of January when the days are hot but the nights

very cool. Neutra designed the house of stone, steel and glass around a central fireplace and sandstone chimney, from which the spokes of his pinwheel design then radiate, including clearly defined zones for guests and staff at a remove from the main living accommodation.

'A well-designed house affects all our senses,' said Neutra, and here he integrated planting and a water garden in the breezeway between the living room and guest quarters. Radiant heating was installed in the floors, walls and ceilings to cope with the cool evenings, and the underfloor system extended out to the terraces around the pool to encourage outdoor use even at night.

The Kaufmann House represented the fruits of a close collaboration between architect and client, with the highly bespoke building moulded to the owners' requirements. A sympathetic restoration in the 1990s by architects Marmol Radziner has returned the building as closely as possible to Neutra and Kaufmann's original vision.

Within this powerful desert setting, the Kaufmann House is a truly alluring and evocative presence. It conjures up many conversations about contextuality, being sleekly manmade and groundbreaking on the one hand, yet so carefully positioned and bound into the environment on the other. Back in the 1940s, Neutra suggested that wellbeing, respect for nature and environmental consciousness could be allied to sophisticated modernity. It is a lesson we are now relearning in the twenty-first century.

Biography

RICHARD NEUTRA (1892–1970)

Neutra was born in Vienna and studied at Vienna Technical University, where Adolf Loos was a mentor, Otto Wagner an inspiration and Rudolph Schindler a friend. Neutra emigrated to the USA in 1923 and settled in Los Angeles. He worked briefly with Frank Lloyd Wright, and then with Schindler, before branching out on his own. His work famously embraced psychology as well as architecture, promoting principles of wellbeing and connections to the natural world.

Key Buildings

Lovell Health House Los Angeles, California, USA, 1929
Miller House Palm Springs, California, USA, 1937
Tremaine House Montecito, California, USA, 1948
Case Study House #20 Pacific Palisades, California, USA, 1948

Against the backdrop of mountains, desert and palm trees, the Kaufmann House is a compound of interconnected elements tied together by breezeways and junction points. With the crowning 'gloriette' roof terrace, and the main rooms – particularly the living room – linking to the gardens and pool terrace, this is the ultimate summer living space.

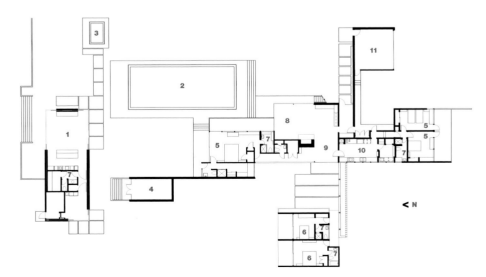

main floor

1 pool house
2 swimming pool
3 spa
4 utility room
5 bedroom
6 guest room
7 bathroom/w.c.
8 living area
9 dining area
10 kitchen
11 carport

< N

The picturesque town of New Canaan in Connecticut, with its easy train access to nearby New York City, became a centrepoint for pioneering Modernist architecture in the 1940s and '50s. Around eighty Modernist houses were built in the area, many of them designed by members of the 'Harvard Five' – Marcel Breuer and four of his former Harvard students, including Eliot Noyes, the first to arrive (he built his family house in 1947), and Philip Johnson, who created his famous Glass House here in 1949 (see pp. 126–131).

The house that Breuer designed for himself, his wife Constance and their young son was a very different building to the first home that he had created soon after his arrival in the States. Breuer House I was built next to Walter Gropius's house in Lincoln, Massachusetts, and on the same generous understanding with benefactor Helen Storrow (see p. 94). It was a modestly sized building, but with a dramatic double-height living room. It was also steeped in the style of the Bauhaus, though Breuer had begun to use natural materials such as stone.

Breuer House II was more ambitious in scope and scale, drawing to some extent on Breuer and Gropius's Chamberlain Cottage in Wayland, Massachusetts – a two-storey wooden box sitting on a fieldstone plinth on a hillside. In both buildings the timber-coated upper storey holds all the key living spaces, while its outline cantilevers beyond the supporting plinth, but in Breuer House II the design is dramatically elongated, with a projecting balcony to the front.

'In our modern houses,' said Breuer, 'the relationship to the landscape is a major planning element. There are two entirely different approaches, and both may solve a problem well: there is the house that sits on the ground and permits you to walk outside at any point, from any room…. And then there is the house on stilts, which is elevated above the surrounding landscape, almost like a camera on a tripod…. My own favourite solution is the one that combines these two opposite sensations: the hillside house.'[1]

Breuer, who was in South America during construction, was faced with a number of technical issues that he deputized to Noyes and Harry Seidler, then working with Breuer, to resolve. In particular, the cantilevered balcony suspended by marine steel cables proved difficult to engineer and a supporting wall was later added underneath, somewhat spoiling the floating effect. Later, too, an extension was added to the rear of the house.

A few years later Breuer and his family moved to a bungalow in New Canaan, but the hillside house remained a photogenic and powerful idea, later seen in Breuer's Caesar Cottage, Stillman House III, Alwarth/Starkey House, and others. Hugely influential as a tutor, mentor, furniture designer and architect, Breuer remains an iconic figure and Breuer House II – in its original conception, at least – one of his most satisfying designs.

1 Quoted in Joachim Driller, *Breuer Houses*, Phaidon, 2000.

Biography

MARCEL BREUER (1902–1981)

Born in Hungary, Breuer studied in Vienna and then at the Bauhaus, later becoming a master at the Bauhaus in Dessau, where he worked on the interiors of the masters' houses and began developing his furniture designs, including the Wassily chair. In 1928 he launched an architectural practice in Berlin. In 1935 he emigrated to London, working in partnership with F. R. S. Yorke and developing furniture designs at Isokon. Two years later, Walter Gropius offered him a teaching post at Harvard; the two also collaborated on a number of architectural projects. In 1941 Breuer founded his own practice, which from 1946 onwards was based in New York. Breuer was one of the key Modernist pioneers, with his work as a furniture designer just as respected as his architecture.

Key Buildings

Doldertal Apartments Zurich, Switzerland, 1936
Breuer House I Lincoln, Massachusetts, USA, 1939
UNESCO Headquarters (with Pier Luigi Nervi & Bernard Zehrfuss) Paris, France, 1958
Whitney Museum of American Art (with Hamilton P. Smith) New York, New York, USA, 1966

Marcel Breuer was drawn to the idea of a raised, long house, sitting on the brow of a hill, with an elevated position offering views of the green setting.

main floor

1 living room
2 dining room
3 kitchen
4 utility room
5 bathroom
6 bedroom

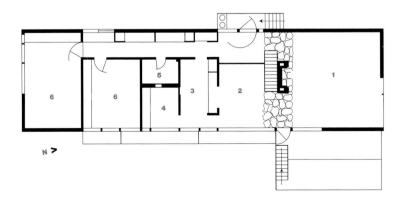

N >

1948

GEOFFREY BAWA

LUNUGANGA DEDDUWA, BENTOTA, SRI LANKA

The estate, buildings and gardens of Lunuganga represented the work of a lifetime for Geoffrey Bawa. He bought the overgrown rubber plantation in 1948, having recently abandoned his first career in law but before studying architecture. Lunuganga then became a project that spanned the decades and is now widely regarded as Bawa's masterpiece.

In 1948 the estate consisted of 25 acres (10 hectares) of plantation and a rather ordinary bungalow. Lunuganga – or 'salt river' – fired Bawa's imagination but initial work was limited, interrupted by his retraining as an architect in London. From the late 1950s to the 1990s, however, Lunuganga gradually evolved as a home, a garden and a landscape, informing and

inspiring other projects, while being shaped by a unique and all-encompassing vision.

Bawa's work, while distinctly rooted in Sri Lanka, is a synthesis of a broad range of ideas, movements and traditions. This can be seen clearly at Lunuganga, where ideas for an Italianate Renaissance garden blend with vernacular principles, with architecture informed by the spirit of Asia but also by a spectrum of European influences, including selected tenets of Modernism, all driven by the impetus of sophisticated, original thought.

Above all – and perhaps this is Bawa's greatest strength – his work was born of a very particular response to the site itself and to nature, the climate and the shifting seasons.

One can also see this in projects such as the Polontawala Estate Bungalow (1965), where the vast boulders of the site are woven into the fabric and structure of the house itself, even helping to support the roof; or at Kandalama Hotel (1994), where the vegetation has merged with the building in striking symbiosis.

The Lunuganga estate rests on two modest hills in a lush region of Sri Lanka bordered by the Dedduwa Lake and Bentota River, plantations, paddy fields and – a mile away – the Indian Ocean. It is a place of astonishing fertility and lush green countryside.

Architecturally, Bawa transformed the bungalow, leaving the shell of the existing house within a remastered building, complete

At Lunuganga, Geoffrey Bawa created a compound of sensitively conceived complementary structures, allied to a series of garden rooms and terraces, cradled by the carefully landscaped trees and vegetation of the cinnamon gardens-turned rubber plantation-turned tropical retreat.

with a series of terraces and verandas. In the 1960s and '70s, he then added a studio, pavilion and guest house, followed by further additions to the main house.

Throughout, architecture and garden have fed off each other, with vistas opened up, viewpoints created and points of reference revealed, including the temple of Katakuliya in the distance. Yet, so natural is the effect, so verdant the gardens, that visitors have imagined that Lunuganga is simply a product of nature and history, not the single vision of a masterful magus of landscape and buildings that tie into one another so solidly and completely – a true fusion of nature and design, for which Bawa will be remembered.

His work has gained renewed attention for its prescient understanding of sustainability and an environmental awareness not just of landscape, but of climate, too, maximizing natural ventilation and the relationship between outside and in. Just as importantly, however, Bawa's work was also focused on pleasure, comfort and beauty. No wonder, then, that Lunuganga is now run as a hotel as well as a centre for the arts.

Biography

GEOFFREY BAWA (1919–2003)
Born in Ceylon/Sri Lanka to Anglo-Asian parents, Bawa studied law at Cambridge, England. After the Second World War he returned to Colombo and practised law but soon tired of it. After a period of travelling, he went to London to study architecture at the Architectural Association. Upon qualifying in 1957, he returned to Sri Lanka, where he became the leading figure of 'tropical modernism' and created a series of houses, hotels and public buildings of extraordinary sensitivity to landscape and place.

Key Buildings

Ena de Silva House Colombo, Sri Lanka, 1962
Bawa House Colombo, Sri Lanka, 1969
Sri Lankan Parliament Building Kotte, Colombo, Sri Lanka, 1982
Kandalama Hotel Dambulla, Sri Lanka, 1994
Jayewardene House Mirissa, Sri Lanka, 1998

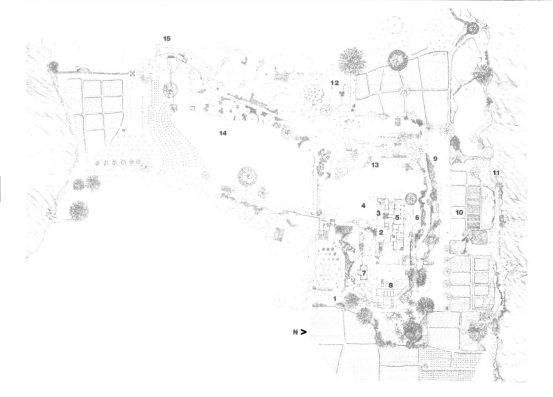

site plan

1   approach
2   entrance area and steps
3   south terrace and entrance to house
4   view towards cinnamon hill
5   house
6   north terrace
7   guest wing and pavilion
8   eastern terrace and galleries
9   cliff
10 broad walk
11 water gardens
12 field of jars
13 western terrace
14 cinnamon hill
15 the house on cinnamon hill

N >

The various buildings at Lunuganga are united by Bawa's cohesive approach and vocabulary, from the entrance to the 'Sandella', or Garden Room, where the architect liked to work.

1949

The setting of the Eames House is a very special one. The house is reached via a private track up in the hills of Pacific Palisades, a suburb of Los Angeles, and it overlooks Santa Monica and the ocean, whose constant rumble carries on the breeze. The house sits in a quiet glade – a meadow that Charles and Ray Eames fell in love with – where eucalyptus trees offer scent and shade. It is this location, as much as anything, that shaped this unique building, which is one of the great international prototypes for a largely prefabricated home, easily assembled from a kit of factory-produced parts.

Famously, the house was one of the brightest stars of the Case Study programme, the hugely influential series of experimental Californian houses commissioned by *Arts & Architecture* magazine and its editor, John Entenza. The Eameses had become closely involved with Entenza and his publication, and they supported the idea of a programme of houses that would serve as inspirational examples: contemporary homes that could – in theory – be both affordable and easily available in the post-war era through industrial methods of production.

Entenza himself bought a plot of land in Pacific Palisades, sectioning off one part for his own Case Study house and selling the other to Charles and Ray Eames. The designs for both houses – which were collaborations with friend and colleague Eero Saarinen – were first published in 1945. But, given the austerity of the post-war period and the difficulties of obtaining steelwork with which to frame the buildings, the years began to tick by.

During this time the Eameses were drawn constantly to the meadow. Their original design was for an L-shaped house and studio that stretched right into the glade, with the main living accommodation contained in a 'Bridge House' cantilevered across the site. But a chance encounter with a similar design by Ludwig Mies van der Rohe left Charles Eames concerned that his home might be regarded as derivative. He therefore radically reconfigured the building, working around the fact that much of the steelwork was already on order.

The resulting house was pushed back into an embankment on the edge of the meadow, and the excavated earth was used to create a landscaped mound to screen it from the single-storey Entenza House. A retaining wall 175 feet (53 m) long was put in place, and the house and studio were positioned in a single line, separated from each other by a modest courtyard. The steel frames went up in just a day and a half. The two-storey structures were then coated in a linear latticework of glazing, Cemesto boards and brightly painted sections to form a Modernist pattern that is sometimes compared to a Mondrian painting. The far end of the house opens up onto a dramatic veranda contained within the overall outline of the building frame, while a line of eucalyptus trees running parallel to the house softens the outline.

Inside, the house suggests a strong Japanese influence and contrasts a soaring double-height living room with more intimate and modest spaces. It also acts as a backdrop to an eccentric and eclectic range of collections and curios. The studio is partially double-height – incorporating a mezzanine – and served as the headquarters of the Eames office for many years until the couple outgrew the space.

For the Eameses, the house was a constant source of pleasure, often evolving and changing. For the rest of us, it has defined many crucial aspects of the contemporary Californian home, with its fluid relationship between inside and out, its sensitivity to light and setting, and its spatial richness. The Eames House also continues to be an exemplar for modular and industrial methods of design, proving that prefabrication techniques do not have to involve compromises or any loss of aesthetic and textural power.

Charles and Ray Eames's calm retreat within vibrant Pacific Palisades is protected and shaded by the eucalyptus trees that have grown to form a green screen. Through this, the Mondrian colours of the façade shine through.

CHARLES EAMES (1907–1978) & RAY EAMES (1912–1988)

The work of the Eameses, a husband-and-wife design partnership, encompassed architecture, furniture, graphics, textiles, exhibition design and film. They became best known for a small number of highly original houses and for their innovative ergonomic furniture in plywood, aluminium and fibreglass. Manufactured by Herman Miller, it was influential around the world.

Key Projects

LCW plywood chair Evans Products/Herman Miller, 1946

DAR chair Zenith Plastics/Herman Miller, 1948

Case Study House #9 (with Eero Saarinen) Pacific Palisades, California, USA, 1949

Max de Pree House Zeeland, Michigan, USA, 1954

670 lounge chair & 671 ottoman Herman Miller, 1956

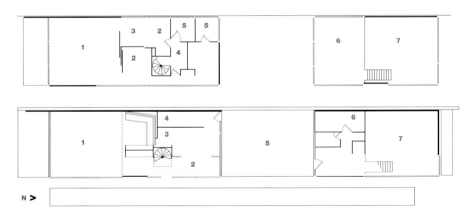

N >

top: first floor	above: ground floor
1 upper part of living room	1 living room
2 bedroom	2 dining room
3 dressing room	3 kitchen
4 hall	4 utility room
5 bathroom	5 courtyard
6 storage deck	6 dark room
7 upper part of studio	7 studio

The interplay between large
volumes and more intimate
spaces is striking. The
studio, with a mezzanine
level approached by
lightweight stairs, is a largely
double-height space, as is
the living room in the main
residence, across a modest
courtyard, with its eclectic
collection of books, furniture
and artwork.

1949

The Glass House is one of the great emblematic buildings of mid-century Modernism. Few buildings have proved so powerful, so provocative, and this one still has the ability to surprise us with its freshness. Indeed, it remains one of the most imitated buildings in the world – the ultimate glass box.

With his design, Philip Johnson created a peerless example of substance born out of simplicity and restraint. Sited on a promontory overlooking the subtly shaped landscape of trees and lake spread out below it, the house is as much a viewing platform as a home. It is a one-storey, open-plan, glass-sided belvedere, punctuated by a brick cylinder holding a small bathroom and services, and it has as its ever-changing 'walls' the countryside beyond.

The Glass House was, however, only one part, or even one room, of a steadily evolving campus of structures, serving – as Johnson put it – as a visual diary of his shifting approach to architecture. The Glass House was mirrored by the nearby Brick House, designed at the same time and serving as a guest house and service block. But where the steel-framed Glass House was open and transparent, the Brick House was enclosed and mysterious in purpose.

Johnson, together with his partner David Whitney, an art curator, was gradually able to extend his estate to 47 acres (19 hectares), and he also added a series of complementary buildings, sculptures and works of land art. New buildings included the subterranean Painting Gallery (1965), the Sculpture Gallery (1970) and a Library/Study (1980). In the water below the house, he also created an extraordinary visual illusion with his Lake Pavilion (1962), a classically inspired temple-like structure in half-scale. These additional 'rooms' allowed Johnson to expand his living and cultural space, while preserving the absolute integrity of the Glass House, which remained unchanged throughout.

Inside the house, Johnson subtly used furniture and rugs to divide the space into zones for sleeping, sitting and dining, but he avoided solid partitions. Much of the furniture was by Ludwig Mies van der Rohe and it is clear that Mies's work and architectural language were key influences on Johnson and the Glass House. Associates and one-time working partners on the landmark Seagram Building in New York, Johnson and Mies were working on the Glass House and Farnsworth

House (see pp. 136–141) at around the same time and, although Farnsworth was completed later, these two highly influential buildings clearly have many key similarities.

'I consider my own house,' said Johnson, 'not so much as a home (though it is that to me) as a clearing house of ideas which can filter down later, through my own work or that of others.'[1] Yet few of Johnson's later buildings, even within the context of his extraordinary estate, achieved the abstract purity of the Glass House.

Famously, he showed himself more than willing to continue to experiment stylistically, though his experiments with Postmodernism and classical references could prove controversial for those who found such power in the Bauhaus-influenced phase of his career. After his death in 2005, and that of Whitney a few months later, the Glass House and the estate passed to the National Trust for Historic Preservation. The beauty of Johnson's greatest and most personal achievement remains undiminished. It is still today a key reference point in the world of contemporary architecture.

1 Quoted in Stephen Fox et al, *The Architecture of Philip Johnson*, Bulfinch, 2002.

The Glass House makes the most of its sublime location. Privacy is no issue on the estate, so the building is open to the light and surrounding nature, changing with the shifting seasons.

Biography

PHILIP JOHNSON (1906–2005)
Born in Cleveland, Ohio, Johnson studied architecture at Harvard under Walter Gropius and Marcel Breuer. He then became director of the Department of Architecture at the Museum of Modern Art in New York. Labelled one of the 'Harvard Five', Johnson was an associate of Ludwig Mies van der Rohe, whose influence was clear upon Johnson's early work. Later buildings exhibited a far broader range of influences and styles.

Key Buildings

Robert C. Leonhardt House Lloyd's Neck, New York, USA, 1956
Seagram Building (with Ludwig Mies van der Rohe)
New York, New York, USA, 1958
New York State Pavilion, World's Fair Flushing Meadows-Corona Park, Queens, New York, USA, 1964
Crystal Cathedral Garden Grove, California, USA, 1980
AT&T Building/Sony Plaza New York, New York, USA, 1984

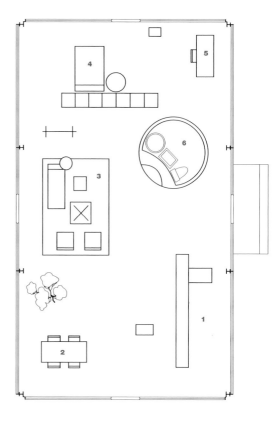

main floor

1 kitchen area
2 dining area
3 living area
4 sleeping area
5 study desk
6 bathroom

The interiors were designed as open-plan, though making use of furniture, rugs and low partitions to help delineate spaces according to function. Only the circular drum containing the shower room and other services offered privacy, though the nearby Brick House discreetly offered many essential domestic functions.

1950

When Harry Seidler arrived in Australia in 1948, he was not at all sure that he would be staying. In America he had studied and worked with the great Bauhaus exiles Walter Gropius, Marcel Breuer and Josef Albers, and on the way to Australia he had spent time working with Oscar Niemeyer in Brazil. After such adventures, post-war Sydney no doubt seemed provincial.

But Australia was an open book, which not only offered Seidler a new start with his family – exiled from Austria just before the war – but also an extraordinary venue for expressing his Modernist beliefs. He had been tempted to Sydney by his mother, Rose, who had offered him a commission to build his first house. With this building, Seidler would lay the foundation for his architectural philosophy, but he would also introduce Australia to a complete and rounded vision of modern, futuristic living.

Seidler found a 16-acre (6.5 hectare) plot at Wahroonga, on the edge of Sydney, opening out to stunning views of the Ku-ring-gai National Park. He brought with him the idea for a house that he had conceived in 1947, while working in Marcel Breuer's office in New York, and whose plan he had published in *Arts & Architecture* magazine. With minor changes and adaptations to site and position, the Rose Seidler House was essentially the same design.

At around 2,150 square feet (200 sq m), the house is tucked into the undulating topography, with the bulk of the building on one raised level, supported by steel columns and sandstone

walls, with garaging and an entrance zone positioned underneath. Raising the house makes the most of the views, while light is maximized by a generous use of glazing, especially to the front of the building, and by a terrace that indents the house's square outline and pushes natural sunlight deep into the main living spaces.

The timber-framed and clad building sits on a suspended concrete floor pad, while the house is connected back to the site by a number of radiating access routes. These include doorways to the higher ground level at one corner of the house and also a rampway extending from the terrace, the ramp later becoming something of a Seidler leitmotif.

Inside, the house has a fluid and highly flexible floor layout. Much of the key living space is open-plan, with bedrooms positioned to the front of the building, overlooking the main approach. Unusually for a first project, the level of detailing is extremely sophisticated and well considered. Seidler even designed some of the furniture himself, and also introduced pieces by Eames, Hardoy and Saarinen.

'There can be no more captive client than a mother,' said Seidler. 'Mother agreed to sell all her Viennese furniture, but refused to part with her elaborately decorated silver cutlery. Whenever I came to dinner, only the Russel Wright stainless steel flatware I brought from New York was allowed to be seen.'[1]

On the terrace, Seidler painted a large mural – echoing Le Corbusier's murals at his Unité de Camping in Cap Martin and elsewhere – using colour notes that pick up on the tones employed within the house itself. The whole comprises a totally cohesive statement of art, geometry, spatial theory, siting, texture, materials and more, all wrapped up in one house.

Later, Seidler added two more buildings for the family on the compound site and ultimately bequeathed the Rose Seidler House to the Historic Houses Trust. Of course, he went on to spend a lifetime in Australia, becoming the godfather of contemporary Antipodean architecture. His impact, however, partly born of the accomplished vision contained in this first house, spread far beyond his adopted country.

1 Quoted in Kenneth Frampton and Philip Drew, *Harry Seidler: Four Decades of Architecture*, Thames & Hudson, 1992.

Biography

HARRY SEIDLER (1923–2006)

Seidler fled his native Austria for England in 1938 after the Anschluss. He was then sent to Canada, where he studied architecture in Winnipeg. At Harvard he was taught by Bauhaus exile Walter Gropius, and later worked with or studied under Josef Albers, Alvar Aalto, Marcel Breuer and Oscar Niemeyer. He followed his family to Sydney, settling there and leading the introduction of Australian Modernism via houses, apartment buildings and other projects.

Raised up on pilotis, with an access ramp, integrated roof terrace and fluid floor plan, the Rose Seidler House conforms to many of the architectural ideals set out by Le Corbusier. The success of the house, however, derives not only from its mastery of Modernist principles, but the way in which it connects so fully and naturally to its site.

Key Buildings

Blues Point Tower McMahons Point, Sydney, New South Wales, Australia, 1962

Harry & Penelope Seidler House Killara, Sydney, New South Wales, Australia, 1967

Australia Square Tower Central Business District, Sydney, New South Wales, Australia, 1967

Waverley Civic Centre Waverley, Victoria, Australia, 1984

Berman House Joadja, New South Wales, Australia, 1999

The surrounding views are best appreciated from the roof terrace, with its discreet sun shading and bold murals. It also acts as a lightwell, introducing sunlight into the semi-open-plan living spaces.

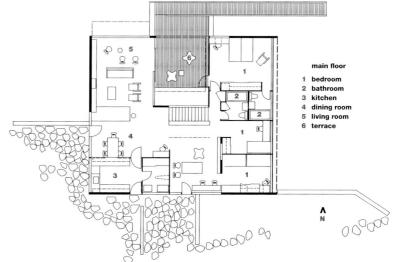

main floor

1 bedroom
2 bathroom
3 kitchen
4 dining room
5 living room
6 terrace

LUDWIG MIES VAN DER ROHE

FARNSWORTH HOUSE PLANO, ILLINOIS, USA

There is a profound irony to the fact that a house so widely seen as a key exemplar of the Modern movement – and International Style – should have been the cause of such a bitter rift between its architect and client. Ludwig Mies van der Rohe's Farnsworth House is a building of extraordinary originality and beauty, situated in a superb landscape, yet its genesis was troubling and greatly at odds with the serene purity of the finished house.

It was undoubtedly a radical structure for its time – essentially, a bespoke, single-roomed, steel-framed, glass pavilion opening out to the landscape. Mies, building on his design for the Barcelona Pavilion of 1929, and on ideas for a 'floating room' and an open, fluid 'free plan', created a house that was a revolutionary departure within any context, but especially within that of American home-building. The avant-garde ambition, aesthetic power and intellectual rigour behind the design have captured the imagination – and provoked debate – ever since.

The house was commissioned by Dr Edith Farnsworth, a Chicago-based kidney specialist, who wanted a weekend retreat of architectural importance. She bought a 7-acre (2.8 hectare) plot of land around 55 miles southwest of Chicago, parallel to the banks of the Fox River, near Plano. At the time, the site was still considered rural, with meadows amongst maples and other trees. From 1945 onwards, Mies developed a design for a one-storey house that would be raised up from the ground by just over 5 feet (1.5 m) to avoid flood risk. Designing along a loose brief that allowed him creative freedom, he also worked together with his client on the evolving plans.

The frame of the 1,500 square foot (140 sq m) house is created by a series of lightweight steel columns that support both the raised floor slab and the flat ceiling, allowing for floor-to-ceiling glass on all sides. Within the overall outline of the house, as much as a third is devoted to a large veranda leading to the entrance, while a secondary terrace runs parallel to the main building. Inside, the pavilion is conceived to be as open and fluid as possible, with largely free-standing units functioning less like solid divisions than like pieces of furniture. The house is a pavilion of monastic simplicity, with a 'core' unit holding kitchen and services, supplemented by a smaller wardrobe cabinet which helps section off the sleeping area.

Importantly, the house opens itself up to the environment and becomes – like Philip Johnson's Glass House (see pp. 126–131) – a frame for viewing the landscape. 'If you view nature through the glass walls of the Farnsworth House,' said Mies, 'it gains a more profound significance than if viewed from outside. That way more is said about nature – it becomes part of a larger whole.'[1]

Dr Farnsworth, however, declared that the house was impractical. While rumours of a short-lived romantic association with her architect further confuse the conflict, Farnsworth did publicly fall out with Mies over the spiralling costs of the building, and a lawsuit – which favoured Mies – underlined the seriousness of the breakdown. The two never met again.

Undoubtedly there were maintenance issues and the continued threat of flooding, which has caused considerable damage over the decades and has necessitated restoration. Dr Farnsworth nevertheless used the house until 1972, when it was sold, and later it became a historic site open to the public.

For Mies and his Modernist disciples, the house was pivotal. It created a prototypical floor plan of lightly zoned yet uninterrupted space, which fed into many later buildings and helped pioneer the shift to open-plan. More than that, it is a house and a pavilion that continues to feed into the collective consciousness, shaping the form and function of new generations of contemporary houses.

1 Quoted in Claire Zimmerman, *Mies van der Rohe*, Taschen, 2006.

The terrace and porch of Farnsworth House interconnect, creating a series of carefully contrived spaces that provide a graduated borderland between exterior and interior.

Biography

LUDWIG MIES VAN DER ROHE (1886–1969)
Born in Germany, Mies van der Rohe worked with Peter Behrens and others before establishing his own practice in Berlin in 1912. He was director of the Bauhaus for three years before its closure in 1933 and emigrated to the USA in 1938, later taking American citizenship. His 'less is more' houses, skyscrapers and furniture were all to have a huge impact, making him one of the most influential and pioneering architects and designers of the twentieth century.

Key Buildings

Barcelona Pavilion/Pavilion of German Representation Barcelona, Spain, 1929
Tugendhat House Brno, Czech Republic, 1930
Chicago Convention Hall Chicago, Illinois, USA, 1954
Seagram Building (with Philip Johnson) New York, New York, USA, 1958
Neue Nationalgalerie Berlin, Germany, 1968

main floor

1 terrace
2 porch
3 kitchen
4 shower room
5 bathroom
6 boiler room
7 fireplace
8 sitting area
9 dining area

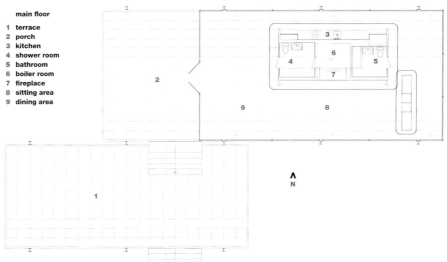

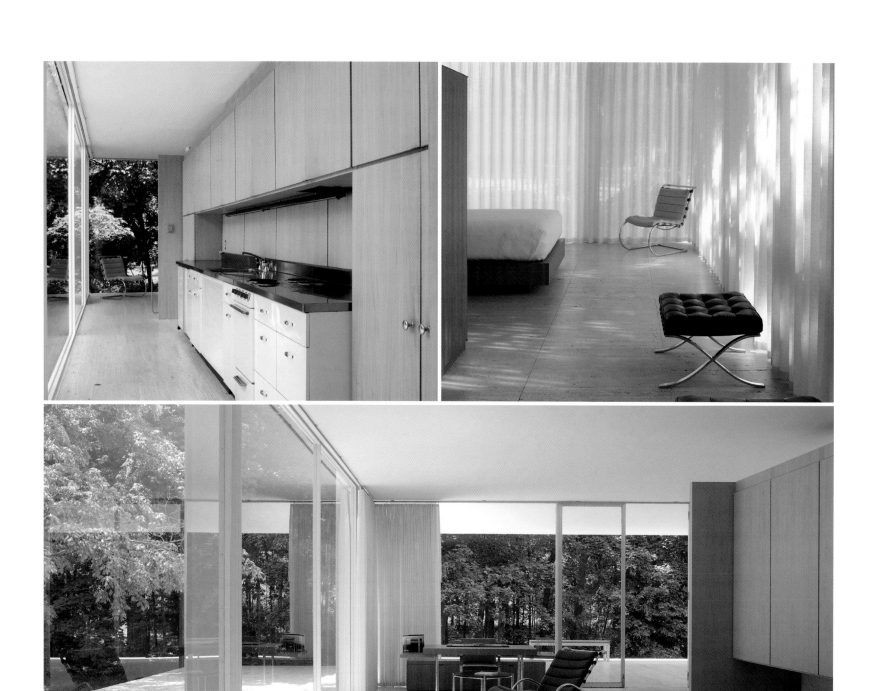

The Farnsworth House helped
pioneer the idea of the free plan
and the domestic service core.
Here one self-contained unit
holds the galley kitchen, shower
room, bathroom, boiler room
and fireplace. The rest of the
house becomes a fluid space,
delineated only by furniture,
flooring and storage units.
Tracked curtains allow for a
degree of privacy – one of
many contentious issues
between architect and client.

FARNSWORTH HOUSE

1954

OSCAR NIEMEYER

CANOAS HOUSE RIO DE JANEIRO, BRAZIL

There is a remarkably contemporary quality to the buildings of Oscar Niemeyer. In an age of increasingly dynamic forms and engineering-led architectural acrobatics, his undulating structures strike a powerful chord. They are all the more impressive for having been conceived long before computer-aided design led to a new era of experimentation and visual extravagance.

'I am not attracted to straight angles or to the straight line, hard and inflexible, created by man,' Niemeyer has said. 'I am attracted to free-flowing, sensual curves. The curves that I find in the mountains of my own country, in the sinuousness of its rivers, in the waves of the ocean, and on the body of the beloved woman.'[1]

This seductive form of architecture has played a large part in forming the image of a progressive, modern Brazil, with Niemeyer's work captured on the tourist-board posters that invite travellers to savour the best of the country's culture. The buildings of Brasília, which Niemeyer did so much to create and define, are a masterclass in architectural

flamboyance and excitement, showing the power of architecture to shape identity itself.

Not all of Niemeyer's achievements have been on the monumental scale of his churches and galleries, however. In their own way, his houses have played a large part in his career and helped to make his work more accessible, bringing out themes and ideas on a domestic scale.

With his own house at Canoas, Niemeyer combined a love of fluid forms with a great sensitivity to site and nature. The main level is low-slung and discreet, with a canopy of trees towering over the curvilinear, almost kidney-shaped roof line, echoed by the form of the modest swimming pool in front.

Much of the main living space is open-plan, with a lightly sectioned-off kitchen to one end, behind a curving timber wall. A subtly positioned staircase leads down to the bedrooms, folded into the hillside in a semi-subterranean arrangement, and peppered with an extraordinary sequence of portholes and crafted windows, like cubist lenses.

The house has ideas in common with Niemeyer's Alberto Dalva Simão House, built around the same time, but the way the Canoas House integrates itself with the hillside gives it a drama and character all of its own. In some ways, the closest point of comparison might be John Lautner's Elrod Residence of 1968 (see pp. 182–187), another building of free-flowing sculpted beauty that seems to have fused with the steep slopes and rock upon which it sits.

'In my view, every architect should have his own architecture and build what he likes and not what others would have him build,' Niemeyer has said.[2] A pioneer in terms of both form and materials, and one of architecture's great humanists, he is a unique presence in twentieth-century design. The Canoas House – like so many of his buildings – seems half a century ahead of its time.

1 Quoted in Alan Hess and Alan Weintraub, *Oscar Niemeyer Houses*, Rizzoli, 2006.
2 Interview with Hattie Hartman, *Architects' Journal*, 22.3.07.

Oscar Niemeyer sculpted concrete to form his distinctive, recognizable buildings, intimately connected to their locations – here a lush forest habitat with the ocean close by.

Biography

OSCAR NIEMEYER (b. 1907)
Born in Rio de Janeiro, Niemeyer studied at the city's
National Art Academy. From 1934 to 1938 he worked
with Lúcio Costa and Le Corbusier on the Ministry of
Education and Health building in Rio. In the late 1950s
he was appointed chief architect of the capital of
Brasília, becoming intrinsically associated with the
city he shaped. In the late 1960s, the changing
political situation led to exile in France, but Niemeyer
returned in 1982 to continue teaching and practising
architecture. Later projects took his work around the
world, and he won the Pritzker Prize in 1988.

Key Buildings

Pampulha Complex Minas Gerais, Brazil, 1940
National Congress Brasília, Brazil, 1958
Metropolitan Cathedral of Brasília Brasília, Brazil,
1959
Niterói Museum of Contemporary Art Niterói, Rio de
Janeiro, Brazil, 1996
National Museum & National Library Brasília, Brazil,
2006

CANOAS HOUSE

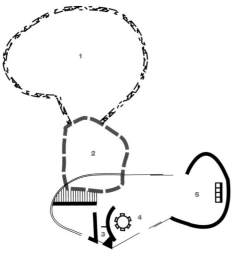
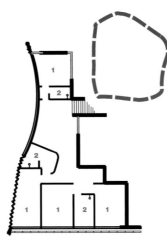

far left: ground floor

1 swimming pool
2 rock
3 kitchen
4 dining area
5 living area

left: lower floor

1 bedroom
2 bathroom

N

A vast rock emerges from the terrace and pushes into the house, but large banks of glass at front and back suggest lightness and transparency.

JEAN PROUVÉ

MAISON PROUVÉ   NANCY, LORRAINE, FRANCE

Jean Prouvé is best known for his experimental work in prefabricated housing and innovative structural building systems, as well as for his pioneering creative collaborations with some of the great Modernist architectural thinkers. Yet his own house in Nancy – perhaps his most influential and highly praised work – was a very individual, personal and one-off project, conceived by him alone and built for his family.

In many senses Prouvé was way ahead of his time. His own workshops produced the prototypes for his experiments with futuristic, mass-produced housing schemes and groundbreaking structural solutions, mainly in steel and aluminium. His prefabricated buildings – largely designed to answer the housing shortages in post-war France – included Les Maisons à Portiques, or 'portable houses', the Standard Houses built in Meudon, and the Maisons Tropicales, destined for Niger and the Congo.

Ultimately his kit buildings failed to catch on, and few designs were built in any significant numbers. In 1952 Prouvé's investors took over and he lost control of his factory in Maxéville; he also lost copyright of many of his own designs. It was a period of desperation but also of rebirth, as he began to rebuild his career and develop new projects. The Maison Prouvé was central to this renaissance, being completely independent, self-penned and self-built.

The site for the house was a sloping hillside overlooking Nancy, the town in which Prouvé had grown up and which remained a constant presence in his life. A small-scale terrace was carved into the hillside, and there the house was anchored at either end by stone walls; in between Prouvé created a typically lightweight structure. The build was low-budget, with the house initially designed to last only a decade. Although a limited number of bespoke elements were used, the house was also partially built with components culled from other recent projects.

The final one-storey pavilion is tied together by an 88 foot long (27 m) corridor, running almost the entire length of the closed section of the house at the rear, contained by a wall of steel panels. This corridor is backed by a continuous cabinet, holding wardrobes and adaptable shelving. Bedrooms and bathroom are modestly sized and placed at one end of the house, allowing space for a large living room with sheet glazing which pushes out from the main axis of the building to meet the landscape beyond.

The façade of Maison Prouvé mixes glazing with a series of 'porthole' panels borrowed from Prouvé's Maisons Tropicales, and then a series of wood-faced wall units borrowed from his Meudon Standard Houses. The roof is made of slim panels of timber coated in aluminium.

Rather than the mass-produced homes of Prouvé's ambitious imagination, it was the Maison Prouvé – this ingenious, singular home, which itself made use of redundant components once destined for mass production – that was to become the great iconic showcase for its creator's talents.

Prouvé went on to produce some of the most striking and innovative buildings of his lifetime – the Pavilion for the Centennial of Aluminium in Paris, also completed in 1954, the House for Abbé Pierre and the mesmerizing Cachat Pump-Room in Évian, as well as other private houses.

The architect himself has become a legendary avant-garde figure, especially for the current generation of High-Tech architects who are, on the one hand, pushing the boundaries of engineering and form, and on the other rediscovering the potential of prefabrication. Maison Prouvé remains the most personal example of its creator's innovative amalgamation of the design disciplines, and it remains a unique testament to a powerful imagination.

Biography

JEAN PROUVÉ (1901–1984)

A designer, manufacturer, entrepreneur, construction consultant, engineering expert and former mayor of Nancy, Jean Prouvé defies categorization. As a designer and producer of both buildings and furniture, he was fascinated by prefabrication and factory production techniques, and managed a series of his own manufacturing workshops and ateliers. Never formally registered as an architect, he carried out much of his architectural work and explored many of his experimental ideas through collaborations with other architects and engineers, including his brother Henri, as well as Le Corbusier, Oscar Niemeyer and Robert Mallet-Stevens.

Key Buildings

Maison du Peuple (with Eugène Beaudouin & Marcel Lods) Clichy, France, 1939

Maisons Tropicales (with Henri Prouvé) Niamey, Niger & Brazzaville, Congo, 1949

Pavilion for the Centennial of Aluminium (with Henri Hugonnet & Armand Copienne) Paris, France, 1954

Maison de l'Abbé Pierre/House of Better Days Paris, France, 1956

Cachat Pump-Room (with Maurice Novarina & Serge Kétoff) Évian-les-Bains, France, 1956

The house was built simply
and economically, recycling
elements from previous
projects, but all the different
components come together
cohesively.

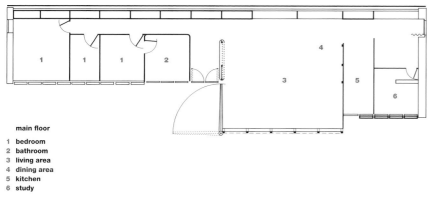

main floor

1 **bedroom**
2 **bathroom**
3 **living area**
4 **dining area**
5 **kitchen**
6 **study**

Eero Saarinen understood, better than most, that architecture could shape identity. This could be the identity of a company, like General Motors, IBM, Bell or John Deere, for all of whom Saarinen designed dramatic buildings, along the way pioneering the idea of the campus office – a collection of buildings suited to different uses. But, of course, architecture also says a great deal about individual identity. This was shown at the Irwin Miller House in Columbus, Indiana – a city with which Saarinen and his father, Eliel, had a particularly close relationship. Indeed, the pair did much to shape the unique character of what is now a mecca of Modernist architecture.

In 1955 Eero Saarinen completed the Irwin Union Bank building under the patronage of the Irwin family, who played a pivotal role in helping to promote and support the development of Modernist architecture in Columbus. The president of the bank, Joseph Irwin Miller, and his wife, Xenia Simons Miller, then commissioned Saarinen to design a house for themselves.

Although we tend to think of some of Saarinen's most famous buildings as masterpieces of organic Modernism, he has also been criticized for having no set style. Part of the reason for the diversity of his work was that he listened to the needs of his clients.

The Irwin Miller House is a large, single-storey building of around 8,000 square feet (745 sq m), with a vast flat roof punctured by translucent skylights in grid formation. Four pavilions stand at each corner of the house, holding both private and service spaces.

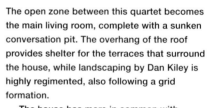

Large expanses of glazing and sliding doors provide strong connections to the natural surroundings of the Irwin Miller House, including the woodlands that border its garden.

The open zone between this quartet becomes the main living room, complete with a sunken conversation pit. The overhang of the roof provides shelter for the terraces that surround the house, while landscaping by Dan Kiley is highly regimented, also following a grid formation.

The house has more in common with Saarinen's 1949 Case Study House #9, designed with Charles Eames, than the more flamboyant sculpted forms of his TWA Terminal and other key buildings. One also sees elements in common with the low-slung Irwin Union Bank building, designed as an open and welcoming glass-faced structure, in contrast to the conventional image of the bank as impregnable fortress.

The Irwin Miller House was a cohesive project, with many pieces of furniture designed by Saarinen himself, but it was also developed in close consultation with the Millers, and a number of schemes were rejected during its genesis. It now embodies the idea of the bespoke, with a programme, form and character intimately suited to the identity of its owners. Beyond this, with its formal simplicity, spatial richness and powerful relationship with the landscape, it remains one of Saarinen's most influential projects. Recently acquired by the Indianapolis Museum of Art, the house will likely remain the best known and best preserved of the architect's few domestic commissions.

Biography

EERO SAARINEN (1910–1961)

Born in Finland, Saarinen moved to the States with his family in 1923. He went to Paris to study sculpture and then studied architecture at Yale. From 1936 onwards he collaborated with his father, as well as working with Charles Eames. From 1950, after the death of his father, he established his own practice in Bloomfield Hills, Michigan. A series of projects remained incomplete upon his sudden and untimely death and were finished by partners Kevin Roche and John Dinkeloo.

Key Buildings

Kresge Auditorium & Chapel, Massachusetts Institute of Technology Cambridge, Massachusetts, USA, 1955
General Motors Technical Center (with Smith, Hinchman & Grylls) Warren, Michigan, USA, 1956
Trans World Airlines (TWA) Terminal, John F. Kennedy International Airport New York, New York, USA, 1962
North Christian Church Columbus, Indiana, USA, 1963
Jefferson National Expansion Memorial St Louis, Missouri, USA, 1968

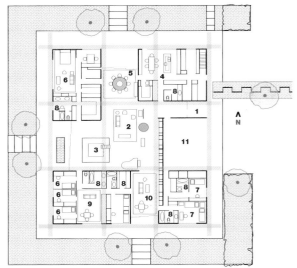

main floor

1 entrance
2 living area
3 pit
4 kitchen
5 dining area
6 bedroom
7 guest room
8 bathroom
9 playroom/children's area
10 den
11 carport

1961

LOUIS KAHN

ESHERICK HOUSE CHESTNUT HILL, PHILADELPHIA, PENNSYLVANIA, USA

The turbulent life-story of Louis Kahn serves as a reminder that the avant-garde is difficult territory for an architect to live and work in. Just as Kahn was born into adversity and struggle, so he seemed to face them again and again throughout his life, and periodically found difficulty securing projects and commissions, and died deeply in debt.

He is best known for his buildings in brick and concrete, colossal structures recalling the immensity of scale and mass seen in temples and other epic buildings of the ancient world. But as well as creating vast campuses, such as the Government Sector project in Dhaka that is widely regarded as his masterpiece, Kahn worked on a series of housing projects and a small number of single-family residences.

The Esherick House was one of the first completed buildings that he designed after a pivotal period in Rome in the early 1950s, where visits to classical sites cemented his ideas of an architecture of modern monumentality.

The 2,500 square foot (230 sq m) house was commissioned by Margaret Esherick, the book-loving niece of sculptor Wharton Esherick, a friend of Kahn's (Kahn designed Wharton Esherick's workshop, and Esherick created the bespoke kitchen in his niece's home). The design of the house establishes a powerful geometrical presence, yet also promotes a number of contrasts, both in terms of materials and space.

The building is made of concrete blocks coated in stucco, while the Apitong timber frames of the large recessed front windows offer a different kind of texture. With regard to layout, the two-storey rectangular building subdivides into two broadly symmetrical units. One is dominated by a double-height living room, complete with integrated bookcases. The other holds a large dining room downstairs and a combined bedroom and study above. Between the two units sits a slim access area, containing front and rear entrances, the

staircase and recessed balconies on the upper level. All service areas are contained within a discreet, more enclosed zone to one side.

The interior finishes are highly crafted, suggesting a strong Arts and Crafts influence and the artisanal touch of Wharton Esherick. They also suggest that the external drama of Kahn's buildings did not come at the expense of a fastidious approach to interior detail. Even though he could be demanding and difficult with his clients, Kahn always retained a sense of the end-user and their needs.

Kahn and his work have been greatly influential, especially for apprentices such as Robert Venturi, who once worked with Kahn; one also sees his ongoing influence in the work of Mario Botta, Tadao Ando and others. In the Esherick House, we find ideas about mass, scale and geometrical precision that were to pervade Kahn's later career, but also a sensitivity to site and need, ergonomics and craft, in a building combining monumentality and elegance.

Louis Kahn's uncompromising designs are structurally experimental and engineer plays between light and darkness, solidity and openness, geometry and nature. Here, the expanses of glazing open the house up to the half-acre (0.2 hectare) gardens.

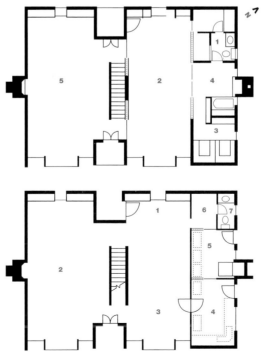

Biography

LOUIS KAHN (1901–1974)

Born into a poor Jewish background in Estonia, Kahn emigrated to the States with his family in 1906. He studied architecture at the University of Pennsylvania before working with a number of practices in the 1920s. Following extensive travels in Europe, he founded his own practice in 1934 in Philadelphia. He also taught at Yale and later at the University of Pennsylvania. Many of his best known projects date from the 1950s onwards and encapsulate his ideas of poetic monumentality; a number of projects were completed after his death.

Key Buildings

Yale University Art Gallery New Haven, Connecticut, USA, 1953
Salk Institute for Biological Studies La Jolla, California, USA, 1965
Kimbell Art Museum Fort Worth, Texas, USA, 1972
Indian Institute of Management Ahmedabad, Gujarat, India, 1974
Government Sector/National Capital Sher-e-Bangla Nagar, Dhaka, Bangladesh, 1983

first floor

1 bathroom
2 bedroom/study
3 walk-in closet
4 sitting room
5 upper part of living room

ground floor

1 entrance
2 living room
3 dining room
4 kitchen
5 utility room
6 utility closet
7 bathroom

To some, Basil Spence was one of the most talented, innovative British architects of the 1960s and '70s, the author of a series of experimental and iconic buildings, including Coventry Cathedral and Hyde Park Cavalry Barracks. To others, he was a serial iconoclast, creating 'brutalist' buildings that alienated those he should have served, including the residents of his Gorbals tower blocks in Glasgow. There are few architects who provoke such division, such contrasting opinions, as Spence.

His admirers pronounce him deeply misunderstood and underrated, unjustly tainted by the failure of his Glasgow housing projects. They point not just to Coventry Cathedral, but also to more modest projects, such as Spence's own family house at Beaulieu. Here, the architect created an elegantly conceived, Scandinavian-influenced home in the Hampshire countryside, overlooking the Beaulieu river.

A keen boatsman, Spence was drawn to the site partly because of the easy access to the river and from there to the waters of the Solent. It is certainly a bucolic and seductive spot, surrounded by mature trees that seem to wish to envelop the house in a green canopy. On this site Spence designed what was essentially a raised timber box, supported by two brick walls, allowing the flat-roofed structure to cantilever over a section of the swimming-pool terrace at the front of the building.

Originally, the first-floor timber unit – which maximizes the views out across the landscape –

contained all the main accommodation, with bedrooms and bathrooms to the rear and living room to the front, dominated by a sculptural fireplace in stone and brick. Spence used the undercroft of the building for workshop spaces and as a storage zone for his boat, thus creating a house of sophisticated simplicity with a strong sense of connection to its riverside site.

Later, recognizing the need for more space, he converted the ground-floor workshops into a dining room and kitchen, while adding an extra bedroom on the upper level. He also designed a spiral staircase, encased in a timber cylinder, which was added to one side of the house to connect the two floors.

Inside, the house was Scandinavian in feel: the living room, for example, mixed timber floors, walls and ceilings with the row of glass windows opening out to the river beyond and overlooking the pool terrace below. The house at Beaulieu has been compared with the work of Alvar Aalto and Arne Jacobsen, and one sees in the building a sensitivity to natural materials and landscape that very much echoes the work of the Scandinavian masters, and seems in contrast to the grand monumentality of some of Spence's public projects and housing schemes.

With great modesty, the flamboyant, cigar-smoking, bow-tie-wearing Spence himself described his country escape – built at the height of his fame and a year after his knighthood – as a 'shack'. In the end, he and his family only used it for around five years, and in the 1970s the architect retired to Yaxley Hall in Suffolk, a country house dating back to the sixteenth century – a curious choice for a Modernist pioneer.

While Spence's 1960s high-rise housing schemes, such as the Gorbals towers, have been widely lambasted and discredited, the house at Beaulieu provokes a very different reaction. Its influence has made itself felt upon the work of a new generation of English architects – including John Pardey, who recently restored the Spence House and added a wing to it for a private client. Original houses by Pardey and others suggest a similar appreciation of context, site and materials, exemplified here by Spence while establishing a novel kind of contemporary English country house. Indeed, the timber 'shack' offers a prime example of sensitive, environmentally aware, rural architecture.

Biography

BASIL SPENCE (1907–1976)

Born in India, Spence studied in Edinburgh and London and worked in the office of Edwin Lutyens. He co-founded his first practice in Scotland – with early work influenced by the Arts and Crafts movement – before serving in the British Army during the Second World War. He founded Spence & Partners in the 1940s, working in a distinctly Modernist and sometimes 'brutalist' style. His crowning achievement was Coventry Cathedral, while later work took him on to an international stage.

Key Buildings

Gribloch House Kippen, Stirling, Scotland, 1939
Coventry Cathedral Coventry, England, 1962
**New Zealand Parliament Buildings Executive Wing/
The Beehive** Wellington, New Zealand, 1964
Hyde Park Cavalry Barracks London, England, 1970
British Embassy Rome, Italy, 1971

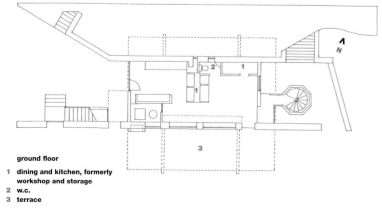

ground floor

1 dining and kitchen, formerly
   workshop and storage
2 w.c.
3 terrace

first floor

1 bedroom
2 bathroom
3 living area
4 balcony

The emphasis on natural materials – especially timber – reinforces the Scandinavian flavour of the house. Spence's design also displays a particular sensitivity to site.

ALISON & PETER SMITHSON

UPPER LAWN PAVILION   TISBURY, WILTSHIRE, ENGLAND

The term 'brutalist', coined by critic Reyner Banham, was first used in the 1950s to describe the work of Alison and Peter Smithson. Their work was full of post-war idealism and hard-fought theory, yet was also uncompromising and at times alienating, as with their Robin Hood Gardens housing scheme in London. Here, they had famously argued for 'streets in the sky', creating balcony walkways to foster a spirit of neighbourly wellbeing – but, while the theory may have been user-specific and laudable, the resulting building proved deeply controversial and divisive.

Like fellow 'brutalist' Basil Spence, the Smithsons achieved fame, even notoriety, not just for their highly formal and structural approach to architecture, but also for their flamboyant attitude to life. Alison Smithson, especially, was an eccentric character with an individual dress sense; she once threw a glass of wine over James Stirling when he mocked her by attempting to tie a bow around her head with the ends of her elongated collar.

The Smithsons' ideas were brought to a wider general public when their designs for a prefabricated, 'plastic-fantastic' House of the Future – inspired by industrial mass production of a kind seen in the car industry – were presented at the 1956 Ideal Home Show.

Upper Lawn Pavilion – or Solar Pavilion – was also experimental but it was relatively simple, personal and highly attuned to its rural site. In the late 1950s the Smithsons bought a small farmstead on the Fonthill Estate with a derelict labourer's cottage and walled yard surrounded by fields and woodland. Here, they designed a weekend and holiday home that made partial use of remnants of the original cottage, preserving a ghost impression of the lost building. Part of one northern stone wall and a chimney buttress, in particular, were retained, and around this the Smithsons designed what was essentially a rectangular observatory, opening out to the extraordinary views. A wooden frame forms the two-storey, flat-roofed structure, with large expanses of glass alongside an outer coating of grey zinc. As with the pair's more ambitious projects, the structure and material integrity of the building is made explicit, with detailing reduced to the minimum.

The upper level of the building became the main living space and viewing platform, a place where the couple could appreciate and record

the passing seasons within their 'Solar Pavilion'. The ground floor features banks of sliding teak and glass doors, which open the house up to the landscape and terraces, one of which also incorporates part of the former cottage wall as a boundary, thus screening the house from the farm track that forms the approach.

Both floors were simply and economically laid out in semi-open-plan style. Facilities were sparse and the Smithsons tended initially to roll out bedding, camping out in the building as though it were a barn or agricultural shed. Indeed, this raw but sensitive agricultural quality has latterly been very important in terms of the evolution of a new type of contemporary country house that mixes both Modernist and rural vernacular influences. So, too, has the idea of retaining and recording the past uses and textures of a site by integrating them within a new building, creating clear linkage and sense of continuity between past and present.

The Smithsons gave up the house in the early 1980s, but recent restoration for the new owners by architects Sergison Bates has fully respected the materials and integrity of the building, while also trying to deal with its poor thermal aspects. The addition of wood-burning stoves, high-spec glazing and underfloor heating have helped mitigate the house's winter failings.

The Smithsons continued to write about, promote and fondly remember Upper Lawn and its place in their careers. Ironically, for all its apparent modesty, it has proved a highly influential architectural statement and plays as significant a role in the Smithsons' canon as some of their larger-scale structures.

Biographies

ALISON SMITHSON (1928–1993) & PETER SMITHSON (1923–2003)

Born respectively in Sheffield and Stockton-on-Tees, the two architects met at the school of architecture in Newcastle. They founded a practice in 1949, having won their first commission, the attention-grabbing Hunstanton School in Norfolk. Outspoken and eccentric, the Smithsons received great praise for their Economist building but great criticism for their Robin Hood Gardens housing scheme. As curators and cultural commentators, they were closely allied with the development of the 1960s Pop Art movement in the UK.

Key Buildings

Hunstanton Secondary Modern School Hunstanton, Norfolk, England, 1954
House of the Future, Ideal Home Show London, England, 1956
Economist Plaza London, England, 1964
Robin Hood Gardens Poplar, London, England, 1972
Hexenhaus Lauenförde, Germany, 2001

The Smithsons reused elements
of the former labourer's cottage
on the site, including the central
stone chimney buttress and part
of the boundary wall. Living
spaces were kept fluid and open-
plan. Recent restoration work
has preserved the upper storey
as the key sitting room, while
adding a new wood-burning stove.

162

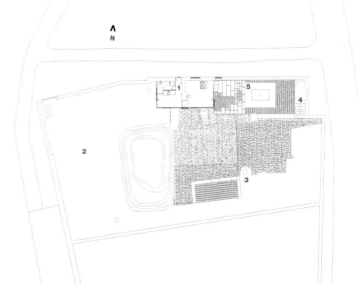

site plan

1 entrance
2 garden
3 well
4 steps leading up to platform
5 terrace

ROBERT VENTURI

VANNA VENTURI HOUSE   CHESTNUT HILL, PHILADELPHIA, PENNSYLVANIA, USA

The house that Robert Venturi completed for his mother in the mid-1960s is a challenging building to pigeonhole. This, however, has proved to be part of the point of this hugely influential home, which attempted to step out from the shadow of Modernist dogma and draw in a rich variety of themes, ideas and symbols from the broader spectrum of architectural history.

As Venturi has suggested in his own commentaries, his design encompasses a series of fascinating contradictions. 'It is both complex and simple, open and closed, big and little,' he wrote. 'Some of its elements are good on one level and bad on another; its order accommodates the generic elements of the house in general and the circumstantial elements of a house in particular.'[1]

Of course, as well as being a manifesto statement, it was also a functioning home built for a special client. Venturi's priorities were 'to express my general ideas about architecture, to please my mother and create a background for her furniture, and to fit in with the site/context'.

Vanna Venturi worked for an interior design firm and had an interest in art and architecture.

After being widowed, she commissioned her son to create a house that would accommodate the many practical necessities of her new life. As Venturi wrote: 'My mother's house was designed for her as an elderly widow with her bedroom on the ground floor, with no garage because she didn't drive, and for a maidservant and the possibility of a nurse – and also as appropriate for her beautiful furniture which I had grown up with. Otherwise she did not make demands … concerning its programme or its aesthetic….'[2]

The design integrates a wealth of experimental ideas in what is, at heart, a modest house. From outside, an initial impression of strong geometric symmetry is purposefully subverted by the irregular pattern of the windows, the asymmetrical entry porch, the off-centre chimney, and so on. Inside, the ground floor is anchored around the combined massing of the stairway and the fireplace, which provides a focal point both to the central living room and the house itself, with the stairs leading up to a second bedroom on a small upper level.

'It connects with ideas of mine of the time involving complexity and contradiction,' said

Venturi; 'of accommodation to its particular Chestnut Hill suburban context, to aesthetic layering I learned from the Villa Savoye, its pedimented roof configuration derived from the Low House of Bristol, Rhode Island, its split pediment derived from the upper pediment of Blenheim Palace, the duality composition derived from the Casa Girasole in Rome and involving explicit applied elements of ornament. But it is a modern house; my mother enjoyed living in it and also entertaining the many young architects who visited it.'[3]

This breadth of referential input, combined with the exuberant originality of the resulting building, established Venturi's career, and the house became an essential reference point for all those who recognized the need for architectural vitality and openness. Much imitated, especially in the Postmodern heyday of the 1980s, the Vanna Venturi House has become emblematic of the power of the unfettered imagination.

1 Robert Venturi, in Frederic Schwartz (ed.), *The Mother's House: The Evolution of Vanna Venturi's House in Chestnut Hill*, Rizzoli, 1992.
2 Robert Venturi, writing in 'Stories of Houses – Vanna Venturi House', www.storiesofhouses.blogspot.com.
3 Robert Venturi, ibid.

Biography

ROBERT VENTURI (b. 1925)
Architect, theorist, writer and lecturer, Venturi was born in Philadelphia and studied at Princeton University. He worked briefly with Eero Saarinen and Louis Kahn before co-founding his first practice in 1960. After his marriage to fellow architect Denise Scott Brown, the firm ultimately became known as Venturi, Scott Brown & Associates. While Venturi's work has defied simple categorization, he is best known for his 'less is a bore' approach to architecture, drawing upon a wealth of influences in search of a richer approach than pure Modernism sometimes allowed for. In 1991 he was awarded the Pritzker Prize.

Key Buildings

Guild House Philadelphia, Pennsylvania, USA, 1964
Sainsbury Wing, National Gallery London, England, 1991
Seattle Art Museum Seattle, Washington, USA, 1991
San Diego Museum of Contemporary Art San Diego, California, USA, 1996
Haute-Garonne Provincial Capitol Building Toulouse, France, 1999

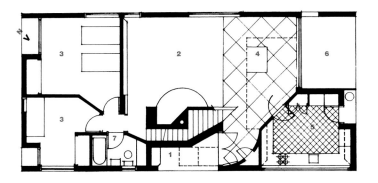

ground floor

1 entrance
2 living room
3 bedroom
4 dining room
5 kitchen
6 porch
7 bathroom

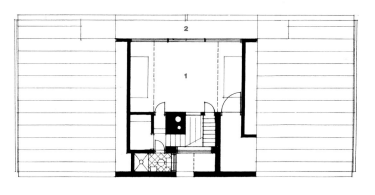

first floor

1 studio/bedroom
2 terrace

1964

ALBERT FREY

FREY HOUSE II PALM SPRINGS, CALIFORNIA, USA

One of the most striking things about Frey House II is its sense of modesty. At less than 1,000 square feet (some 90 sq m), largely on one level, it is pushed discreetly into its mountainside site. Much of the house is open-plan, with bedroom, lounge and space for a raised dining/drawing table merging into one. The compact layout and the built-in, space-saving, mahogany plywood furniture make it in some ways reminiscent of the simple wooden cabanon at Cap Martin, near Monaco, the self-designed and much favoured retreat of Frey's mentor, Le Corbusier.

Yet this is a house of contrasts, because at the same time that it is modest it is also a site of great drama and impact. Built 220 feet (67 m) above Palm Springs, in Tahquitz Canyon, it commands a spectacular spot with views across the city – spread out below in the valley basin like a texture-rich carpet – and the desert communities beyond. Banks of glass open the house up to this breathtaking vista, while inside a large boulder pushes its way into the main living space, and beyond the mountainside continues its impressive ascent.

By the time Albert Frey built this, his second home in the city, he was already moving into semi-retirement and was able to pick and choose his projects. Throughout his career – largely centred on the booming Palm Springs of the 1940s and '50s – he had at times experimented with more flamboyant structures and statement engineering, as in the Tramway Gas Station – now a visitors' centre – with its soaring, cantilevered roof greeting drivers as they enter Palm Springs on Route 111 from Los Angeles. But Frey House II was perhaps the ultimate expression of a more subtle strand of Frey's career as a pioneering Desert Modernist.

With earlier projects, such as the Raymond Loewy House of 1946 and the Carey House of 1956, Frey had shown an unusual sensitivity to site and context. With Frey House II he developed this appreciation and understanding even further, moulding his home to the topography and views. It becomes a belvedere, opening out to the city and desert, with a form and positioning born – typically – from very careful observation of the conditions of the plot.

'I studied the position of the sun for a whole year,' Frey said. 'My partner and I put up a ten-foot pole and we measured the shadow from it and made a diagram so we knew where the sun

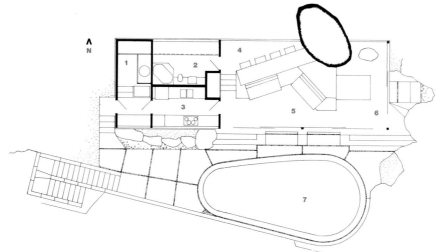

main floor

1 utility room
2 bathroom
3 kitchen
4 dining room
5 living room
6 bedroom
7 swimming pool

was at this location at any time of the year. The plan was designed so that, for instance, the glass walls are not exposed to the sun in the heat of the summer. That's what determined these overhangs. In winter, when the sun is much lower, it comes in and heats the house.'[1]

A platform, or deck, holding a small teardrop-shaped swimming pool, sits to the front of the house and is made of a coloured concrete to help it blend in with the mountainside. Similarly, the ribbed metal roof and the aluminium exterior siding – sitting on a steel frame – are coloured to integrate with the rock, while the floor plan is designed around the way the adopted boulder protrudes into the building.

Despite its uncompromising modernity in form, layout and materials, Frey House II does its best to harmonize with the landscape in which it bathes. There is no hubris to this house, but a respect for the terrain that Frey came to so admire and enjoy.

As such, the house – which he bequeathed to the Palm Springs Art Museum situated at the base of the hillside below – became a key exemplar not just of Desert Modernism but of a fresh and sensitive approach to landscape, drawing on lessons from vernacular architecture and making the most of economic and commonsense methods to mitigate issues such as solar gain – a major factor in the desert climate. Through such masterpieces, Frey's influence spread well beyond the city that he made his own.

1 Interview with Jennifer Golub, in *Albert Frey: Houses 1 & 2*, Princeton Architectural Press, 1999.

ALBERT FREY (1903–1998)
Born in Switzerland, Frey worked in the Paris atelier of Le Corbusier – contributing to Villa Savoye (pp. 64–69) – before emigrating to America in 1929. A commission took him, after a period in New York, to the desert city of Palm Springs, where he was to make his home and which was to prove pivotal to his future work. Frey became the leading light in the development of Desert Modernism, as the city became a fashionable retreat for the Hollywood and Los Angeles elite.

Key Buildings

Movie Colony Hotel (formerly San Jacinto Hotel)
Palm Springs, California, USA, 1935
City Hall Palm Springs, California, USA, 1957
North Shore Yacht Club Salton Sea, California, USA, 1959
Valley Station, Palm Springs Aerial Tramway Palm Springs, California, USA, 1963
Tramway Gas Station Palm Springs, California, USA, 1965

CHARLES DEATON

SCULPTURED HOUSE GENESEE MOUNTAIN, GOLDEN, DENVER, COLORADO, USA

Every now and then a building seeps into popular culture. One thinks of John Lautner's Elrod Residence (see pp. 182–187) playing a part in the Bond film *Diamonds Are Forever*, or George Wyman's Bradbury Building in *Blade Runner*. Such was the case with Charles Deaton's Sculptured House, which played a starring role in Woody Allen's 1973 sci-fi comedy, *Sleeper*. The house, emblematic of the future and instantly recognizable to many, became widely known as the 'Sleeper House'.

Today, the importance of the architecture, quite apart from the iconicity of the building, is recognized. The sculpted, sinuous form was certainly way ahead of its time; indeed, the Sculptured House feels very contemporary in an era of architectural dynamism, when fluid forms are an increasingly common thematic thread.

Deaton initially began designing a sculptural entity, formulating its organic, pod-like shape for a spectacular 15-acre (6 hectare) hillside site in Colorado's Rocky Mountains. Detailing and floor plans followed, as he turned the form into a house for himself. It was the only residential

project of his career but it was one that tied in closely with the futuristic forms of some of his other work, particularly his Key Savings & Loan Association building in Englewood, Colorado, designed at around the same time.

'I felt, first of all, the shape should be strong and simple enough to stand in a gallery as a work of art,' said Deaton. 'I knew, of course, when I started the sculpture that it would develop into a house. There was, however, no attempt to simply wrap a shell around a floor plan. In fact, no scale was set until the sculpture was done.'[1]

Like a clam shell, opening up to the undulating landscape spread out below, the house was a polar opposite to the rectilinear Case Study aesthetic being developed to the west. Instead, it had more in common with Lautner's experimental approach to form, or the pioneering concrete structures of Félix Candela. Anchored to bedrock with a steel and concrete cylindrical pedestal, it had a steel and wire cage construction on top, coated in pumped concrete, plus a final layer of Hypalon blended with walnut shells and white pigment.

'On Genesee mountain,' proclaimed Deaton, 'I found a high point of land where I could stand and feel the great reaches of the Earth. I wanted the shape of it to sing an unencumbered song.'

Although this house of the future earned itself a blaze of publicity, as well as a film role, Deaton never fully completed the interiors and he sold the building in the late 1980s. It then languished for some years in a poor state until being fully renovated at the turn of the millennium, with a large Deaton-designed addition – which triples the available living space – completed by his daughter Charlee Deaton and son-in-law Nicholas Antonopoulos.

Today, the fully restored and refreshed Sculptured House – a symbol of the future when it was built, and a bona fide Colorado landmark – is perhaps as close to Deaton's original vision as it could ever be. It has taken the architectural world more than forty years to catch up with the architect's vision, but today the house still continues to inspire practitioners, who, in an age of sophisticated engineering and structural experimentalism, are increasingly looking to nature and organic forms.

1 Quoted in Philip Jodidio, *Architecture Now! 3*, Taschen, 2004.

Biography

CHARLES DEATON (1921–1996)
Born in New Mexico, Deaton was a self-taught designer. He specialized in architecture and engineering, funding his studies with work as a commercial artist. Much of his early architectural work focused on designs for banks. From 1955 he based himself in Denver; innovative stadium work followed. Deaton had a parallel career as a designer of board games, patenting a number of products. He also worked in industrial design.

Key Buildings

Central Bank & Trust Denver, Colorado, USA, 1960
Wyoming National Bank Casper, Wyoming, USA, 1964
Key Savings & Loan Association/Colonial Bank
Englewood, Colorado, USA, 1967
Arrowhead Stadium & Kauffman Stadium (with Kivett & Myers) Kansas City, Missouri, USA, 1972

The sinuous, moulded aesthetic
carries through to the interiors.
Staircases, walls and windows
echo the organic outer shell.
These powerful spaces have
elements in common with the
work of John Lautner in the
States, Félix Candela in Mexico
and Antti Lovag in France.

CHARLES GWATHMEY

GWATHMEY HOUSE & STUDIO AMAGANSETT, HAMPTONS, LONG ISLAND, USA

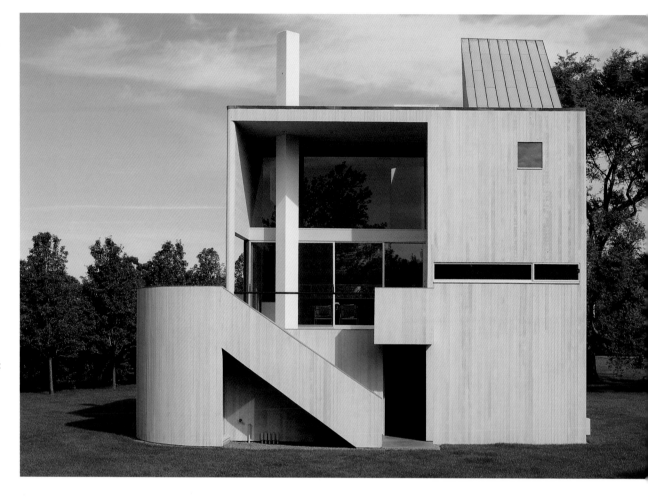

Designing this radical house in the Hamptons for his parents launched Charles Gwathmey's career and inspired a host of beach- and resort-house imitations across Long Island and beyond. In many ways, it is a modest building and modestly made, yet its impact was out of all proportion to its limited $35,000 build cost.

After finishing his studies, Gwathmey toured Europe, including a stint in France where he visited the buildings of his spiritual mentor, Le Corbusier, before working in the office of Edward Larabee Barnes. However, in his mid-twenties, he gave up his job to concentrate on the commission from his parents, Robert and Rosalie Gwathmey, a painter and a photographer-turned-textile designer.

Back in the mid-1960s, the Hamptons was still an unspoilt backwater – the preserve of farmers and painters – and the Gwathmeys cheaply secured a 1-acre (0.4 hectare) site near Amagansett to build a home. They set the build budget and laid out the most basic requirements of living space, master bedroom and space enough for four grandchildren, otherwise effectively offering carte blanche.

Gwathmey designed a highly sculpted object – a combination of intersecting cubes and spheres – sitting on the flatlands of dunes and scrub. Realizing that building in concrete would be too expensive, he designed the house with a timber frame and vertical cedar siding, but still the lowest build estimate came in at nearly twice the projected budget. So he became the lead contractor himself, working with a builder, and balanced constructing the house with teaching at the Pratt Institute in New York.

Importantly, Gwathmey was able to raise the house up to three levels to take advantage of the ocean views. The highest point is 40 feet (12 m) – a level no longer permitted under local codes. The entire house is only 1,200 square feet in area (110 sq m), and 24 by 28 feet wide (7.3 x 8.5 m), but within that outline Gwathmey packed a great deal, while allowing for generous interior spaces and constant connections to the exterior and its views.

On the ground floor sits a bedroom, originally separated by a cabinet with bunk beds on either side for the grandchildren; a small galley-style studio for Gwathmey's mother was tucked under the curving stairway. The living room is on the floor above, with a small terrace within the overall outline of the structure, bordered by a large bank of glass which allows light to flood into the house. A mezzanine level above contains the master suite.

A year later, Gwathmey added a separate but complementary structure – in the same simple and restrained palette of materials – with a guest bedroom on the ground floor and a painting studio above for his father.

The house became – and remained – Robert and Rosalie Gwathmey's main residence, while the Hamptons transformed around them into a fashionable weekender community. Charles Gwathmey and his wife later inherited the building, making only subtle changes, including the addition of a small number of new windows in the main house, marble floors, a hedgerow to frame the house and a line of linden trees to one side of the site.

Locally the house proved controversial at first, but was soon accepted as it won critical praise and its architect's career blossomed. Some commented on the silo-like quality of the house and its flavours of reinvented vernacular largely born of its use of timber and traditional materials, but for Gwathmey the key importance lay in the experiment with form and volume.

Biography

CHARLES GWATHMEY (b. 1938)

A member of the highly influential 'New York Five' – along with Richard Meier, Peter Eisenman, Michael Graves and John Hejduk – Gwathmey studied at Yale and was strongly influenced by Le Corbusier. In 1968, after a stint working with Edward Larabee Barnes, he founded Gwathmey Siegel & Associates with Robert Siegel. The practice adopts a holistic approach to its projects, which have included many educational and cultural works, as well as high-profile residential commissions.

Key Buildings

Haupt House Amagansett, Hamptons, Long Island, USA, 1979
American Museum of the Moving Image Astoria, New York, USA, 1988
Fogg Art Museum Library, Harvard University Cambridge, Massachusetts, USA, 1990
Disney World Convention Center Orlando, Florida, USA, 1991
Solomon R. Guggenheim Museum addition & renovation New York, New York, USA, 1992

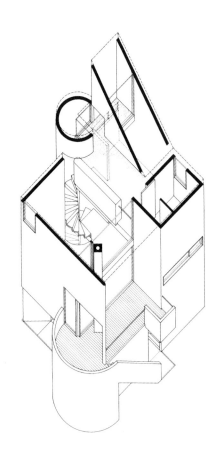

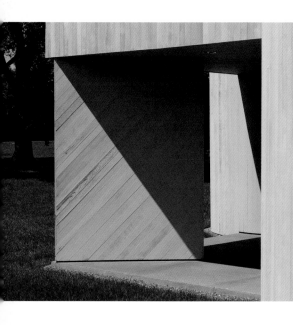

Despite its relatively modest size, the house has a generous feel to its spaces. Gwathmey created an elevated terrace on the upper storey, and also made the most of the building's height by incorporating a mezzanine gallery on the upper level, holding the master bedroom.

1966

Centred on a former sheep farm, overlooking the Pacific, the community of Sea Ranch is a pioneering eco-centric settlement. It is situated around 100 miles north of San Francisco, near the small Californian town of Gualala. Its idyllic clifftop setting is rich in natural beauty and, since the community's inception in the mid-1960s, part of its ethos has been to respect and preserve its unique surroundings.

There are no pristine landscaped gardens or picket fences around the houses and apartment buildings here; instead there is a policy of native planting, and a naturalistic approach to the creation of interconnected gardens and communal spaces, with much of the feeling of a wild reserve. Utilities are buried underground and outside lighting is restricted. The architecture, too, is characterized by sensitivity to the site.

Sea Ranch was born in 1963 when architect and planner Al Boeke began working with developers Oceanic California, Inc., on the purchase and master planning of the 4,000-acre (1,600 hectare) plot. Boeke worked closely with landscape architect Lawrence Halprin on a careful study of the area and then in developing a cohesive, long-term strategy for the new community, founded upon principles of sustainability and an intrinsic understanding of the topography. The main idea was not to impose a new community on this seductive stretch of coastland but to work with the landscape, while mitigating the impact of the building work that was to follow.

The early buildings on the site were commissioned out to Charles Moore, Donlyn Lyndon, William Turnbull and Richard Whitaker of MLTW Architects, and also to Joseph Esherick, these men collectively becoming the architectural founding fathers of the community. Their early work was to be crucial in the development of what became known as the 'Sea Ranch Style', governed by a strict set of self-imposed building codes.

The principles of Sea Ranch sat well with Esherick, who believed in site-specific buildings that responded to the needs of client and location alike, without shouting the signature of the architect. He developed a series of demonstration houses, as well as the Sea Ranch Store, along the line of one of the windbreak hedgerows planted on the farmland back in 1916. These shingle-clad Hedgerow Houses were deeply influenced by the vernacular tradition of barns and farmsteads, but Esherick reinterpreted this aesthetic to create buildings that were contemporary, flexible and linked in to the land.

The very last and smallest of the sequence was Esherick's own Sea Ranch home, now also known as the Friedman/Stassevitch House – a modest, three-bedroomed dwelling pushed into a sloping site, with a small stream to the front, traversed by a small bridge, and meadows to the rear.

Esherick packed a great deal into this compact, 875 square foot (81 sq m) home, which is essentially all on one level but for the third bedroom on a mezzanine. Downstairs, the kitchen leads onto a generous terrace with ocean views; to one side of the kitchen is a porch entrance, to the other a master bedroom with a private terrace. A large living room runs along much of the length of the rear of the house.

Typically for Esherick, this was a building of great subtlety and order, integrated with the land in which it snugly sits. As with the other Sea Ranch homes, the Esherick House suggested an innovative approach to sustainable living and respect for the landscape – crucial themes for a new generation of architects. 'The ideal kind of building is one you don't see,' Esherick once said, and his own house leads the way.

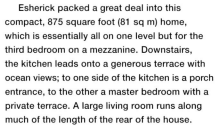

The discreet and cohesive style of Sea Ranch is made possible by a self-imposed set of guidelines and building codes. Houses are of unpainted timber and shingles, roofs are free of overhangs, and there are no perimeter fences or formal gardens.

JOSEPH ESHERICK (1914–1998)

Born in Philadelphia, Esherick served an apprenticeship with his uncle, Wharton Esherick, an artist and furniture maker. He then studied architecture before moving to the Bay Area of California and founding his own practice in 1953. He also taught architecture at the University of California, Berkeley, and co-founded the College of Environmental Design there. In 1972 he and three associates set up Esherick Homsey Dodge & Davis, later known as EHDD Architects, winners of the 1986 Architecture Firm Award. Esherick was awarded the American Institute of Architects Gold Medal in 1989.

Cary House Mill Valley, California, USA, 1960
Wurster Hall, University of California Berkeley, California, USA, 1964
The Cannery San Francisco, California, USA, 1968
Garfield School San Francisco, California, USA, 1981
Monterey Bay Aquarium Monterey, California, USA, 1984

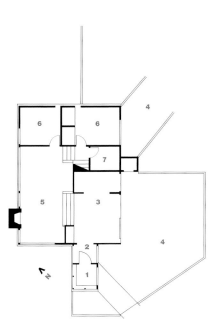

ground floor

1 porch
2 cloakroom
3 kitchen/dining area
 (below mezzanine bedroom)
4 terrace
5 living room
6 bedroom
7 bathroom

The compact house makes the most of its oceanside location, and internally it makes the most of the available space with many built-in and bespoke elements, including the additional bedroom tucked away in the mezzanine.

Luis Barragán, in his acceptance speech for the 1980 Pritzker Prize, talked of the importance of the romantic, the poetic and the artistic values of architecture: '... the words Beauty, Inspiration, Magic, Spellbound, Enchantment, as well as the concepts of Serenity, Silence, Intimacy and Amazement. All these have nestled in my soul, and though I am fully aware that I have not done them complete justice in my work, they have never ceased to be my guiding lights.'[1]

In a profession that is prone to excessively intellectual theory, Barragán's work offers a powerful reminder of the more profound and emotional possibilities of architecture. While his work was grounded in Modernism, it was also deeply rooted in the history, culture and art of Mexico. Drawing on this wealth of inspiration, he became one of the great regional Modernists and the godfather of new Mexican architecture.

In Barragán's work one sees the reinvention of particularly Mexican and Hispanic themes, such as the monumental textured wall, the vibrant use of colour, and a sensitivity to nature and landscape, including the use of water features within gardens and courtyards conceived in full sympathy with the buildings themselves. The old convents, churches and haciendas of Mexico were revisited and reinterpreted for a new era. 'I have always been moved by the peace and wellbeing to be experienced in those uninhabited cloisters and solitary courts. How I have wished that these feelings may leave their mark in my work.'[2]

Barragán's most famous and best loved project, San Cristóbal, stemmed from this rich context, but was also inspired by a shared love of horses on the part of the architect and his client, Folke Egerström. Still very much a working stables, San Cristóbal is a fresh kind of hacienda, enriched by water pools, fountains

and a stunning use of vivid colour, which seems to act as a bridge between nature and architecture, drawing the two together.

Designed in collaboration with Andrés Casillas, San Cristóbal consists of house and stables located at Los Clubes on the outskirts of the epic sprawl of Mexico City. Barragán, a passionate horseman from his early years, was inevitably drawn to clients and projects where horses were part of the equation, and indeed he kept his own horses at Los Clubes.

He talked of ranches and haciendas as one of his deepest sources of inspiration, taking in the high stable walls, compound enclosures, water troughs and horse ponds that were a necessary part of the ranch configuration. His San Cristóbal compound is essentially rectangular and holds the house and swimming pool, along with stables, hay barn, paddocks and horse pool. The house is a white, cubist composition, contrasting with the rich pinks seen along the walls of the stables and the central courtyard of the compound.

While Barragán established a highly complementary relationship between the domestic building and the domain of the horses, perhaps his greatest success was the way in which he cohesively wove both elements with the landscape, integrating gardens, courtyards and patios, unified by a common language and enlivened further by the use of colour and water.

The classic image of a thoroughbred horse against a vast fuschia wall has become a defining image of twentieth-century architecture at its most seductive. Barragán's work was to have a profound influence on Mexican architecture, especially the work of Ricardo Legorreta, but it also had an impact around the world, combining what might be considered a minimalist approach with an imaginative response to shade and light, colour and texture, water and landscape, in such a way as to suggest a richness and romance.

'Underlying all that I have achieved, such as it is,' said Barragán, 'are the memories of my father's ranch where I spent my childhood and adolescence. In my work I have always strived to adapt the needs of modern living to the magic of those remote nostalgic years.'[3]

1 Luis Barragán, acceptance speech, The Pritzker Architecture Prize, The Hyatt Foundation, 1980.
2 Ibid.
3 Ibid.

Biography

LUIS BARRAGÁN (1902–1988)
Born in Guadalajara, Barragán studied engineering
at the Escuela Libre de Ingenieros. His talents as an
architect, artist and landscape designer were largely
self-taught. He travelled to Europe and North Africa
in the 1920s and attended lectures by Le Corbusier,
although his work was always as rooted in Mexican
culture as in the Modernist movement. He founded his
own architectural practice in Guadalajara in 1927 and
later moved to Mexico City.

Key Buildings

Luis Barragán House Tacubaya, Mexico City, Mexico,
1948
Gálvez House Chimalistac, Mexico City, Mexico, 1955
The Towers of Satellite City (with Mathias Goeritz)
Querétaro Highway, Mexico City, Mexico, 1957
Chapel and Convent of the Capuchinas
Sacramentarias del Purísimo Corazón de María
Tlalpan, Mexico City, Mexico, 1960
Gilardi House Chapultepec, Mexico City, Mexico,
1975

Form, function and beauty unite
within a seamless and seductive
composition. In the central
courtyard, the fountain-fed
horse pool offers a sense of
contrast with the monumental
walls. The purity of Barragán's
work – rich in colour and texture
but stripped of ornament and
excess – creates a powerful
backdrop to the daily life of the
ranch.

ELROD RESIDENCE PALM SPRINGS, CALIFORNIA, USA

As an architect, John Lautner turned his back on boxes. For him, they were fit for jails and dog kennels, not for houses. While many of his Californian mid-century contemporaries spent their time defining the classic flat-roofed, glass-fronted, rectangular dream home, Lautner let his imagination and his passion for engineering take him in other directions.

Lautner's houses are great adventures in form, some with scarcely a true right angle to be found. These are buildings of a different kind of geometry – hexagons, cones and spheres, and sensual, organic curves, expressed in concrete and timber. They owe some debt to the lessons of Frank Lloyd Wright, with whom Lautner once worked. But Lautner's vision was fresh and unique, liberated by the benign Californian climate in which he worked, the region's openness to experimentation, and his desire to integrate architecture and landscape.

The Elrod Residence is one of Lautner's most famous houses and among the greatest expressions of his art. Perched on Smoke Tree Mountain, overlooking the desert city of Palm Springs, the house cannot be seen easily from below, tucked as it is into the mountainside like a bunker. From the outside, it has a certain modesty, its concrete shell merging into the sun-kissed rocks.

It is within that the Elrod Residence reveals its true beauty, particularly in the extraordinary circular living room, 60 feet (18 m) across. Here, a vast concrete ceiling is formed from a series of giant concrete panels intersected by fan-shaped ceiling lights. These heavyweight petals appear to float, like a hovering flying saucer, and they contrast with a large, curving, retractable wall of glass that gives access to the swimming pool and also opens up to reveal the landscape and the city spread out below.

The house was commissioned by Arthur Elrod, interior designer to the stars. Lautner later wrote: 'After showing me the site, Elrod said: "Give me what you think I should have on this lot." As a very knowledgeable interior designer, Elrod was capable of designing something really good for himself, but he wanted the architecturally exceptional.'[1]

The building is largely sheltered from the access roadway and is entered via a large pivoting copper gate. A sculpture garden lies ahead, and then a large glass doorway leading into the dramatic living room. The kitchen is recessed to the rear, with a black slate floor and a large integrated concrete fireplace to one side. Noting large outcrops of stone, Lautner dug down around 8 feet (2.4 m) to expose them, and integrated them into the design of the house.

The organic quality of these slate and stone outcrops contrasts with the great slabs of concrete and the light touch of the glass. 'At night, with the house lights dimmed,' Lautner wrote, 'the black slate floor in the living room seems to disappear into the night and one finds oneself in space viewing the sparkling lights of Palm Springs.'[2]

Later, Elrod commissioned Lautner to add a separate guest wing. Shaped like a great ship's bow, this is largely self-contained in a separate structure that sits down the hillside from the main house. On seeing the finished development, Bob and Dolores Hope asked Lautner to design one for them nearby, within the same gated community. The Elrod house also played a backdrop role in *Diamonds Are Forever*.

Lautner's houses tend to be shaped by one big, defining idea, and with the Elrod Residence it is the high drama of the flowering concrete ceiling and the way the landscape is brought into the main living room as though through a giant lens. But Elrod also encapsulates the great spatial as well as visual originality of Lautner's work, setting up a series of discoveries and excitements within its sequence of contrasting, complex and extraordinary spaces.

1 Frank Escher (ed.), *John Lautner: Architect*, Artemis, 1994.
2 Ibid.

The living-room ceiling offers one of the most remarkable architectural devices – and images – of the era. The roof, supported by discreet concrete piers, appears to float, while a glass wall retracts to open up the panoramic view.

Biography

JOHN LAUTNER (1911–1994)
Like Rudolph Schindler, Lautner was a protégé of Frank Lloyd Wright who slowly but successfully emerged from his mentor's shadow to establish his own unique, extravagant and innovative style. He is best known for a series of highly original houses, mostly in California, whose spectacular fluid forms open themselves up to the landscape or the ocean.

Key Buildings

Malin Residence ('The Chemosphere') Los Angeles, California, USA, 1960
Reiner Residence ('Silvertop') Los Angeles, California, USA, 1963
Sheats/Goldstein Residence Los Angeles, California, USA, 1963/89
Zimmerman Residence Studio City, California, USA, 1968
Arango Residence Acapulco, Mexico, 1973

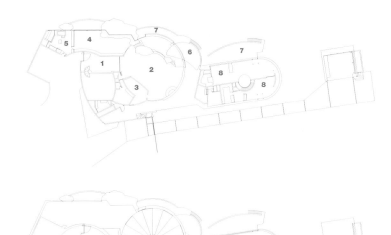

ground floor

1 entrance area
2 living room
3 kitchen
4 master bedroom
5 master bathroom
6 swimming pool
7 terrace
8 guest room

roof level

1 courtyard garden
2 roof deck

The bold concrete shell allows
for sculpted interior spaces
and plays of light. The floral
additions in the kitchen by glass
artist Dale Chihuly add notes of
rich colour.

This house, situated in a green enclave of southwest London, was one of Richard Rogers's first commissions after the dissolution of his Team 4 partnership with Norman and Wendy Foster and Su Rogers. Team 4 had spent six years designing and building Creek Vean in Cornwall – a highly tailored and complex house of crafted concrete blocks on a sloping hillside site overlooking the creek below – for Su Rogers's parents.

When it came to the commission for Richard Rogers's own parents, a very different kind of house evolved, but one that was to have an enormous influence on the shape and direction of the architect's career. The ideas and themes brought to the house ultimately fed into later major projects, including the Pompidou Centre.

Dr Nino and Dada Rogers had emigrated from Italy in 1939, with Richard, and lived for many years in the suburbs of Surrey. But they retained a passion for architecture, contemporary design and modern art, and in the 1960s they commissioned their son to build a house for their retirement – a house more suited to their way of living and their interests. Having found a long narrow garden site, opposite Wimbledon Common, they asked for a one-storey home to avoid any need for stairs, with a small consulting room for Dr Rogers, a pottery studio for Dada Rogers and two bedrooms.

Rogers had toured many of the Case Study houses in California after a year spent studying at Yale and had been inspired by the steel-framed Eames House, as well as by the work of Craig Ellwood, Raphael Soriano and Rudolph Schindler. He liked the adaptability of their buildings and wanted to bring this attitude to bear on the Wimbledon house, using easily sourced, industrially made materials.

The house, then, consists of a simple and exposed steel frame, with a high degree of transparency provided by banks of steel-framed glass to front and back. Solid side walls, abutting the site's boundary, are made of prefabricated panels of aluminium and plastic, bonded together by neoprene. Inside, the house is highly flexible and largely open-plan, with any partitions being moveable. The exposed frame and fixed elements, such as the kitchen, are painted in bright, vivid tones. Beyond the courtyard garden and closer to the nearby roadway, a secondary pavilion was constructed holding the pottery studio and a guest room.

'It was very much a prototype,' says Rogers. 'You can make a direct link between the Wimbledon house and the Pompidou Centre. It's all there – the exposed steel frame, the bright colours and the flexible, adaptable space. The idea was that the house could easily grow as well as change.'

The house was also prototypical in that it set out ideas for homes that could be reproduced on a larger scale, meeting mass housing needs – a theme that has continued to be a point of exploration for Rogers's practice.

For Rogers, one of the biggest surprises was the way in which his mother integrated house and garden, so maximizing the transparency of the structure and the connections between outside and in, rather in the manner of the Case Study houses. 'It's one of the most successful elements of the building,' he commented.

The house is now home to Rogers's son, designer Ab Rogers and his young family, and has thus proved its flexibility. 'The critical words we use,' says Richard Rogers, 'are transparency, flexibility, adaptation, insulation, the relationship between inside and outside. I always compare buildings to children – you can't have a favourite child. But the buildings I have enjoyed most are: my parents' house, because it had these embryo ideas which influenced us ever since; the Pompidou Centre; Lloyd's; and then Madrid Airport. There is a very direct link between them.'

Flexibility was always a key element of the design, and the house has not only endured well but has consistently proved its ability to adapt to shifting circumstances.

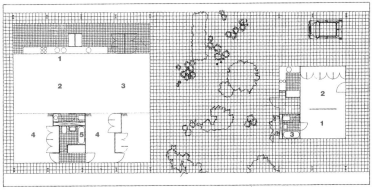

main house

1 kitchen
2 dining area
3 sitting area
4 bedroom
5 bathroom

studio

1 pottery studio
2 guest room
3 bathroom

1970

Emerging from the construction industry and shaped by his field experience, Craig Ellwood came at the business of architecture from an engineering-led perspective. He was, however, able to combine his knowledge of construction and his talent for structural innovation with a sophisticated sense of the unique, glamorous potential of Californian Modernist architecture.

Ellwood combined a search for the structural simplicity of the glass pavilion – embodied by the Barcelona Pavilion and Farnsworth House (see pp. 136–141) by Ludwig Mies van der Rohe, always a significant influence on Ellwood's work – with his intrinsic understanding of West Coast style. He himself was caught up in the lifestyle ethos that he catered for, living well and driving fast in a Ferrari or Lamborghini. He truly understood the Hollywood-influenced, post-war, Californian dream. He was, as some have called him, 'the Cary Grant of architecture'.

Many of Ellwood's best known houses, packaged, photographed and publicized by the architect himself, explored variations on the Californian Modernist classic – the sleek, steel-framed, glass pavilion opening out to the landscape and the great outdoors. But certain houses also explored other themes – courtyard living, for instance, exemplified in the Palevsky House of 1970, one of the last but also one of the most accomplished of Ellwood's career.

Ellwood had known Max Palevsky for some time. In the mid-1960s, Palevsky's Scientific Data Systems (S.D.S.) had established itself as one of the leading hi-tech computer companies in the States, and Ellwood was commissioned to design a production plant. The two men became good friends and, when Palevsky and his wife decided to build a vacation house in the fashionable desert resort of Palm Springs, Ellwood was the obvious choice of architect.

Palevsky already owned an apartment in Palm Springs, in a building designed by A. Quincy Jones, but he craved more privacy and decided on a walled compound to be built in a prime position at the edge of the city. 'Craig said that Moroccan walled houses were well known,' recalled Palevsky, 'And so we went to Morocco with Craig and Gloria [Ellwood].... We looked all over the country and then we went to Tunisia.... We looked at a lot of houses.'[1]

Ellwood, working closely with his associate Alvaro Vallejo, created a rectangular compound of around 655 x 295 feet (200 x 90 m). Within this he positioned the steel-framed main residence overlooking the terrace and pool in front and the open desert beyond, unfolding below the small plateau on which the house was situated. To the rear was added a separate guest house, with two bedrooms back to back, and garaging. This courtyard arrangement allowed for privacy while still opening the residence up to natural light and views of the rugged landscape.

'This house has been a wonderful place for me,' said Palevsky, who carefully layered it with artwork by Andy Warhol, Roy Lichtenstein, Alexander Calder, and others. 'It's very simple. It takes very little care. Things don't break.... I couldn't be more pleased with this house.'[2]

So pleased was Palevsky that he gave Ellwood $10,000 in stock of the new company he was setting up, having sold S.D.S. to Xerox. The new company was called Intel, and five years later Ellwood cashed in his holding for a healthy profit, which helped fund a divorce and facilitated his decision to close his practice down and move to Italy to adopt a different way of life.

1 Quoted in Neil Jackson, *Craig Ellwood*, Laurence King, 2002.
2 Ibid.

Biography

CRAIG ELLWOOD (1922–1992)

Born in Texas and christened Jon Nelson Burke, Ellwood initially studied architecture at night school while working in the construction industry by day. He met John Entenza, editor of *Arts & Architecture* magazine and originator of the Case Study house programme, when he was working as a cost estimator; after founding his own architectural practice in 1948, he went on to design three Case Study houses and to develop a series of stylish Modernist buildings. A glamorous figure and media favourite, Ellwood closed his practice in 1977 and moved to Tuscany to develop his work as a painter.

Key Buildings

Hale House Beverly Hills, Los Angeles, California, USA, 1949

Case Study House #16 Bel Air, California, USA, 1953

Case Study House #18/Fields House Beverly Hills, Los Angeles, California, USA, 1958

Rosen House Brentwood, California, USA, 1962

Art Center College of Design Pasadena, California, USA, 1976

Palevsky House is arranged within a walled compound reminiscent of North African farmsteads or Mexican haciendas. Here, however, the walls feature openings that frame the views, and to the front, beyond the pool terrace, the barriers are lightweight and transparent, allowing for an open vista across the desert.

The main residence is designed with a fluid layout that allows for continuous expanses of glass to front and back along neatly conceived access corridors. Room dividers are kept to a minimum, with semi-partition walls used only to separate the kitchen and master bedroom, while the dining area and sitting room remain open-plan.

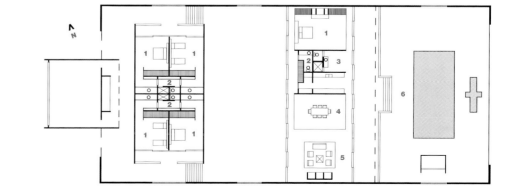

guest house

1 guest bedroom
2 bathroom

main house

1 bedroom
2 bathroom
3 kitchen
4 dining area
5 sitting area
6 pool terrace

AGUSTÍN HERNÁNDEZ

CASA HERNÁNDEZ MEXICO CITY, MEXICO

'To be a creator, you have to be original,' says Agustín Hernández. There is no doubting that his voice is one of the most original in Mexican architecture, with a series of epic sculpted buildings to his name. Fusing the influence of pre-Hispanic cultures with the lessons of Modernism and a good dose of futuristic sci-fi imagery, Hernández has created a range of monumental structures in Mexico City and beyond.

In many of his key projects, including the Heroic Military College in Mexico City and a meditation centre in Cuernavaca, the past, present and future seem to collide in the most dramatic of abstract forms. 'I tried to be different,' he says. 'I tried to look for a real Mexican architecture, to look for a way to revisit the pre-Hispanic roots of our history. It was about looking for identity. It's about a synthesis of all the different cultures around Mexico. And I love science and science fiction.'

Chief among Hernández's projects is his own house and studio in the leafy Bosques de las Lomas residential district of Mexico City. True to his maxim that 'geometry is my god', here the architect and sculptor has created a vast tower crowned by a dynamic concrete spaceship. The building is embedded into a hillside, with its single supporting column reaching down into the sloping bank and the entrance bridge close to the top of the structure's concrete flower, where it meets the road sited at the summit of the hill. This abstract, spacious crown – with views out across the valley below – holds both living spaces and Hernández's atelier.

Casa Hernández – or Taller de Arquitectura (Architectural Atelier) – is one of a small sequence of 'floating machine houses', which include the Casa en el Aire of 1991, built for Hernández's cousin. These are extraordinary structures, with an unclear purpose to the passer-by, and resembling some kind of hi-tech facility. Many of the components reinforce the impression of machine-age drama: the vast metallic entrance doors, for example, or the coiled steel-plate staircase that looks like a giant spring or cog buried within an epic engine.

The house was conceived as a cohesive entity, with the bespoke and largely fitted interiors and furniture designed by Hernández himself to suit the highly unusual spaces. 'Structure, form and function have to come together,' he says. 'It's about unity.'

The structural integrity of Hernández's tower has been tested more than once, during the earthquakes that periodically affect the city, and the house has barely suffered a crack. Casa Hernández will surely long remain among the most captivating of Mexican buildings.

Biography

AGUSTÍN HERNÁNDEZ (b. 1924)
Born in Mexico City, Hernández studied architecture at the National Autonomous University of Mexico. One of his hometown commissions was for the Folkloric Ballet School set up by his sister, the choreographer Amalia Hernández. A number of later commissions – futuristic, monumental sculptures – dot the city. Recent work has taken Hernández to Guatemala and other parts of Latin America.

Key Buildings

Mexican Pavilion Osaka Expo, Japan, 1970
Heroic Military College Mexico City, Mexico, 1976
Meditation Centre Cuernavaca, Mexico, 1984
Casa en el Aire Mexico City, Mexico, 1991

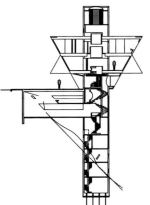

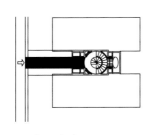

entrance level

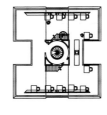

level 1

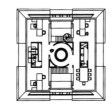

level 2

level 3

The work of Paulo Mendes da Rocha is rich with grand gestures on a monumental, some might say heroic, scale. His structures tend to become abstract sculptures, with a raw and industrial quality enlivened by giant beams, towering columns, vast windows or monolithic walls. Often, the great slabs of his buildings appear to float impossibly, as at the Brazilian Sculpture Museum or the Chapel of St Peter in São Paulo.

On a domestic scale, such a methodology can sometimes seem alienating and intense, recalling factory floors and warehouse stores, and there are good reasons why Mendes da Rocha is usually placed within the brutalist school of architecture. Yet his are also spaces of high drama, born of a sense of scale and openness. Impactive engineering combines with a minimalist approach to finishes and colour, with the textures of concrete and polished cement being allowed to stand in their raw state.

Mendes da Rocha's own single-storey home, completed in 1960, employed prefabricated and industrially produced concrete component parts. The Millán House of 1970, however, works on a rather grander scale.

The house was designed for art dealer Fernando Millán, a close friend of the architect. It has a courtyard garden and sheltered swimming pool to the front, while a series of steps leads up to a roof terrace complete with fish pond. The street exterior is a simple concrete façade, almost completely devoid of windows or standard doorways, as though it were some kind of monolithic repository, sitting in this leafy enclave of São Paulo.

Inside, the house is a tour de force, with comparatively enclosed single-height volumes contrasting with soaring double-height spaces, toplit from skylights above. The centrepiece is a sweeping spiral staircase that leads upwards from the double-height section of the main living room, with balcony landings looking down into the heart of the structure.

The house was sold to another art dealer, Eduardo Leme, and he has worked with Mendes da Rocha on a renovation and modest update. Bedrooms have been enlarged and extra windows added to the upper level. The house has, however, kept its sense of monastic purity, with its bare, unpainted walls well suited to the display of artwork. Indeed, somewhat like the more recent work of John Pawson and Claudio Silvestrin, though lacking the concentration on natural materials and crafted finishes (see p. 240), the minimalism of the Millán House has an art gallery feel. Ornament has been stripped away and the grand bones of the house have been laid bare. Perhaps the spiritual cousins of such a house are the converted lofts and 'found spaces' in cities like London and New York, whose industrial heritage is exposed and made explicit, and whose artistic association becomes significant, with such places usually colonized initially by avant-garde artists.

Mendes da Rocha's spaces have influenced – and continue to influence – a younger generation of architects interested in, on the one hand, this raw, unfettered approach to concrete construction and, on the other hand, the mastery of contrasting space and light. Today, an updated interpretation of the raw brutalist beauty that Mendes da Rocha created can be seen in many urban centres.

The rectangular concrete block of the Millán House is pushed into a sloping site. Its sense of luxury comes not from fine materials or elaborate decoration, but from pure spatial grandeur.

PAULO MENDES DA ROCHA (b. 1928)

Born in Vitória, Brazil, Mendes da Rocha studied at the Mackenzie University School of Architecture in São Paulo. He opened his practice in 1955. Since then, much of his work – residential, cultural, commercial – has been in the city. It is sometimes referred to as 'Paulist brutalism', and has an emphasis on structural monumentality and innovative engineering. Mendes da Rocha has also been a teacher and lecturer for many years, as well as a furniture and set designer. He was awarded the Pritzker Prize in 2006.

Paulistano Athletics Club São Paulo, Brazil, 1957
Mendes da Rocha House São Paulo, Brazil, 1960
Chapel of St Peter São Paulo, Brazil, 1987
Brazilian Sculpture Museum São Paulo, Brazil, 1988

The avant-garde quality that
persists in Mendes da Rocha's
work comes from its extreme,
monumentality.

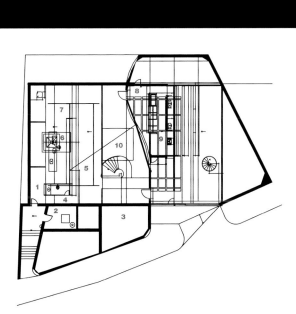

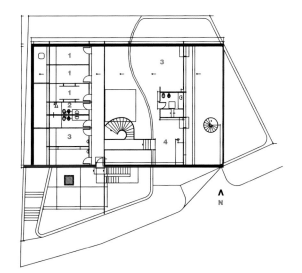

far left: ground floor

1 entrance
2 pump room
3 swimming pool
4 w.c.
5 living room
6 fireplace
7 library
8 dining room
9 kitchen
10 winter garden

left: first floor

1 office
2 bathroom
3 bedroom
4 studio

N

1972

The Goulding House is an elevated sculpture, hovering above the waters, its transparent aspect contrasting with its cedar cladding.

There are certain houses for which the siting adds a whole new dimension to the architecture, becoming a key part of the statement. When one thinks, for example, of Amancio Williams's bridge-like House over the Brook in Mar del Plata, Argentina, or Frank Lloyd Wright's Fallingwater (see pp. 100–105), or many of the gravity-defying houses of John Lautner (see p. 182), one realizes the extent to which an imaginative response to topography can shape a building and transform the ordinary into the extraordinary.

Scott Tallon Walker's Goulding House is a classic case in point. This eyecatching rectangular box of a house cantilevers out from a river bank over the rushing waters of the River Dargle, in Enniskerry, Ireland, in a way that

looks almost impossible at first glance. The steel-framed building, clad with a mix of cedar and glass, becomes a startling belvedere floating over the wooded landscape.

The building was commissioned by businessman, art collector and gardener Sir Basil Goulding. He and his wife Valerie had spent much time and effort developing the extensive gardens at their Enniskerry estate, and now wished to build a summer pavilion, without any planting being ruined by building work.

Ronald Tallon of Scott Tallon Walker designed a pavilion, with acknowledged echoes of Ludwig Mies van der Rohe and Craig Ellwood, but elevated it up above the gardens, pushing the building – with the help of engineers Ove Arup & Partners – out across the river.

The five-bay house was discreetly anchored to the hillside at its entrance point. Two of the bays along the cantilever were supported by iron legs anchored into the rock bed on the river bank below. The last three bays pushed further out across the water, with the furthest two glazed to side and front (this created a viewing platform so dramatic that Goulding had to be dissuaded from ordering the floor to be glazed as well).

Inside, the service core just beyond the entrance area originally contained a kitchenette and utility services, while corridors around the core led to the large open-plan space that forms the majority of the pavilion.

'At the opening night we danced on the outer space of the cantilevers and I was surprised by how well sprung the floor was,'

says Tallon. 'But my greatest pleasure was to be in the building at different seasons of the year. The building embraces the season and its discipline contrasts delicately with the organic forms around it.'

The building eventually became derelict, but the new owners of the Goulding estate recommissioned Scott Tallon Walker to restore the summer house as a guest pavilion, while updating and adding to the service and storage core so as to include a new galley kitchen and fold-down bed.

For all of its echoes of Mies van der Rohe's Farnsworth House (see pp. 136–141) – and also his 1934 design for a Glasshouse on a Hillside – the Goulding House bravely strikes its own course. The gesture of elevation is simple, but a bold and confident precursor to an age of highly engineered pieces of tectonic theatre.

Biography

SCOTT TALLON WALKER (founded 1960)
Ronald Tallon (b. 1927) studied architecture at University College Dublin, and in 1960 formed Scott Tallon Walker with Michael Scott (1905–1989) and Robin Walker (1924–1991). Their firm became the leading Irish Modernist practice, designing a series of commercial and industrial buildings as well as occasional houses and cultural buildings. The company has continued to flourish with the arrival of a new generation of directors.

Key Buildings

Knockanure Church Moyvane, County Kerry, Ireland, 1964
Carroll's Tobacco Factory Dundalk, Ireland, 1969
Central Remedial Clinic Clontarf, Ireland, 1970
Tallon House Foxrock, County Dublin, Ireland, 1970
Bank of Ireland Headquarters Dublin, Ireland, 1975

The key living area, pushing
out over the river and drawing
in leafy greenery through its
banks of glazing, forms an
extraordinary viewing platform.

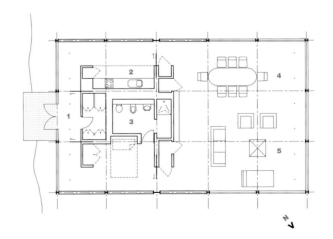

main floor

1 entrance
2 kitchen
3 bathroom
4 dining area
5 sitting area

1972

Jørn Utzon's first house in Majorca was completed just before the opening of the world-famous project that dominated, and indeed overshadowed, his career – Sydney Opera House. Twenty years in the making, the Opera House finally opened without Utzon's name even being mentioned in the opening ceremonies. Sydney has done its best to make up for this in recent years, waking up to the unique value of a masterpiece building that has come to define the city, and arguably the country itself.

The protracted process of the design and build of the Opera House took a considerable toll upon the architect. But, of course, he worked on other projects both large and small, public and private, around the world, drawing on a rich breadth of global architectural influences filtered through the precepts of Modernism. These projects included a series

of houses for his family and himself in Denmark, Australia and Majorca.

Utzon and his wife Lis discovered Majorca in the late 1960s, after leaving Australia where Utzon had been living while working on the Opera House. The couple, who were both drawn to the sea, fell in love with the island and bought a plot of land, sitting among myrtle and pine trees, right on the coast near the village of Porto Petro. Here Utzon designed a family summer house, which he named after his wife.

Before designing the house – models of which Utzon liked to assemble in sugar lumps at a café table in Porto Petro – he would go to the clifftop and scramble down towards the sea, where he would find himself in a cave. This sense of an unfolding view, plus the feeling of shelter and solidity, is what he sought to recreate in the design of Can Lis.

Essentially, it is composed of a line of four stone pavilions – with their face to the ocean and their back to the nearby access road – complemented by a series of courtyards and terraces. The most dominant building of the sequence holds the dining room and kitchen and opens out to a large courtyard that faces the sea, flanked by two loggias pushing out towards the water. The neighbouring pavilion is the tallest structure of the quartet, holding a double-height sitting room. The final pair of structures hold the family bedrooms and separate guest quarters. Thus the site becomes a compound with a carefully composed assembly of buildings, all opening out to the seascape.

All are made with the local sandstone, sourced by Utzon from quarries spotted on bicycle trips around the island. The roofs are made of concrete beams topped with pantiles,

With its solidity and formation, Can Lis suggests in some respects Jørn Utzon's long fascination with courtyard houses and also with the monumentality of pre-Hispanic South American architecture. But it is also a specific response to the site and Majorcan context.

again locally sourced. The large and uniform *marés* sandstone blocks give the house that feeling of cave-like solidity, while holding great thermal mass, and in summer natural cross-ventilation helps to keep the place cool.

Ultimately, the Utzons tired of the exposed position of the site and the attentions of architectural students and tourists coming to see 'the home of the architect of the Sydney Opera House'. In 1994 Can Lis was passed on to Utzon's grown-up children and their own families, while he designed another house – Can Feliz – in a more secluded position elsewhere on the island.

Can Lis, however, has proved a model for a new approach to – in particular – the Mediterranean home, with its contextual attitude to materials and site invigorated by a fresh reinvention of courtyard living. The compound formation, especially, is one that has proved inspirational. Many other contemporary Mediterranean hotels and homes – one thinks, for example, of Carlos Ferrater's Casa Tagomago on Ibiza – have since recognized the advantages of the creation of separate structures within one home, offering a perfect combination of privacy and communal space.

Biography

JØRN UTZON (1918–2008)

The son of a naval architect, Utzon was born in Copenhagen and studied at the city's Royal Academy of Fine Arts. He worked with Alvar Aalto in Finland and established his own practice in Copenhagen in 1945. In 1957 he won the Sydney Opera House competition, although the landmark project proved controversial and Utzon resigned from the job in 1966 (the building went on to be declared a World Heritage site in 2007). In 2003 he was awarded the Pritzker Prize. His sons, Jan and Kim, continue the architectural practice, Utzon Architects, today.

Key Buildings

Kingo Courtyard Housing Helsingør, Denmark, 1958
Melli Bank Tehran, Iran, 1962
Sydney Opera House Sydney, Australia, completed 1973
Bagsværd Church Bagsværd, Denmark, 1976
National Assembly of Kuwait Kuwait City, Kuwait, 1982

Divided according to function, the pavilions are separate and independent, requiring journeys across courtyards and terraces, but each is united with the others by materials and approach.

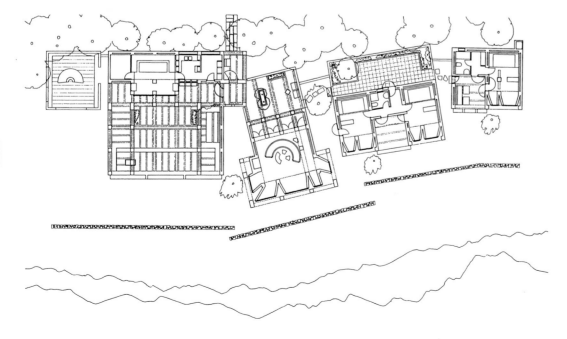

MARIO BOTTA

HOUSE AT RIVA SAN VITALE   TICINO, SWITZERLAND

Our perception of an iconic building is usually filtered through the medium of architectural photography. Such images help to define what a building is all about and articulate the grandest gestures of the architect. In the case of Mario Botta's House at Riva San Vitale, it is the image of a red steel bridge spanning a void from mountain side-path to abstract sculpted platform, with a mountain range towering in the distance, that has come to sum up this dramatic intervention.

Rather like Richard Meier's Douglas House on the banks of Lake Michigan (see pp. 214–217), coincidentally built the very same year, this is a building on a steeply sloping site accessed from the rear by a bridge and then unfolding from the uppermost point downwards. The house becomes a viewing platform, with Lake Lugano spread out before it like a shimmering bowl. Its form, however, can only fully be appreciated from less accessible vantage points further down the slopes of the San Giorgio mountain or from the banks of the lake.

From below, the house reveals itself as an abstract cubist tower – an isolated and almost industrial object, such as a water tower or grain store, sitting in the landscape. Yet the structure is punctured by great openings and voids that erode the pure symmetry of the overall outline and question the building's purpose even further. Botta has become world-renowned for such exercises in geometrical spectacle, taking cubes and cylinders and turning them into sculpted, monumental objects, rich with texture and bound into traditions of material expression and artisanal craftsmanship.

The house was commissioned by a couple who had known Botta since he was a student and had refurbished a village apartment for them. They asked him to design this new home in the canton of Ticino – where Botta also lives – to house them and their two children.

The site, which the clients inherited, is in an area of great natural beauty, dotted with 'roccoli', old bird-hunting towers, some of which have been converted into homes. From the beginning, Botta and his clients wished to preserve the natural setting and avoid landscaping or shaping the site. The idea of a tower suggested a way to create a large family home with minimal impact upon the countryside, and it also suggested a unique programme for family living.

Built with double-layered cement blocks, the house progresses downwards, from the entrance hall and studio at the top of the building, to three main levels below, holding – from the highest to the lowest point – the master bedroom, the children's bedrooms and the main living, dining and kitchen areas. The basement holds services.

Certain spaces become double-height as the interiors unfold and retract, arranged around a spiral staircase that runs up the centre of the house like a spine. The large apertures in the shell of the structure create deep openings that act as a 'filter' and also allow space for sheltered, semi-enclosed terraces.

The house helped establish Botta as an original voice, and commissions moved from private houses to large-scale projects, including the porphyry-clad Tamaro Chapel, also in Ticino and again perched on the mountainside. This chapel explores on a far grander scale some of the ideas first expressed at Riva San Vitale, with a processional bridge once again reaching out to a mesmerizing landscape.

entrance level: studio

± 0,00

level 1: master bedroom

– 2,46

level 2: children's bedrooms

– 4,92

level 3: living/dining/kitchen areas

– 7,38

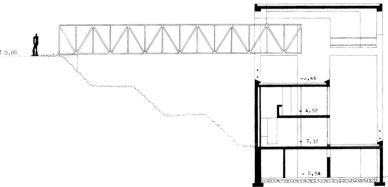

Biography

MARIO BOTTA (b. 1943)

Born in Mendrisio in Switzerland, Botta served an
architectural apprenticeship in Lugano and studied in
Milan and then at the University Institute of Architecture
in Venice under Carlo Scarpa. He worked briefly with
Le Corbusier and Louis Kahn, and founded his own
practice in 1970 in Lugano. As well as designing
buildings around the world, including a series of
powerful sacred spaces that fuse contemporary and
traditional ideas, Botta has founded a new academy
of architecture in Ticino.

Key Buildings

San Francisco Museum of Modern Art San Francisco,
California, USA, 1995

Évry Cathedral/Cathedral of the Resurrection Évry,
France, 1995

Chapel of Santa Maria degli Angeli Monte Tamaro,
Ticino, Switzerland, 1996

Cymbalista Synagogue & Jewish Heritage Centre
Tel Aviv, Israel, 1998

Tschuggen Bergoase Spa Arosa, Switzerland, 2007

The design is sensitive but also has a bold, abstract, elemental power, framed by the landscape which it honours. Inside, white walls and terracotta tiles set off a rich sequence of spatial contrasts.

213

RICHARD MEIER

DOUGLAS HOUSE HARBOR SPRINGS, MICHIGAN, USA

It is a remarkable juxtaposition: a pristine composition of glass and light within a frame of pure white, set against a dramatic hillside landscape, coated in dense conifer trees and reaching down to the shoreline of Lake Michigan. While Richard Meier's earlier Smith House, which overlooks Long Island Sound in Connecticut, toyed with the power to be gained from the contrast of the man-made and the natural, the Douglas House relies upon the sheer surprise of the mix, in an extraordinary site, to create an iconic image in itself.

Beyond this, the Douglas House is one of the most ambitious and influential buildings of Meier's early years. It helped refine and evolve ideas that he first explored in the Smith House and that he subsequently employed on an increasingly ambitious scale as he moved into museum and other cultural projects.

Perhaps, above all, this is a house of light, in which Meier's trademark emphasis on a richness of natural sunlight is explored to its fullest extent. The front of the house, facing the waters of the lake, is enlivened by a sequence of linear glazing, creating a significant sense of transparency, but Meier also introduced a large rooflight at the top of the house, which brings sunlight deep into the building via a complex sequence of double- and triple-height voids that act as light wells.

A series of terraces at one corner, and a sun terrace on top of the building, help further to connect the house to its setting, as though it were a ship with decks open to the passing scenery. The influence of Le Corbusier on Meier's work has often been mentioned, but here one is also reminded of Eileen Gray's E-1027 (see p. 17), its own maritime motifs played out upon the shores of the Mediterranean.

The Douglas House functions as a belvedere, looking out into nature and yet purposefully set apart from its setting – a stirring contradiction. It is simultaneously a highly conspicuous statement, especially when viewed from the lake, and a very private, even discreet house, pushed as it is into the hillside. From the access road behind the building only the upper two levels of the four storeys are visible, and an entry bridge, or gantry, is needed to bring one to the main entrance at the top of the house.

Bedrooms and service areas such as the bathrooms and kitchen are positioned at the back, separated off by a series of aligned landings running the length of the building. Two staircases at opposite corners encourage flexibility and fluidity, one being inside the building and the other pushing out from the terraces of the northeast corner. A discreet access ladder beneath can be used to reach a path down to the dunes and the beach.

In another note reminiscent of the Smith House, the fireplace and its flues are placed right at the front of the house. The fireplace anchors the living room, and the flue stack is transformed into funnel-like cylinders that climb the front elevation.

'The residential commission allows one to formulate ideas and develop a set of principles that, one hopes, will inform future work for a long time to come,' Meier once said. With the Douglas House (and Smith, too), one sees a direct line between the open, light, pure and precise spaces of the home and those similar qualities played out in much larger, more ambitious terms in Meier's later work. Beyond that, such crisp and sophisticated Meier houses – bathed in sunlight and opening like a lens onto their environment – have had an international impact and have become shorthand reference points for a wave of imitators.

Biography

RICHARD MEIER (b. 1934)
Born in New Jersey, Meier was educated at Cornell University. He went on to work in Marcel Breuer's office before establishing his own practice in 1963. A key member of the 'New York Five' group, he first made an impact with a series of private residences before moving on to large-scale projects – particularly cultural centres in the United States and abroad.

Key Buildings

Smith House Darien, Connecticut, USA, 1967
High Museum of Art Atlanta, Georgia, USA, 1983
Frankfurt Museum of Decorative Arts Frankfurt, Germany, 1985
Canal Plus Headquarters Paris, France, 1992
The Getty Center Los Angeles, California, USA, 1997

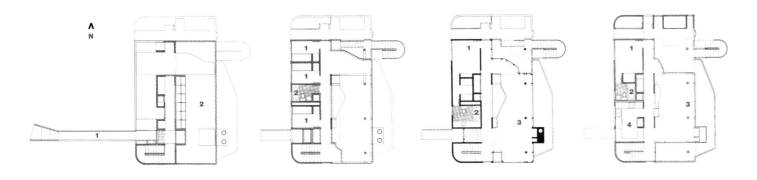

from left to right

roof level:
1 bridge
2 terrace

upper level:
1 bedroom
2 bathroom

middle level:
1 bedroom
2 bathroom
3 living room

lower level:
1 bedroom
2 bathroom
3 dining room
4 kitchen

Purity of geometrical form and the striking use of natural light within crisp, white structures are the hallmarks of Meier's architectural practice. Here, the double-height living room looks down upon a triple-height dining area, while the terrace to one side dissolves the line between indoors and out, and forms part of a walkway that continues down to the beach.

PETER EISENMAN

HOUSE VI   WEST CORNWALL, CONNECTICUT, USA

Peter Eisenman is an architect who has made a career out of challenging convention, preconception and tradition. In his writings, and particularly in his extraordinary Berlin Memorial to the Murdered Jews, his philosophy has been powerfully articulated, pinned upon ideas of subverting expectations of architectural form so as to unsettle and incite the observer. But when applied to the house, that most fundamental and functional of buildings, Eisenman's practice has exposed him to a flurry of controversy.

'I am looking for ways of conceptualizing space,' he said, 'that will place the subject in a displaced relationship because they will have no iconographic references to traditional forms of organization. That is what I have always been trying to do – to displace the subject; to oblige the subject to reconceptualize architecture.'[1]

House VI was commissioned by art historian Suzanne Frank and her photographer husband.

The story of the build goes some way towards underlining the extraordinarily intimate and complex relationship that develops between architect and client as they go on the long and highly personal journey of designing and constructing a home. While the resulting house may achieve the status of an artwork, it is also of course meant to be a practical, working building devoted to day-to-day living.

Suzanne Frank was initially trusting and sympathetic to Eisenman's intellectual vision. She had worked with him in the early 1970s and, in commissioning the weekend house to a loose brief, set herself out as a firm supporter of his ideas. Yet this small post and beam, plywood and stucco, two-storey country house, set in 6 acres (2.4 hectares) of bucolic woodland, became something of a cause célèbre.

The adventure of designing, building and living in this high-concept residence was captured in a book, *Peter Eisenman's House VI*,

with commentary from both Frank and Eisenman. What became clear was that, while the house was an undoubtedly pioneering building full of richly applied theory that turned Modernist assumptions of space, form and function upside down, it was also a challenging and often impractical space in which to live.

'My first four houses were essentially variations on white cubes,' wrote Eisenman. 'They were hermetic self-contained environments. While it was not apparent at the time, they contained many preconceptions which upon reflection seemed to me to be culturally conditioned. The inversion of these preconceptions in House VI seemed to make it possible to look at the nature and meaning of, say, a façade or a plan in a new way, and thus to cast some light on aspects of architecture previously obscured.'[2]

House VI subverts the idea of the white cube in almost every way, with the exteriors even

House VI is a home that invites constant questions and has become a high watermark for the Deconstructivist canon. Its disjointed form is punctured by irregular windows, large and small, and walls seem to serve little purpose, accompanied by floating, non-supporting beams.

painted grey in a complex colour-coding system. Function becomes secondary: a second ghost staircase leading nowhere echoes the first; a slot window cuts the master bedroom in two and continues along the floor, apparently seeking to divide the marital bed. The house becomes, as Frank put it, a sculpted, cubist concept of 'spatial opposites'.

While professing her great fondness and respect for the house, Frank describes how it took three years to build, with a struggling contractor, only to end up leaking and structurally compromised. A considerable and costly rebuilding process resulted, which was not always completely in tune with the architect's vision, though ultimately he affirmed his pleasure at the sensitivity of the renovations.

'During the ... years my husband and I have lived in the house and seen its fragility and its development, we have had numerous differences with Eisenman, but the house itself has been a continuous source of aesthetic delight, if not always a place that protected us from the rain and snow.'[3]

House VI is 'a superb cultural object', as Frank put it, and an important one in a larger process of reassessing architectural assumptions. Yet it also suggests that the avant-garde is no easy place for the home-maker to inhabit.

1 Quoted in Philip Jodidio, *Contemporary American Architects*, Vol. II, Taschen, 1996.
2 Writing in Suzanne Frank, *Peter Eisenman's House VI*, Whitney Library of Design, 1994.
3 Ibid.

Biography

PETER EISENMAN (b. 1932)
A member of the 'New York Five', and well-known as a theorist and experimentalist associated with the Deconstructivist and Postmodern movements, Eisenman has proved a controversial and divisive figure. Educated at Cornell, Columbia and Cambridge, he is a lecturer and writer, as well as a practising architect. His abstract and unsettling Memorial to the Murdered Jews of Europe in Berlin has thus far proved the apotheosis of his theories of dislocation and displacement.

Key Buildings

Wexner Center for the Visual Arts, Ohio State University Columbus, Ohio, USA, 1989
Greater Columbus Convention Center Columbus, Ohio, USA, 1993
Aronoff Center for Design and Art, University of Cincinnati Cincinnati, Ohio, USA, 1996
Memorial to the Murdered Jews of Europe Berlin, Germany, 2005
University of Phoenix Stadium Glendale, Arizona, USA, 2006

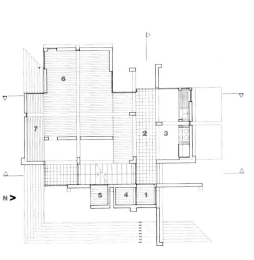

ground floor

1 entrance
2 dining room
3 kitchen
4 closet
5 storage area
6 living room
7 study

N >

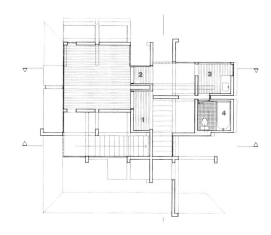

first floor

1 bedroom
2 closet
3 bed alcove
4 bathroom

1976

MICHAEL & PATTY HOPKINS

HOPKINS HOUSE HAMPSTEAD, LONDON, ENGLAND

When it was designed and built in the mid-1970s, the Hopkins House served as much more than just a home. It was a studio for Michael and Patty Hopkins's new architectural practice, a showcase of their work to be presented to prospective clients, and an experimental building that proved a key stepping stone in the couple's innovative approach to structure and building technology.

Michael and Patty Hopkins and their three children were fast outgrowing a house in nearby Highgate when they came across the site for a new house on a traditional street in Hampstead, lined with Georgian houses. The site had been created by partitioning the garden of a neighbouring house, and its ground level – in this village of steep hillsides – was 10 feet (3 m) below that of the road and pavement beyond.

The design of the house was driven not only by an interest in structural innovation but also by very pragmatic considerations, such as cost. Having spent the value of their former property

on buying the site alone, the Hopkins needed to build on the tightest of budgets.

'We definitely wanted to build a steel-framed house; that came very early on,' says Patty Hopkins. 'We wanted to build a little villa and were keen on things like the Eames House and the Farnsworth House. Those things were in our minds and it all fell into place. Also, we already had a timber-framed house in Suffolk which we used at weekends and, although it was completely different, we enjoyed the idea of an exposed frame. This was like doing a modern equivalent.'

The two-storey, flat-roofed house is discreetly positioned, becoming almost invisible from the road beyond, from which it is accessed via a footbridge directly into an entrance on the upper level. Only from the garden elevation does the ambition of the house – a lightly made pavilion with banks of glass opening it up to its garden setting – become clearer.

Laid out on a simple six-bay grid, the lightweight steel frame creates a highly flexible structure, coated to the sides in metal panels but with alternately sliding sheets of glass to front and back. Building and enclosing the frame cost just £20,000.

Stand-alone pods containing bathrooms were inserted on each floor, with a prefabricated spiral staircase connecting the two levels. Beyond this, the house was initially kept as open-plan as possible (partitions were later inserted to create three bedrooms, one upstairs and two down). Having just founded their practice, the Hopkins used much of the upper level as their studio. Eventually the house, having proved its flexibility and resilience, returned to fully residential use, and is still home to Michael and Patty Hopkins today.

For all its neighbourly discretion, the house is highly emblematic of the 1970s surge in High-Tech architecture and the push towards fresh, adaptable and lightweight building systems; in this, it shares a number of themes with the house Richard Rogers designed for his parents in Wimbledon (see pp. 188–191). Michael Hopkins went on to develop the Patera framing system, used in the main London offices of his practice, and he also developed building systems on a far larger scale, such as the design for the new-generation steel and glass 'super shed' for the brewers Greene King in Suffolk.

Within the Hopkins House one detects a sensitivity to site and context that came partially to define later work. A more striking statement could have been made by adding another floor and glazing the side elevations, but this might have compromised privacy as well as provoked local controversy. Balancing the demands of the site with the powerful message of innovative modernity ultimately created a more successful and enduring home.

Biographies

MICHAEL HOPKINS (b. 1935) & PATTY HOPKINS (b. 1942)

The son of a builder, Michael Hopkins studied at the Architectural Association and worked in the office of Basil Spence before going into partnership with Norman Foster. He went on to co-found Hopkins Architects with his wife Patty in 1976. An initial emphasis on structural and technological innovation was later augmented by renewed interest in contextuality and the reinterpretation of more traditional materials.

Key Buildings

Mound Stand, Lord's Cricket Ground St John's Wood, London, England, 1987
Schlumberger Cambridge Research Centre Cambridge, England, 1992
Glyndebourne Opera House Sussex, England, 1994
Saga Group Headquarters Folkestone, Kent, England, 1998
Portcullis House Westminster, London, England, 2000

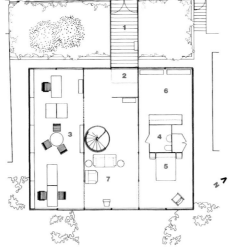

far left: street level

1 bridge
2 entrance
3 studio
4 shower room
5 bedroom
6 dressing room
7 sitting room

left: garden level

1 bedroom
2 library/bedroom
3 kitchen
4 dining room
5 sitting room
6 shower room

Frank Gehry is, arguably, the best-known and most influential architect of the early twenty-first century. His cultural buildings have reached wide audiences, films have been made about him, and he manages to reach out to those who might not even recognize the names of any of his architectural contemporaries.

Perhaps most famously, his sinuous, titanium-clad Guggenheim building in Bilbao gave rise to the 'Bilbao effect' – the idea that the eyecatching architecture of a new and high-profile cultural institution could help regenerate an entire city by encouraging tourism and inward investment. Ever since, many communities around the world have been seeking out their own catalytic Bilbao effect.

The new level of public recognition that Gehry attained with Bilbao was a long time in coming. For many years his best-known projects were a handful of residences, for which he developed ideas that were later explored on a far larger canvas. There was the sculpted Winton Guest House, in Wayzata, Minnesota, in 1987, sitting alongside a house by Philip Johnson, and a house for Marna and Rockwell Schnabel in California. But above all there was his own house in Santa Monica. The fact that this was not a new-build, but a revision of an existing building, makes its impact all the more surprising.

In 1977 Gehry and his wife Berta bought a two-storey, timber-framed house on the corner of a Santa Monica street. This pink-painted house was unremarkable, similar to many others in the area. Gehry's radical reinvention involved extending the building but, more importantly, partially covering it with a new and unusual skin.

Using an ad hoc combination of a Christo-like structural wrapping process and a process akin to mounting the hoardings on a construction site, Gehry remodelled the old house to the north and east with outer layers of corrugated metal sheeting. These new walls, standing at irregular angles and tilts, continue beyond the house to partially enclose a private courtyard, while two crumpled glass cubes form a link between the old house and its new coat.

The result is essentially a house within a house, with the outline and character of the original 1920s building still visible beyond its surreal blanket. Inside, parts of the original house were also stripped back to reveal the skeletal lathe below, as though deconstructing the structure and uncovering its bones.

The Gehry House – much influenced by the art world on many levels – touched upon key themes that became all the more apparent in the architect's work later on. There was the sculpted form of the new building expressed in raw and semi-industrial materials, and the idea of dynamic movement suggested by the new interventions' irregular and fluid forms. The house seems like a rough and ready prototype of buildings – such as the Bilbao Guggenheim and the Disney Concert Hall – that were to follow many years later, in which the surfaces are as sinuous and finely honed as an airplane fuselage and the metallic finishes are gleaming and polished.

In the early 1990s, once Gehry's children had grown up into teenagers, he undertook a further updating of the house, which was now a star attraction on architectural tours. As well as increasing the family's privacy and extending key internal spaces, he converted the garage into a guest lodge and games den, and added a lap pool.

For all its raw aesthetic, the Gehry House was a signpost to a new way of thinking and a new direction in architecture, ultimately given impetus by the rise of computers in architects' offices. The house has become a shrine to the power of Gehry as the supreme North American shape-maker.

FRANK GEHRY (b. 1929)
Born in Toronto, Gehry studied architecture at the University of Southern California and at Harvard. He founded his own practice in Los Angeles in 1962. Using computer-aided design technology, he has been at the forefront of the reinvention of architectural form in terms of fluid, sculpted buildings. He was awarded the Pritzker Prize in 1989.

Key Buildings

Schnabel Residence Brentwood, California, USA, 1990
Guggenheim Museum Bilbao Bilbao, Spain, 1997
Experience Music Project Seattle, Washington, USA, 2000
Walt Disney Concert Hall Los Angeles, California, USA, 2003
Hotel Marqués de Riscal Elciego, Spain, 2006

The wrapping and realignment
of the original house creates a
level of abstraction as well as a
wholesale reassessment of the
building. The fluid and original
nature of the reinvention
presages the Gehry buildings
that have made the architect
world-renowned.

'When you look at Japanese traditional architecture, you have to look at Japanese culture and its relationship with nature,' says Tadao Ando. 'You can actually live in a harmonious, close contact with nature. This is very unique to Japan. Japanese traditional architecture is created based on these conditions. This is the reason you have a very high degree of connection between the outside and inside....'[1]

Certainly, one of the most fascinating aspects of Ando's work is the complex way in which he combines a passion for monumental, abstract, geometrical forms – usually in concrete – with a sensitive respect for the natural world. His buildings, for all their dramatic power, are not simply imposed upon a landscape but emerge from a deep understanding of the site. 'You have to absorb what you see around you, what exists on the land, and then use that knowledge along with contemporary thinking to interpret what you see.'[2]

Indeed, a number of Ando's buildings have woven themselves into their sites by forming 'landscrapers', bound into the land itself. This is especially true of the Honpukuji Water Temple and the Naoshima Contemporary Art Museum, which partially disappear into the topography.

It can also be said of the Koshino House. This is not organic architecture: the rectangular forms of the house clearly contrast with the forms of nature. But it is an example of what Ando calls 'site-craft' – a careful integration of house and setting.

The house, created for a fashion designer, was pushed into a lush green hillside, partially encircled by trees. 'The goal,' says Ando, 'was a house in which the power of nature that penetrates it is made conspicuous by a thorough purification of the architectural elements.'[3]

The building is divided into two rectangular concrete blocks, sitting parallel to one another but of different sizes and dimensions. The two-storey block holds the entrance, main living spaces and master bedroom above, with a highly minimal living room on the lower level. The other block, accessed by a subterranean walkway, sits a little lower on the site and originally held a sequence of bedrooms. Typically for Ando, the interiors are pared down to the extreme, creating an emphasis on light, shadow, texture and those all-important but edited views of the land.

In 1984 Ando added a – mainly submerged – atelier to one side of the site. In 2006 he was asked to remodel the bedroom unit, given that the owner's children had grown up. This part of the house was reinvented as a largely independent two-storey guest house.

Koshino House's evolution has not undermined its central themes and architectural presence. It remains, like so much of Ando's work, a building of great order which lends itself to deep contemplation. It embodies a particularly Japanese sense of purity, which has had a profound effect on the Minimalist movement in general, and also on the trend towards reduction in favour of textural richness and the play of light. That this is done in concert with site and setting further enriches Ando's achievement.

1 Interview with Robert Ivy, *Architectural Record*, May 2002.
2 Ibid.
3 Writing in *Tadao Ando: Houses & Housing*, Toto Shuppan, 2007.

Biography

TADAO ANDO (b. 1941)

Born in Osaka, where he still lives and works, Ando was raised by his grandmother. He worked in a carpentry shop and a glass factory before becoming a professional boxer, always maintaining an interest in design. In the early 1960s he began a process of self-education in architecture, culminating in a 'Grand Tour' around the world which lasted four years. In 1969 he founded his own practice in Osaka. A number of his projects have been focused on the city, but increasingly his work has taken him abroad. He was awarded the Pritzker Prize in 1995.

Key Buildings

Church on the Water Tomamu, Hokkaido, Japan, 1988
Church of the Light Ibaraki, Osaka, Japan, 1989
Modern Art Museum Fort Worth, Texas, USA, 2002
4 x 4 House Kobe, Hyogo, Japan, 2003
Stone Hill Center, Clark Art Institute Williamstown, Massachusetts, USA, 2008

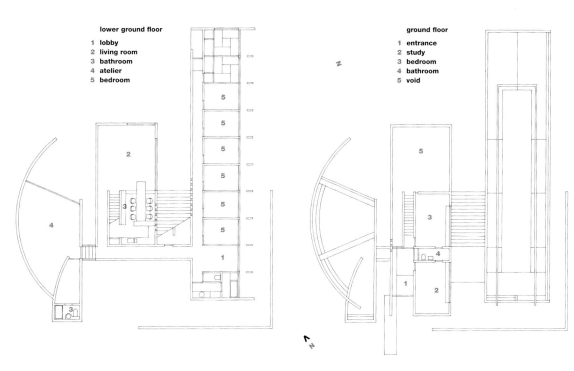

lower ground floor

1 lobby
2 living room
3 bathroom
4 atelier
5 bedroom

ground floor

1 entrance
2 study
3 bedroom
4 bathroom
5 void

1984

The Benthem House can be seen as an important chapter in the ongoing story of the prefabricated home. Throughout the twentieth century and beyond, many architects have experimented with prefabrication, including Jean Prouvé, Richard Buckminster Fuller, Richard Rogers and Shigeru Ban. The goal of a well-designed, well-made, longlasting, affordable and flexible home has proved a tough challenge, with few prototypes making it into mass production.

Jan Benthem's prefab house was the result of a competition to design 'unusual homes', with the five winning entries being offered parcels of land for five years' duration in the neighbourhood of De Fantasie in the Almere quarter of Amsterdam, overlooking the Weerwater. Given that the houses were intended to be temporary, they were free from many of the usual building restrictions and regulations. Indeed, they had a remit to be experimental.

Since the houses needed to be removable or recyclable, they had to touch the site as lightly as possible and they had to be lightweight and adaptable. Benthem's cuboid house raises itself off the ground on a series of steel struts connected to four discreet concrete floorpads. The house is glazed with supporting reinforced glass on the front and on much of the sides, being closed only at the rear. The walls, floors and internal partitions are constructed from a sandwich of plywood wrapped around a layer of polyurethane foam. Stabilizing fins help strengthen the glass panels, and steel tension cables aid in securing the roof.

'This house was prefabricated,' says Benthem, 'because that was the best means of getting the lightest and strongest materials, and to be able to build it myself in a very short time. The house had a very limited period to be spent on the site so it had to be very cheap or relocatable.'[1]

The simple outline of the house is reminiscent of an extraordinary ship, with gantries used to access the raised structure, and with internal and external rear doorways resembling bulkhead entry ways. Meanwhile, the floor plan is extremely flexible and simple, featuring a large, open living space with sliding glass doors that give onto the raised balcony at the front of the building, overlooking the flat countryside and the nearby waterways.

To the rear of the building sits a line of cabins, or pods. These contain two bedrooms, a bathroom and a small galley kitchen.

'I wanted to make it the most simple house I could think of,' says Benthem. 'It needed to be light though strong, and I left out everything that was unnecessary, not only in the plan but also in the materials and detailing. Being one of our first built projects the house taught me how to focus.'

The competition was deemed such a success that the houses were allowed to remain on site, and Benthem and his family have made this 700 square foot (65 sq m) house their home ever since. The addition of a shipping container in the garden has provided extra storage.

That such a lightweight and flexible structure could not only age well but also prove versatile has increased the influence of this modest home, which still has the feeling of transience, as though it were about to be freed from its moorings. In its construction and its visual power, this unusual residence has given so much more than its initial five-year lifespan could ever have suggested.

1 Quoted in Allison Arieff & Bryan Burkhart, *Prefab*, Gibbs Smith, 2002.

Biography

JAN BENTHEM (b. 1952)
Benthem grew up in Amsterdam and studied architecture in Delft alongside Mels Crouwel, with whom he formed a practice in 1979. The forward-thinking and often experimental Benthem Crouwel team place an emphasis on contemporary materials and technical innovation within user-friendly buildings that at times also have a lively and playful quality.

Key Buildings

Sculpture Pavilion Sonsbeek, Netherlands, 1986
De Pont Museum Tilburg, Netherlands, 1993
Schiphol Railway Station, Schiphol Airport
Amsterdam, Netherlands, 1995
IJburg Bridges Amsterdam, Netherlands, 2002
GEM Museum of Contemporary Art The Hague, Netherlands, 2003

While the outline of the Benthem House may be reminiscent of a ship, the structure also has something of the look of a lunar lander or transportation system. Raising the house has many benefits, including maximizing views and protecting the building from flood risk. The hatch-like doorways suggest a further borrowing of themes from ships, trains and planes.

The transparency and open-plan nature of the bulk of the living space allow an extraordinary degree of integration between inside and out, the division blurred further by the slim balcony running along the front of the house.

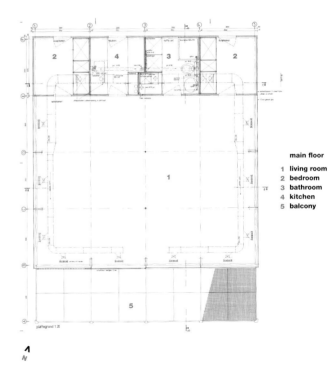

main floor

1 living room
2 bedroom
3 bathroom
4 kitchen
5 balcony

N

1985

Pierre Koenig was experimental and pioneering in many respects. He became one of the leading lights of Californian mid-century Modernism through his intoxicating, much-photographed houses, with their free-flowing floor plans and deep-rooted connections between inside and out. His passion for steel-framed housing over traditional timber construction is well known; so, too, his interest in using prefabrication and factory production to create affordable, well-designed homes. Now, however, his contribution to the environmental movement is also being reassessed and credited.

Koenig's buildings may have been photogenically alluring, but they were also built without air conditioning; in fact they benefited from a presciently careful approach to solar gain and natural cooling techniques. Such energy-saving principles have become cornerstones of sustainable architecture, but for Koenig these were commonsense, instinctive choices.

Koenig paid great attention to his sites and the positioning of his buildings, painstakingly working out the movements of the sun over the course of the day and the seasons, as well as noting the effects of breezes and wind movements. As he remarked, it was 'essential' for him to be able to cool his designs naturally. He ensured that his houses were sited and fenestrated to avoid overheating by solar gain, and he employed organic ventilation methods to keep his buildings cool in summer.

These ideas were developed in his much-publicized Case Study Houses #21 and #22, key designs in John Entenza's famed Case Study programme. Case Study #21, aka the Bailey House, was a highly transparent, open-plan home but conceived to block out the heat in summer and to capture solar gain in winter. Shallow reflecting pools around the house were also used to provide evaporative cooling, helped by water spouts feeding the pools from the roof. This was not a new idea, indeed it was

a very traditional one in some parts of the world, but its application in such a modern context was groundbreaking.

When it came to designing a home for himself and his wife Gloria in Brantwood in the 1980s – the second home Koenig had designed for his own use – he had refined his ideas about natural ventilation and about creating domestic micro-climates even further, and had also taught them to his students. In addition, he had the advantage of having lived in a previous building on the long narrow suburban site for many years, and hence knew it intimately.

The design of the steel-framed house took account of the slender plot and the need to introduce natural light into all parts of the building, while mitigating the power of the afternoon sun. Towards the roadway Koenig created a single-storey studio and office, partially separated from the rest of the house by a courtyard garden. The house then begins to step upwards, rising to two storeys and then a triple-height atrium – a pivotal point, from which all other living spaces radiate. On ground level, this includes the kitchen and library, and on the floor above this includes bedrooms and a study, with a bridge linking the accommodation on either side of the dramatic atrium, which continues upwards to be crowned by a clerestory and an aluminium-coated ceiling. Garaging is to the rear of the site, beyond the back garden, accessed via an alleyway.

The atrium acts as a major cooling conduit for the house. In a natural ventilation cycle, a wind doorway on the lower level sucks in air from outside, while open windows at the top of the atrium draw out hot air. The aluminium-clad house – with its carefully positioned windows worked out in sun-angle diagrams – is thus kept cool throughout the summer.

Such thinking goes hand in hand with a sophisticated and ambitious, yet fluid and adaptable layout and a clearly thought-out building system – with the prefabricated steel frame erected, according to Koenig's step-by-step instructions, in just one day.

'Pierre's method was to think about a building for a year before putting pencil to paper,' says Gloria Koenig. 'His work was incredibly precise and poetic: he welded steel together to form a kind of golden mean. There is a certain serenity that everyone feels when here.'

The triple-height living room, with the kitchen to one side and the music room to the other, acts as an ingenious ventilation stack and is the dramatic heart of the house.

PIERRE KOENIG (1925–2004)

Born in San Francisco to parents of French and
German descent, Koenig studied architecture at the
University of Southern California. While still a student,
he designed and built an avant-garde, steel-framed,
low-budget house for himself in Glendale, California.
He later worked briefly with, among others, Raphael
Soriano, and then founded his own practice. A leading
light in the Case Study programme, Koenig
established himself as a master of mid-century
Modernism with his innovative work in steel-frame
construction and his sensitivity to climate and site.

Koenig House #1 Glendale, California, USA, 1950
Lamel House Glendale, California, USA, 1953
Bailey House/Case Study House #21 Los Angeles,
California, USA, 1958
Seidel House Los Angeles, California, USA, 1960
Stahl House/Case Study House #22 Los Angeles,
California, USA, 1960

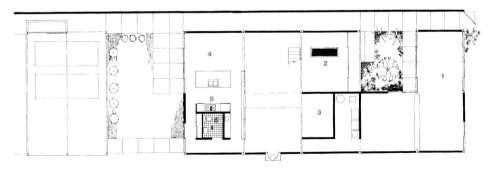

ground floor

1 studio/office
2 parlour
3 library
4 dining room
5 kitchen
6 w.c.

first floor

1 bedroom
2 study
3 bathroom

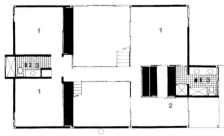

HOUSE AT KORAMANGALA BANGALORE, INDIA

'In India, the sky has profoundly affected our relationship to built form and to open space,' Charles Correa has said. 'For in a warm climate, the best place to be in the late evenings and in the early mornings is outdoors, under the open sky. Hence to us in Asia, the symbol of education has never been the Little Red Schoolhouse of North America, but the guru sitting under the tree. True Enlightenment cannot be achieved within the closed box of a room – one must be outdoors, under the open sky.'[1]

For Correa, terraces, verandas and courtyards have become essential architectural tools, and not just for single-family houses but for the large-scale, low-cost housing projects to which he has often devoted himself. He has argued the great value of outdoor space for the most sophisticated buildings as well as the simplest.

While remaining informed and inspired by traditional Indian architecture, he has also learned from Le Corbusier and others. Like Luis Barragán and Ricardo Legorreta in Mexico, Correa is one of the great regional Modernists, whose buildings are rooted in a very specific response to the climate, history, materials, colours and craftsmanship of their own country.

All of these preoccupations – including the emphasis on a close relationship between indoor and outdoor living – come together at Correa's house and studio in Koramangala. Here the architect was looking at the example of traditional Hindu houses in Tamil Nadu and Goa, which are arranged around a small central courtyard planted with greenery. This courtyard is not only a pivotal point for the circulation pattern of the house, but also helps introduce light and fresh air to the rooms around it.

Correa needed studio and office space, so one part of the house became dominated by areas for work and the other by areas for living. Even after construction began, the family made a number of changes to the programme, which meant that the designs evolved throughout. 'The only thing that they all had in common,' says Correa, 'was the courtyard in the centre. That never varied and it seemed to allow the rest to keep changing, right until the end.' These successive rounds of decision-making

have generated a complicated layering ... like the subtle ambience of an old town that has grown organically over time.'[2]

The vernacular influence is clear, yet this is a house that fuses tradition and modernity, along with a dynamism partially born of the ongoing design changes. There is also an element of spiritual richness, with reference to the emotional importance of both the courtyard and the nearby *kund* – an abstract sacred space, made of cubist blocks of granite. It is with such exceptional fusions that some of the most inspiring and richest architecture comes into being.

1 Writing in *Charles Correa*, Thames & Hudson, 1996.
2 Ibid.

Much of the House at Koramangala is single-storey, though two upper-storey elements hold additional bedrooms. Key spaces such as the living room open on to the courtyard, enlivened by a large Champa plant. There is also a surrounding garden, a veranda shared by the living room and master bedroom, and a roof terrace.

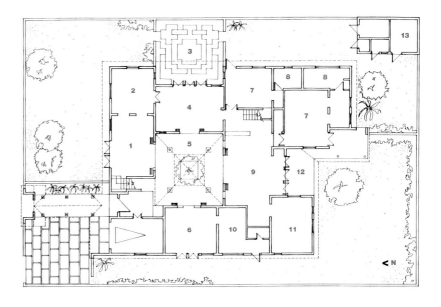

main floor

1. office
2. architect's room
3. *kund*
4. studio
5. courtyard
6. dining/conference room
7. bedroom
8. bathroom
9. living room
10. kitchen
11. weaving room
12. veranda
13. servants' quarters

John Pawson and Claudio Silvestrin have established themselves as major architectural figures within an international design movement that has come to be recognized as 'Minimalism'. It is a movement of architectural purity that is largely devoid of ornament, embellishment or clutter, coming down to the essential lines, proportions and rhythm of a building, together with a clear understanding and appreciation of the texture and quality of materials and finishes.

For obvious reasons, the Minimalist style particularly suits art galleries, fashion stores and sacred spaces, becoming a neutral yet carefully conceived backdrop. But it has also been applied across a certain kind of domestic canvas, particularly in the 1990s when, arguably, the movement was at its height. Pawson, in particular, was seen as an advocate not just of a particular kind of pure architecture but of a carefully defined way of living that reduced the domestic arena down to its bare essentials and a Japanese-inspired level of calm and order. After the perceived excesses and outlandish style statements of the 1980s, the Minimalist philosophy gained ground on account of its sense of austerity and restraint, coupled as it was with an emphasis on a sophisticated approach to high-quality design.

In the late 1980s Pawson and Silvestrin briefly joined forces and entered into joint practice, before once again heading in separate directions. The chief result of their collaboration was this house in Majorca for German art dealer Hans Neuendorf and his wife Carolina and family. Neuendorf, in his wish to create a very different kind of holiday retreat, wanted to go well beyond the traditional rustic style of architecture then favoured on the Balearics.

'In order to get the house passed by the bureaucrats, we had to first start building it in the rustic style, which is really no style at all but some form of kitsch,' explains Neuendorf. 'Then there were numerous changes during the building process. Among other items, I insisted on windows for the bedrooms, which Pawson/Silvestrin did not deem necessary. We settled on very small windows.'

The resulting house is a typical reduction down to a series of essential elements, like an abstract artwork but one in which the quality of light is all-important. The building essentially becomes a large, punctured cube among the

almond and olive trees, with a series of steps leading to a slim entrance fracture in an almost blankly monumental wall, through into an internal courtyard that forms much of the ground-floor plan. The main living space sits to one side of the courtyard, with bedrooms on the floor above.

The exterior render was mixed with ochre pigment to give the house a more organic quality suited to the rural location, while local limestone was used for interior flooring and to create bespoke tables and benches. Some years later, Silvestrin added a sunken tennis court alongside the entrance walkway to the house.

'We worked very closely and fought about many details,' says Neuendorf. 'But the main elements of the design, like the location of the pool and the idea of the 110-metre wall which separates the land from the garden, as well as the submerged tennis court, were all their ideas.'

The absence of visual noise gives the house a wonderful calmness and serenity, while at the same time allowing for the dramatic play of the light. It is a spiritual house, never mundane.'

The monumental simplicity of the house echoes the work of Luis Barragán and Ricardo Legorreta, among others, while also helping to define the ethos of the Minimalist house. As well as being a key project in the careers of the two architects, Neuendorf House continues to be a widely imitated model within the architectural genre of the abstract, sophisticated, pared-down, modern home.

Biographies

JOHN PAWSON (b. 1949)
Born in Yorkshire, Pawson travelled in Japan after a stint at the family textile business. On his return he studied at the Architectural Association in London, and founded his own practice in 1981. His partnership with Claudio Silvestrin lasted from 1987 to 1989. Pawson has become established as one of the leading proponents of the Minimalist style.

CLAUDIO SILVESTRIN (b. 1954)
Born in Italy, Silvestrin studied in Milan and at the Architectural Association in London. He established his solo practice in 1989, mixing domestic commissions and larger-scale international projects, including worldwide work for Giorgio Armani.

Key Buildings

JOHN PAWSON
Novy Dvur Monastery Touzim, Czech Republic, 2004
Baron House Skåne, Sweden, 2005

CLAUDIO SILVESTRIN
Museum of Contemporary Art Turin, Italy, 2002
Victoria Miro Private Collection Space London, England, 2006

A slim swimming pool seems to emerge from a wall of the house, drawn into the enclosed courtyard via the largest opening of the structure and bordered by terracing. Other openings, particularly on the upper floor, become slots neatly cut into the building.

The enclosed living quarters are modest in scale when compared with the overall outline of the building, much of which is devoted to the internal courtyard. Inside, the Minimalist aesthetic continues, within a philosophy of sophisticated simplicity.

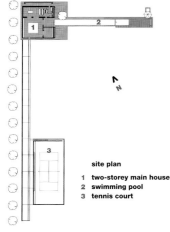

site plan

1 two-storey main house
2 swimming pool
3 tennis court

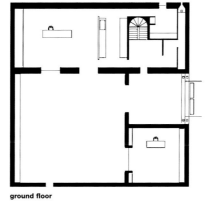

ground floor

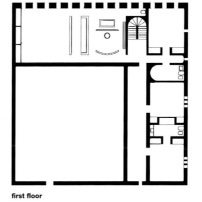

first floor

1989

From above, the Palais Bulles looks like some extraordinary sea creature, complete with random blinking eyes, making its way back into the ocean. It is a vast collection of organic, sinuous capsules, or shells, periodically dotted with sky domes and 'oculi', seemingly rounded by the waves of the Mediterranean, which it overlooks. Its architect, Finnish-born Antti Lovag, initially studied naval design and employs some of its language when describing his work, but the Palais Bulles – as with his other highly distinctive bubble houses – has nothing conventionally nautical about it.

Lovag, along with Pascal Häusermann and Charles A. Haertling, was a pioneer of a futuristic form of organic architecture, mostly associated with the 1960s and '70s, which refused to be limited by the right angle or by the tenets of the International Style. Instead, it sought inspiration from the natural world. Lovag's curvaceous capsule houses, largely built in southern France, were designed to flow over a site, shifting according to the topography of the land – cellular dream homes with echoes of troglodyte caves and igloo villages. They were part of a total philosophy of living which argued that, ergonomically, curves created the most comfortable homes.

'I began to think about improvised buildings, cobbled together on site and adapted to a particular person's desires or idea of a house,' Lovag said. 'Instead of construction based on prefabricated panels, I began experimenting with frameworks that could be bent and changed, and with techniques of concrete surfacing. That way, forms could move again.'[1]

On a hillside location, looking out over the Côte d'Azur between Cannes and St Raphaël, the Palais Bulles was begun in the early 1970s as a project for an industrialist who died before the house was completed. Fashion designer Pierre Cardin then stepped in, ensuring that work on the 28-bedroomed house continued in typically flamboyant style. 'I've always been fascinated by circles, spheres and satellites,' he explained. 'When I heard about a project to construct a house entirely out of round surfaces, I knew it would correspond perfectly with my universe.'[2]

Cardin likened his convention-defying pleasure palace to the human form, with its exotic assemblage of curves, limbs and eyeballs, and certainly its effect is quite surreal. Given the completely fluid nature of the house – which spreads over at least 16,000 square feet (1,500 sq m) within a much larger compound of gardens and grounds – most of its furniture and fittings needed to be bespoke. Cardin designed much of it himself. Colours tend towards earthy browns and reds, contrasting with the blue of the sea and the swimming pools (the large oval window of the main living room opens up to allow access to the adjoining pool).

Although the main building campaign was completed in 1975, Palais Bulles was not declared finished until 1989, when an outdoor theatre was added. Many locals initially opposed the house, arguing that it should be covered over so no one would have to see it. But it has become perhaps the ultimate expression of an idealistic, futuristic strand of twentieth-century organic architecture, which has fed into a more sophisticated and continuing concern with how architecture lives with and learns from the environment, the landscape and nature.

1 Quoted in 'Vive la Différence' by Bruno de Laubadre, *Interior Design* magazine, January 2002.
2 Quoted in 'Double Bubble' by Jonathan Wingfield, *GQ* magazine, September 2000.

ANTTI LOVAG (b. 1920)
Born to Russo-Scandinavian parents and raised in Finland, Turkey and Sweden, Antti Lovag studied naval architecture in Stockholm before working with Jean Prouvé in Paris. He later worked in Sardinia, and finally began to concentrate on his own practice in southern France. Inspired by the natural world, he developed a distinctive architectural approach expressed in a series of houses that are organic, futuristic and highly sinuous.

Key Buildings

Maison Bernard Port-la-Galère, France, 1971
Maison Gaudet Tourette-sur-Loup, France, 1989

Built on a grand scale, immersed within the landscape, and with porthole windows complemented by other rounded openings framing ocean views, the Palais Bulles is a subversive organic sculpture.

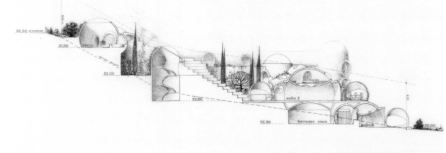

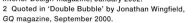

The infinity-style swimming pool lends a further layer of surreal abstraction to the house. Inside, the collaboration between Antti Lovag and Pierre Cardin has resulted in equally unexpected interiors.

RICARDO LEGORRETA

GREENBERG HOUSE LOS ANGELES, CALIFORNIA, USA

Mexican architect Ricardo Legorreta is a standard-bearer for a powerful form of regional architecture. Its influences are disparate, drawing upon colonial Hispanic and pre-Hispanic references, as well as the lessons of Modernism – a rich infusion of the architectural background of the hacienda, the pueblo and the courtyard house, and an appreciation of a typically Mexican approach to structural monumentality and vibrant use of colour.

'My work is very much influenced by Mexican culture,' says Legorreta, whose mentors were Luis Barragán and José Villagrán García. 'Sometimes it's more superficial things, such as the use of colour or plaster, but it runs far deeper than that. For me, the elements which are especially Mexican are the use of scale. In Mexico we have the combination of two cultures – the Hispanic and the Indian – which has led to a very special sense of scale. We are used to ample spaces, sometimes almost frightening spaces....'

Legorreta's highly individual and recognizable style was played out on a suitably large canvas early on with the Camino Real Hotel in Mexico City. Here we saw not only vast spaces, regal courtyards, great expanses of textured walls and a rich approach to pigment, but also mastery in the manipulation of light. These features and qualities were to become apparent in Legorreta's domestic projects, too, both in Mexico and in California – itself, of course, once part of Mexico.

The Californian houses began with the Hollywood home of Mexican actor Ricardo Montalbán in 1985, Legorreta's first project in America. This was followed some years later by the Greenberg House for attorney Arthur N. Greenberg and his family.

The Greenberg House, essentially, masters two traditions in one building. To the front, an irregular two-storey structure creates a courtyard entrance, with simple planting of cacti and palms around a composition of sandy walls, punctured to allow the through-flow of light while preserving a largely private and closed face to the visitor. Then to the rear the building opens up dramatically, creating a strong interplay between house, terracing, pool and gardens.

The outline of the house is dominated by two towers at either side, anchoring the building to its undulating site and holding respectively a studio and a library plus master suite. These

towers also help to cradle the main terrace, accessed by easy flow from the main living room, which then steps down to the elongated pool and lower garden, with landscaping by Mia Lehrer.

Arthur Greenberg says: 'There is a dynamic between indoor and outdoor which we constantly enjoy. There is an incredible quality of light, wonderful colours, human-scale rooms, amazing views, and a very warm and gracious atmosphere. The beautiful landscaping makes us feel as if we are walking through a garden even when we are indoors.'

On plan, the Greenberg House reads as a complex building full of ideas, but the ultimate effect – as with much Mexican architecture – is of simplicity and restraint, with a sense of grandeur derived from scale and line rather than from flamboyant finishes or costly materials.

Above all, perhaps, this is a house that, rather than unfolding every secret in one move, offers a progressive journey of discovery as it shifts from enigmatic entrance to open spaces, twin towers and finally the vivid topography of the garden. 'We love surprises, we love mystery,' says Legorreta. 'Even in our way of being in Mexico we are rather mysterious.'

Biography

RICARDO LEGORRETA (b. 1931)
Born and educated in Mexico City, Legorreta initially worked with José Villagrán García before co-founding Legorreta Arquitectos in 1963. The early success of his groundbreaking Camino Real Hotel in Mexico City led to a series of commissions for hotels and houses, as well as major commercial and cultural buildings. While remaining firmly rooted in the regional Mexican tradition, Legorreta has increasingly worked in the States and beyond. In 2000, the practice was renamed Legorreta + Legorreta to mark a new partnership between the architect and his son Victor.

Key Buildings

Camino Real Hotel Mexico City, Mexico, 1967
Renault Factory Gómez Palacio, Durango, Mexico, 1985
Montalbán House Hollywood, Los Angeles, California, USA, 1985
Metropolitan Cathedral Managua, Nicaragua, 1993
San Antonio Main Library San Antonio, Texas, USA, 1995

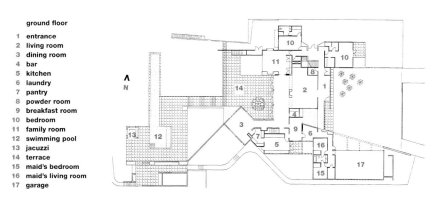

ground floor

1 entrance
2 living room
3 dining room
4 bar
5 kitchen
6 laundry
7 pantry
8 powder room
9 breakfast room
10 bedroom
11 family room
12 swimming pool
13 jacuzzi
14 terrace
15 maid's bedroom
16 maid's living room
17 garage

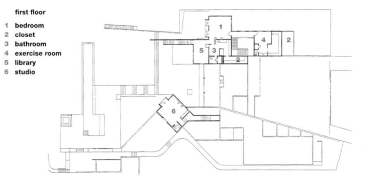

first floor

1 bedroom
2 closet
3 bathroom
4 exercise room
5 library
6 studio

1991

The punctured wall is a recurrent motif in Legorreta's work. Here, the regular lines of slot windows establish a rhythm, while also creating extraordinary plays of light within the interior.

GREENBERG HOUSE

The building opens up
dramatically to the rear, with
key living spaces leading
out to the terracing, gardens
and pool. The vibrant form of
the house is dominated by
the two towers at either side,
one containing a library and
master suite, the other a studio.

1992

ALBERTO CAMPO BAEZA

CASA GASPAR ZAHORA, CÁDIZ, SPAIN

The work of Alberto Campo Baeza has been categorized as falling into the camp of 'Minimalism', but the architect takes issue with the term. He prefers the word 'essentiality', which suggests the innate richness – rather than reductiveness – in his approach to design and sensitivity to context and composition.

Campo Baeza speaks of 'more with less' rather than 'less is more' – 'a more which keeps human beings and the complexity of their culture firmly at the centre of the created world, at the centre of architecture. And a less which, leaving all questions of Minimalism aside, distils the essence of a design by using a "precise number of elements" to translate ideas into physical reality.'[1]

Another way of putting it is to stress that, while Campo Baeza's work represents a pared-down method, devoid of excess and ornamentation, the architect is also a romantic with a poetic view of form and space. His designs are particularly concerned with capturing and filtering light, creating a modern interpretation of the crisp white Iberian home.

Casa Gaspar, situated within an orange grove near Cádiz, was conceived in a poetic spirit of distillation. The architect had to build on a tight budget while balancing, on the one hand, a request for privacy and enclosure, and, on the other, a need for openness, light and fluidity between inside and outside spaces.

The client was a schoolteacher who wanted, above all, seclusion. Campo Baeza's solution was to create a pavilion within a walled garden, borrowing from the classic compound formation of Iberian and North African farmsteads and secret gardens, but bringing the idea very much up to date. High blank white walls, 60 feet long and 12 feet high (18 x 3.5 m), create a square compound, accessed by a simple doorway to the eastern side. Within the enclosure, Campo Baeza established a formal grid with a simple pavilion at its heart.

The pavilion contains a high-ceilinged living and dining room, bordered by modest spaces to either side, containing a bedroom and a kitchen. The pavilion – with a high outline visible over the top of the compound walls – opens out to sheltered patios on either side, planted with a quartet of citrus trees, while a water pool adds another element to the western terrace.

The succinct plastered walls, the clear formal outline, the stone floors flowing inside and out, all suggest the philosophy of romantic essentiality and create a sanctuary of quiet, contemplative calm. 'I was trying to synthesize the spirit of Andalusian houses – a shadow between two patios, crossed by the light,' says Campo Baeza. 'Everything is important when you are using a reduced number of ingredients – light, shadow, white walls, water, trees. You can't leave any of them aside.'

This small but highly significant house helped define Campo Baeza's architectural image and led to ongoing experiments within a series of houses that owed much to the patterns laid down at Gaspar. Casa De Blas, Casa Asencio, Casa Guerrero and others all echo the idea of the crisp pavilion and sheltered courtyard, and also play on the many contrasts between light and shadow, solidity and transparency, openness and enclosure, anonymity and exposure.

More widely, such houses have helped to redefine the concept of the contemporary, Neo-Modernist, Iberian and Mediterranean home, creating an updated version of the escapist retreat and the white outline sitting in the landscape. Such sophisticated simplicity offers a refreshing alternative to the occasional excesses of the Iberian coastline.

1 Quoted in Antonio Pizza, *Alberto Campo Baeza: Works and Projects*, Gustavo Gili, 1999.

The featureless exterior walls of Casa Gaspar immediately encourage a sense of mystery about the building, which appears of such indistinct purpose from without.

Biography

ALBERTO CAMPO BAEZA (b. 1946)

Born in Valladolid, Campo Baeza studied architecture in Madrid, where he also taught for a number of years, as well as lecturing abroad. He is well known for his commercial, cultural and public buildings, but also for his series of innovative Spanish houses, which led to commissions in the United States and elsewhere. Among many projects, the most representative is his design for the offices of Caja de Granada, a building conceived around a spectacular atrium.

Key Buildings

Fene Town Hall Fene, Coruña, Spain, 1980
Turegano House Madrid, Spain, 1988
Casa De Blas Sevilla la Nueva, Madrid, Spain, 2001
Caja de Granada Granada, Spain, 2001
Casa Asencio Chiclana, Cádiz, Spain, 2001

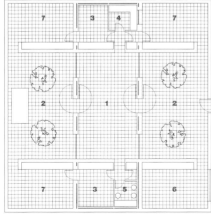

main floor

1 living/dining room
2 patio
3 bedroom
4 kitchen
5 bathroom
6 garage
7 courtyard

The house both maximizes privacy and tempts discovery, unfolding as one enters the perimeter and travels through the sheltered compound from patios to pavilion.

1992

SIMON UNGERS

T-HOUSE WILTON, SARATOGA SPRINGS, NEW YORK, USA

The relationship between art, architecture and home is a complex one, and never more so than when it comes to a house that is as much sculpted artwork as living space. In his work, architect Simon Ungers constantly explored the blurred line between homestead and sculpture, art and architecture, and benefited from a radical cross-pollination of themes and ideas in his achievements in these different fields. His finest buildings – the T-House, and later the Cube House – were striking and abstract artworks, placed within extraordinary and vibrant landscapes, like titanic pieces in a sculpture park.

Sitting in a wooded, rural location in upstate New York, the T-House is a vast, three-dimensional cruciform, partially pushed into the ground and coated in plates of rusting Cor-ten steel. This protective, weathering coat of rust gives the house the quality of a Richard Serra sculpture, but also, despite its industrial qualities, gives the house an organic flavour that ties it into the surrounding woodlands.

The house was designed for writer and academic Lawrence Marcelle and his wife. Marcelle wanted a rural escape that would house his vast library of 10,000 books. The resulting building was a collaboration between Simon Ungers and fellow architect Tom Kinslow.

The base of the building was designed as a long, loft-like room. This ground floor has a largely open-plan feel, though it is lightly divided into four sections by a fireplace, kitchen and other units.

The double-height library is on an upper level and forms a great T-shaped bar that cantilevers out over the site like a giant cross, with a sequence of distinctive slit windows allowing views across the woods. The books are tucked into mezzanine cages, protected from the sun, while the 'deck' of the main house below can be accessed and used as a roof terrace.

'It was my hope that the house would provide a kind of protection and distance from the outside world,' says Lawrence Marcelle. 'I wanted the house as a place to live and work, and asked Simon to provide a distinct sense of space between the living and work areas, and that the house should be unusual. It also shows that what we mean by a "house" is not something fixed and settled but is open for contestation. Since the word "home" runs very deep in our language, this is not a trivial reminder.'

The T-House, exemplifying the talent and imagination of an architect whose career was cruelly cut short, became hugely influential on many levels. As one of the first Cor-ten buildings in America, it set a dramatic precedent for other architectural practices, including Shim-Sutcliffe and Messana O'Rorke, who went on to explore the aesthetic power and beauty of the material. Perhaps more importantly, the house fitted into a strand of late twentieth-century, artistically fuelled architecture that has since pushed abstraction to new levels, questioning the adage that form follows function and pushing into new realms of creative expression.

One now sees the power of abstraction – and sculpted Minimalism – in the 'domestic' architecture of Mathias Klotz, Bearth & Deplazes, Pezo von Ellrichshausen, and others. Here, too, abstraction allied to an extreme or exceptional landscape only intensifies the boldness and power of the statement being made.

The monumental quality of the T-House is all the more extraordinary for being a home and place of work that fulfils its brief so successfully. 'I underestimated just how imposing the finished structure would be,' says Marcelle. 'But others have expressed surprise at how warm the interior space is, and it is surprising that when you enter a steel house you have such a homely and safe feeling.'

Biography

SIMON UNGERS (1957–2006)
Son of German architect O. M. Ungers, Simon Ungers came to America in the 1960s, when his father was teaching there, and studied at Cornell University. He formed UKZ Design with two partners in 1981 and founded his own practice in 1992; he also collaborated with Tom Kinslow. An artist and sculptor as well as an architect, Ungers designed buildings that took on the abstract quality of vast sculptures in the landscape.

Key Buildings

Hobbs House Lansing, New York, USA, 1982
Hermann J. Wiemer Vineyard Addition Dundee, New York, USA, 1982
Knee Residence Caldwell, New Jersey, USA, 1984
Cube House Ithaca, New York, USA, 2001

In a way, it is books that help define the extraordinary and powerful form of the T-House. The cross-bar of the steel-plated structure is dominated by the library and study. At the same time, the library's elevated position offers woodland views, as though placing the viewer within the tree canopy itself.

T-HOUSE

The double-height library's
ingenious stacking system
allows books to be catalogued
and stored in the raised gallery,
while the lower floor area is left
clear. The main 'body' of the
house is simply designed,
with the openness and semi-
industrial aesthetic of loft living.

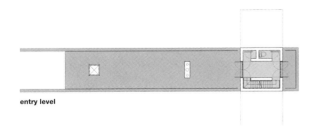

entry level

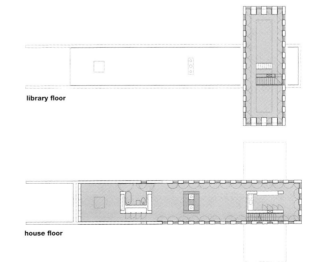

library floor

house floor

1993

LAWSON-WESTEN HOUSE BRENTWOOD, CALIFORNIA, USA

A master of twisted geometry, Eric Owen Moss creates buildings of a sculptural and abstract nature. His structures – hard to define and difficult to categorize – are highly inventive and original. Well versed in deconstruction, Moss continually defies both convention and expectation, rethinking the component parts of his buildings and reassembling them in powerful, fresh combinations.

For Moss, house commissions have been a rarity, given his ongoing work in Los Angeles's Culver City and his large-scale buildings beyond. But the Lawson-Westen House has created a strong impact, with its subversion of traditional and Modernist Californian architecture, and its radical ambition in creating new forms and new ways of living. Linked with the LA School – a term used to cover the formal experimentation of Frank Gehry, Morphosis, and others – Moss's practice is indicative of a substantial shift towards a new kind of architecture, wherein form is liberated by the latest developments in engineering and materials and by pure unfettered imagination.

The Lawson-Westen House was commissioned as a family home by Linda Lawson and Tracy Westen. A key factor in the four-year development was the clients' insistence on the kitchen as the central point of the house. While many contemporary American homes place the kitchen close to garaging for easy access, the Lawson-Westen House places the kitchen literally at the heart of the home, with all other spaces, such as dining room and living room, radiating from it in largely open-plan fashion.

Lawson and Westen had other stipulations, too: 'We said we didn't want the house to be boring. We wanted it to be fun, warm and visually stimulating, even startling. We wanted a house that was itself a work of art, not a series of boxes or rooms in which to hang art. We wanted to live inside a sculptural work.'

Moss designed the house broadly as a parallelogram, with a large circle pushing into its centre, holding the kitchen. In a complex volumetric spectacle, this circle is then carried upward into a soaring cylinder, the void intersected by bridges, stairways and beams, all bathed in natural light. Around the cylinder, Moss created a four-bedroomed, two- and three-storey home with a strong sense of connection to its garden setting.

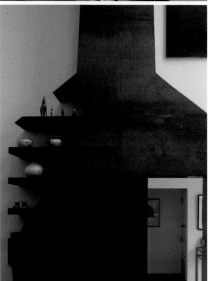

During the 18-month design process, the brief was significantly adapted, with a dining room and extra bedroom added, and the living room moved. While the overall feel of the house remained the same, these evolutions were marked by the purposeful integration of 'ghost' elements of previous schemes, heightening the abstract nature of the spaces.

Materials including concrete, glass and birch were juxtaposed with elements like the steel fireplace in the living room, further underlining the semi-industrial or machine-like quality of the building. Meanwhile, the irregular window pattern encourages plays of light across the key living spaces, while framing views of the garden, and the cathedral-like nature of the main space creates acoustics well suited to the musical performances and events that are occasionally held at the house.

This expressive, bespoke building marks a highly individual collaboration between architect and client. 'There are very few art forms in which a "patron" can participate in the creative process,' say Lawson and Westen. 'But a house invites collaboration, because you have to live in it. The collaborative process with Eric was one of the greatest experiences of our lives.'

Clients Linda Lawson and Tracy Westen said of Eric Owen Moss's complex and startling composition: 'There are so many spectacular angles that you can stay in the house for weeks and keep discovering new vistas or qualities.'

Biography

ERIC OWEN MOSS (b. 1943)
Having studied architecture at the University of California and Harvard, Moss opened his practice in 1973 in the Culver City district of Los Angeles. He has been involved in a series of projects in this former manufacturing district under the patronage of developers Frederick and Laurie Samitaur Smith. With these and other buildings, Moss has explored ideas of deconstruction and the reinvention of form within fluid and unconventional structures layered with unexpected materials and interjections.

Key Buildings

Petal House West Los Angeles, California, USA, 1984
Central Housing Office, University of California
Irvine, California, USA, 1989
The Box Culver City, Los Angeles, California, USA, 1994
Stealth Culver City, Los Angeles, California, USA, 2001
Beehive Culver City, Los Angeles, California, USA, 2002

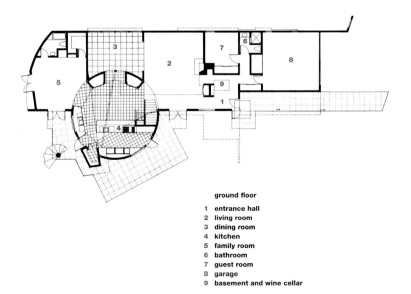
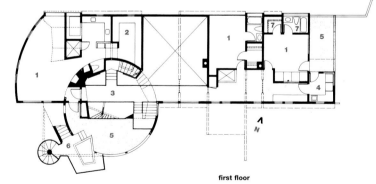

ground floor

1 entrance hall
2 living room
3 dining room
4 kitchen
5 family room
6 bathroom
7 guest room
8 garage
9 basement and wine cellar

first floor

1 bedroom
2 dressing room
3 bridge
4 laundry room
5 deck
6 jacuzzi
7 bathroom

ANTOINE PREDOCK

TURTLE CREEK HOUSE DALLAS, TEXAS, USA

Context is all-important to Antoine Predock. His best known work is grounded in New Mexico and the desert, where his buildings seem to rise up from the earth itself. They splice inspiration from pre-Hispanic cultures and vernacular adobe settlements, though key projects such as the American Heritage Center in Wyoming – a remarkable cone rising out of the ground – are also futuristic and formally striking. The Turtle Creek House combines these ideas in a building carefully tailored to site and client.

The house was commissioned by Rusty and Deedie Rose, keen ornithologists, who were drawn to the site because of its nearby creek. This quiet enclave, with its mix of woodland and water world, is part of a rich birdland habitat and a major point of convergence for birds crisscrossing the country.

'We wanted a place where we could live happily with contemporary art, be able to watch birds in a variety of habitats, and have a real home that would function well for an event for three hundred and for two people with two dogs,' says Deedie Rose. 'The most unique quality of the house is the way it unfolds and doesn't reveal itself all at once, and the way it integrates into nature and allows you to see the natural world in new ways.'

Beyond the elemental entrance point, Predock has set up a series of dynamic routes

through and beyond the main living zones. Above all, one is carried onto a dramatic sky-ramp, which projects outwards and upwards from the back of the house. While leading to nowhere, this extraordinary viewing platform – echoing a desert sky-way at Predock's earlier Zuber House in Arizona – carries one out into the treetops to savour the views out across the creek. At the same time the sky-bridge and its axis create a split in the building between what Predock terms a 'north house' and a 'south house'.

A vast polished reflective steel panel set into the rear aspect of the building offers an extraordinary mirror for the sky-bridge and the surrounding landscape, establishing a stage for optical games and surreal illusions. Another highlight of the house, which is arranged on three levels, plus roof terraces, is the cylindrical, towering drum at the rear containing a raised dining room with views out across the sky-bridge and the countryside beyond.

As Predock has said: 'There is a purely phenomenological impulse toward the use of that convex mirror – how light strikes it and the juxtaposition of this opaque mirror with the transparent, yet mirror-like quality of the living area glazing. Overlaying that intention, though, is the compressed and distorted reflection of the house.... This notion of dematerialization and destabilization, in a polemical not a

perverse way, is part of the intention of the mirrored piece.'[1]

Predock has created here a home that is specifically crafted to its owners and their way of life, but, as with the work of Agustín Hernández, Eric Owen Moss and others, he has also challenged the notion of what a house should be, what it should do and what it should look like.

1 Writing in *Turtle Creek House*, Monacelli Press, 1998.

Biography

ANTOINE PREDOCK (b. 1936)

An artist as well as an architect, Predock studied as a painter under Elaine de Kooning. He attended the universities of New Mexico and Columbia, before founding his architectural practice in 1967, now with offices in Albuquerque, Los Angeles and Taipei. He is best known for his work in New Mexico and the desert states of America, although he has also executed commissions much further afield.

Key Buildings

Zuber House Phoenix, Arizona, USA, 1989

Nelson Fine Arts Center Arizona State University, Tempe, USA, 1989

Las Vegas Library & Museum Las Vegas, Nevada, USA, 1990

American Heritage Center Laramie, Wyoming, USA, 1993

Ventana Vista Elementary School Tucson, Arizona, USA, 1994

Turtle Creek has two faces, each with very different personas. To the street, the house appears as a stone ziggurat, a monumental relic of a forgotten pre-colonial age. But beyond the entrance cut into this stone mass, a very different house unfolds – one that is decidedly modern, open and formally experimental, thrusting out into the landscape.

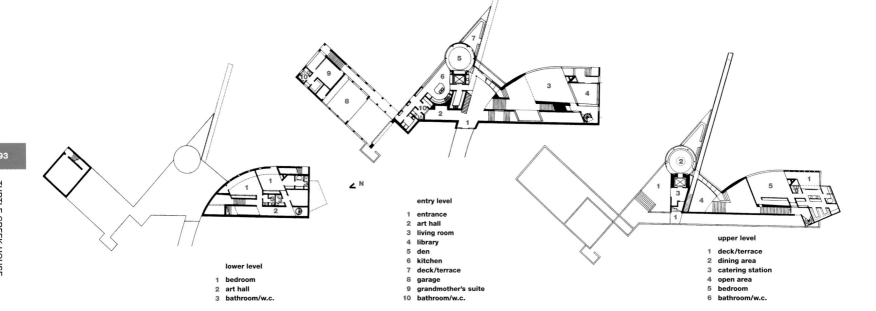

N

lower level

1 bedroom
2 art hall
3 bathroom/w.c.

entry level

1 entrance
2 art hall
3 living room
4 library
5 den
6 kitchen
7 deck/terrace
8 garage
9 grandmother's suite
10 bathroom/w.c.

upper level

1 deck/terrace
2 dining area
3 catering station
4 open area
5 bedroom
6 bathroom/w.c.

The house becomes a game of contrasts between the epic solidity of one face and the blurred, open nature of its opposite. At the same time, the encroaching woodland and verdant tree canopies dissolve the boundaries between house and landscape even further.

1994

ANTHONY HUDSON

BAGGY HOUSE CROYDE, DEVON, ENGLAND

As one of the first of a new generation of English country houses, Baggy House helped re-energize a flagging tradition. Although Serge Chermayeff, Berthold Lubetkin, Patrick Gwynne, Maxwell Fry and others had successfully created something of a pre-war Modernist tradition of English country houses, in the austerity years after the Second World War this was almost forgotten. When country house building did finally restart in any significant manner, the look was dominated by pastiche and Neo-Classicism.

In the 1990s, however, there were finally signs of what could ultimately prove to be a renaissance. A resurgence of interest in Modernist design in Britain was accompanied by an increasingly broad and international frame of reference among a sophisticated and enlightened client base. Here, at last, were patrons willing to battle through the planning system and a bias of conservatism in the hope of creating innovative and pioneering houses that linked back to the days of the 1930s English Modernists, while also paving a new way.

One of the first results of this movement was Anthony Hudson's Baggy House. With a patient and design-conscious patron behind him, Hudson was able to create a dramatic new kind of rural home, infused with a contemporary spirit yet referencing both the Modernist movement and – with its bold white outline reminiscent of the age of Mackintosh and Voysey – touches of the Arts and Crafts era.

The site is an extraordinary one – a clifftop position on the Devon coast, overlooking the Atlantic. The house was intended as a holiday and weekend retreat. Set in this seductive context, it needed to open itself out to the coast and the sea. There was a previous building here on Baggy Point, an undistinguished nineteenth-century house built for a local newspaper baron. Later this was used as a hotel, and Hudson's clients at first had an idea they might convert the existing structure, until they faced up to its many intrinsic shortcomings, particular the lack of a sea view from the main living rooms.

'The brief from the client was straightforward,' says Hudson. 'They wanted an informal family house, approximately six bedrooms, with provision for guests, and to make the most of a spectacular location. They had no fixed ideas of how the building might be; in fact they were courageously open to all possibilities.'

The finished house has two distinct faces. The more private side, facing rising ground to the north, has a solid and monumental aspect, with thick masonry walls protecting the structure and providing solid enclosure. To the south, the house has been opened up, with key living spaces spilling out onto terraces that make the most of the stunning views. In the dining area and 'sea room' the glass walls retract into the floor in summer to form a seamless transition to the terrace and Barragán-inspired swimming pool.

This sophisticated retreat is a paradigm of a modern way of rural living. The attention it garnered attracted new clients, and Hudson has since experimented in other rural contexts, drawing on the vernacular of barns and timber-framed houses. But Baggy was the building that set a standard of ambition not only for his career but for the new breed of English country home.

The complex but fluid three-storey plan of Baggy House makes the most of the rugged Devon topography, with the raised living room as the hub of the home. The plan draws on very disparate influences, including the designs of Adolf Loos, Islamic patterns of circulation and Palladio's Villa Rotonda, but it offers a clarity of form and an imposing presence that is all its own.

Biography

ANTHONY HUDSON (b. 1955)

Born in Norfolk to a farming family, Hudson studied architecture at Cambridge and Westminster. He worked in India and for Connor, Powell-Tuck and Orefelt in London before founding his own practice in 1985. Ten years later he joined forces with architect Sarah Featherstone, but resumed his own practice in 2002 with the creation of Hudson Architects. With offices in London and Norfolk, he has made his greatest impact to date with a series of crafted and considered private houses and conversions, while increasingly developing larger public projects.

Key Buildings

Drop House Northaw, Hertfordshire, England, 1999
Cedar House North Elmham, Norfolk, England, 2005
Barsham Barns Walsingham, Norfolk, England, 2005
Light House Belper, Derbyshire, England, 2006
Stoneleigh Road Managed Workspace Tottenham, London, England, 2007

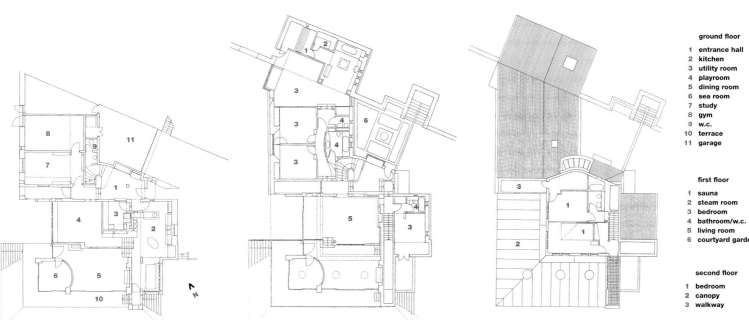

ground floor

1 entrance hall
2 kitchen
3 utility room
4 playroom
5 dining room
6 sea room
7 study
8 gym
9 w.c.
10 terrace
11 garage

first floor

1 sauna
2 steam room
3 bedroom
4 bathroom/w.c.
5 living room
6 courtyard garden

second floor

1 bedroom
2 canopy
3 walkway

The rich variety of references are all delivered in a spirit of considered restraint. There are nods to the seaside setting with porthole windows, to the distant past with the stone pillar, and to foreign exoticism with the Barragán-like colours of the pool area.

For Glenn Murcutt, designing the Simpson-Lee House was an unusually intense, time-consuming but ultimately rewarding experience. He was first approached in 1986 by economist and academic Geelum Simpson-Lee and his wife Sheila, a potter, when they wrote to him requesting 'a sanctuary for a retired couple of intellectual and reclusive leanings', a home with 'a minimalist pared-down approach',[1] to be built on an impressive site close to the Blue Mountains National Park, about 95 miles northwest of Sydney.

'With every good building, as Mies van der Rohe said, there was a very good client, and with this house that has to be acknowledged from the outset,' says Murcutt. 'But Geelum was extremely demanding and we argued the whole way through about every design decision. It was an extraordinary process.'

It took a total of six years for the house to be designed, to get through a lengthy planning process and to be built. The Simpson-Lees asked for a lightweight structure, located in the forest. This was very much in tune with Murcutt's highly influential approach to design, which fuses the lessons of Californian and Scandinavian Modernism with the inspiration of Australian vernacular buildings such as wool sheds, barns and farmsteads, to create a new model for a contemporary country house that sits lightly and integrates with the surrounding landscape. But client and architect came close to breaking

point when Geelum Simpson-Lee suggested that Murcutt had designed him a 'battleship'.

'I was very angry,' says Murcutt, 'and wrote a letter of resignation and hung on to it for a week. [Geelum] rang me and said, "Are you angry with me?" I said that would be an understatement, and he said we'd better meet....'

The problems were resolved by commissioning non-standard, bespoke components and steelwork at extra cost but satisfying the Simpson-Lees' desire for the lightest possible touch upon the landscape. The resulting building is a pavilion tucked into its site, surrounded by silver-trunked eucalyptus trees and forestry.

The house sits on a modest, discreetly positioned ledge in the hillside, and is divided into two separate elements. One holds a garage and pottery studio for Sheila. The other holds the main living accommodation and two bedrooms. The two elements are unified by scale, design and materials, sharing a steel-framed structure coated in corrugated iron that has been painted with a silvery aluminium paint referencing back to the eucalyptus. Each structure has a dramatic sloping roof, sending rainwater into seven recycling tanks.

Between the two structures – which are connected by a bridge – sits a dam that collects excess rainwater. This pool can also be used for damping down and firefighting in case of forest fires, which are an occasional threat. The main

building features a frontage of sliding glass doors, which can be retracted to create a belvedere open to the landscape.

For Murcutt, the house marked a turning point. As well as being a test of the client/architect relationship, the long design process prompted him to question and hone his principles. At one and the same time the building appears simple but is also highly disciplined and sophisticated in its fluid relationship with the natural world and the lightness of its touch. It is this unique version of sophisticated simplicity, together with the great respect shown for setting and environment, that have given the house an international resonance.

Geelum Simpson-Lee died in 2001, but Sheila continues to use the house and Murcutt has often visited. The building stands as a powerful expression of the architect's craftsmanship, eye for detail and sensitivity.

'[The Simpson-Lees] were exceptional clients who made huge demands, on me personally and my time and my intellect, and in the end there was an amazing bond. At the end of the job Geelum put his arm through my arm – we became like father and son – and said, "You know, Glenn, there's one huge disappointment in this project: the process is over."'

1 Letter to Glenn Murcutt, quoted in Kenneth Frampton et al, *Glenn Murcutt, Architect*, 01 Editions, 2006.

The axial route into and through the house follows the path of a historic aboriginal 'songline', while the outward modesty of the pavilion, almost disappearing into the greenery of the woodlands, suggests an intrinsic respect for the surroundings.

Biography

GLENN MURCUTT (b. 1936)

A key figure for environmentally aware architects and designers, Murcutt has made an international impact while continuing to work as a sole practitioner in his native Australia. His buildings fuse Modernist influences from Pierre Chareau, Alvar Aalto, Ludwig Mies van der Rohe and others with ideas from rural vernacular architecture, to form true originals that fully respect the landscape and context.

Key Buildings

Marie Short House Kempsey, NSW, Australia, 1975
Magney House Bingie Point, NSW, Australia, 1984
Marika-Alderton House Yirrkala Community, Eastern Arnhem Land, Australia, 1994
Arthur and Yvonne Boyd Art Centre Riversdale, West Cambewarra, NSW, Australia, 1999

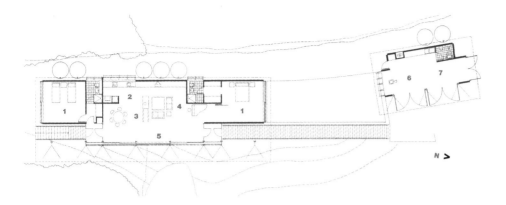

1 bedroom
2 kitchen
3 dining area
4 sitting area
5 veranda
6 pottery studio
7 garage

The Simpson-Lee House defines the architectural notion of 'touching the earth lightly', with its gentle footprint and limited impact upon the environment. The building opens itself up to the landscape quite literally, with its retractable glass walls, which also help with natural ventilation.

1995

SHIGERU BAN

PAPER HOUSE LAKE YAMANAKA, YAMANASHI, JAPAN

The two great themes of Shigeru Ban's work have been transparency on the one hand and structural innovation on the other. The Paper House is possibly the greatest example of a Ban building in which the two themes intersect in one sublime but outwardly simple pavilion.

Ban has become the great explorer of the contemporary architectural world, pushing at the boundaries of both construction and convention. Some of his work has appeared eccentric; some strikingly beautiful, with the sculpted purity of an art installation. All his work has been powerfully original and imaginative, with each successive experiment building upon the last. 'Each of the projects is related to one another,' he says. 'Ideas get developed further and further.'

The theme of transparency and the erosion of conventional divisions in the home have been explored in key buildings, including the Curtain Wall House, the Naked House, the Picture Window House, and perhaps above all the Wall-Less House, where on a hillside site a concrete floor curves upwards against the rise of the slope to anchor the building into position, while its roof is supported by the most slender of columns, and glass panels to three sides retract, leaving the house fully open to the landscape.

Ban has, famously, developed the use of new and unusual materials as structural building tools. With the Naked House, layers of polycarbonate sheeting and polyethylene noodles gave the house a translucent quality. In the Furniture House sequence, bookcases and cupboard units became part of the structure, forming outside walls and partitions as well as supporting the roof.

Most famously, Ban's strong, rugged tube structures – made of recycled paper – have been put to a whole range of uses. They have formed pavilions, churches, disaster relief shelters for the Kobe earthquake, and more. 'Even in disaster areas, as an architect I want to create beautiful buildings,' says Ban. 'I want to move people and to improve people's lives.'[1] The tubes have also formed the temporary office on top of the Pompidou Centre in Paris, which Ban has used while working on the second Pompidou building in Metz.

The Paper House – or 'Paper Tube Structure 05' – marks the first use of structural paper tubes in a permanent building. This weekend home, in a rural area with views of Mount Fuji, consists of 108 cardboard tubes in an S-shaped formation, some of which help to support the roof. The paper tube structure developed here was integrated into the Japanese building code.

The winding S-shape of tubing sits largely within a square pavilion – though also pushing out into the garden at points – with sides of 3 feet (10 m) each. As at the Wall-Less House, glass panels to three sides mark the boundaries of the pavilion and retract to open the building up to terraces and the surrounding landscape.

Inside, the tubes create an organic, fluid screen that partially separates a multifunctional living area, or 'universal space', from access and bathing areas. This womb-like central core can be subdivided with sliding screens to create a private sleeping zone – a familiar convention in the traditional Japanese home.

In some ways, the house is a radical re-interpretation of the traditional home spliced with the model of Mies van der Rohe's Farnsworth House, one of Ban's favourite buildings (see pp. 136–141). With the Paper House, Ban has proved that the most unlikely of materials can result in the most beautiful of buildings.

1 Writing in the introduction to Emilio Ambasz and Shigeru Ban, *Shigeru Ban*, Laurence King, 2001.

Biography

SHIGERU BAN (b. 1957)
Born in Tokyo, Ban studied architecture in the United States, graduating from the Cooper Union School of Architecture. He worked with Arata Isozaki before establishing his own practice in Tokyo in 1985. He has taught at Keio University for many years and served as a consultant to the UNHCR on disaster relief projects.

Key Buildings

Takatori Paper Church Kobe, Japan, 1995
Curtain Wall House Tokyo, Japan, 1995
Paper Log House-Kobe/Paper Tube Structure 07
Kobe, Japan, 1995
Wall-Less House Karuizawa, Nagano, Japan, 1997
Naked House Saitama, Kawagoe, Japan, 2000

Retractable glass walls disappear to expose the central idea of the paper tubes, which help to separate out the living zones and also create a sinuous contrast to the crisp outline of the structure, sitting on its pristine platform.

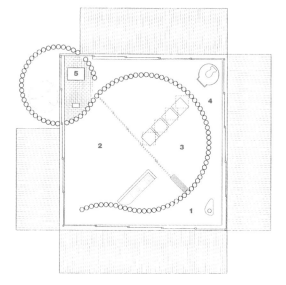

main floor
1 **entrance**
2 **living/dining/kitchen area**
3 **bed corner**
4 **corridor**
5 **bathroom**

O. M. UNGERS

UNGERS HOUSE III COLOGNE, GERMANY

It is well known that an architect's own home is generally regarded as a laboratory of ideas and a manifesto statement. In the case of Oswald Mathias Ungers, however, his homes in Cologne are even more than this. They are, certainly, instalments of an evolving and open-minded architectural approach, drawing on a breadth of architectural traditions and marking different phases in a long career, but – less commonly – they are also autobiographical buildings of which Ungers always retained ownership, and as such the homes evolved with the man himself.

Ungers's first house in Cologne – initially categorized as 'brutalist' – was completed in 1959, but was then radically extended thirty years later when the Cube House was added alongside. A complex of interconnected buildings was thus created. This functioned as home and office, and also housed – principally in the Cube – an extraordinary and wide-ranging collection of architectural books, models, artworks and sculptures, acquired by Ungers and his wife Liselotte over many years. The combined buildings earned comparison with Sir John Soane's home in London – both architectural statement and gallery.

From the 1980s onwards, after periods of teaching and a phase of competition work, Ungers saw his career revive, and he sought to expand his living space once again. Ungers House III, also known as Haus Kämpchensweg, represented a further refinement, indeed the apotheosis, of Ungers's thinking.

He was drawn towards an architecture of geometrical purity, abstraction and minimalist essentiality that stripped away everything but the most precise and powerful architectural elements. 'The new house is cold, rational, monochrome and pared to the bone,' he wrote. 'It is a question of scraping off the superfluous, arriving as close as possible to the core, to the essential. Stopping all decoration, leaving out all redundancy, letting the pure form emerge.'[1]

While the existing house and the Cube addition were devoted to Ungers's architectural practice and also served as gallery, library and archive, the new building was conceived as a working home, devised around a central double-height studio that also held part of the architect's collection of first editions.

The building was positioned within a hidden garden – a 'hortus conclusus' – formed by tall box hedging around 10 feet (3 m) in height, thereby becoming a highly abstract white presence within a background of greenery. This pure white box, with an invisible flat roof, is punctured by a series of window and doorway openings that are strikingly uniform. Ungers also placed equal emphasis on all routes into the house, declining to delineate a specific entrance area.

Inside, the plan is arranged around the central studio, bordered by arterial walls to either side holding stairs, service spaces, galley kitchen and storage. A living room sits at one end of the ground floor and a kitchen/ dining area at the other; these spaces are echoed by two large studio bedrooms above. A swimming pool is concealed below ground.

'In this restricted space are concentrated modules and elements of existence,' Ungers wrote. 'An arsenal of utilitarian tools and notions, a spiritual retreat, with the most important books, drawings, drawing board, bed, easel and reading desk – and mementos. A personal microcosm, squeezed into a minimal space. At the same time: the mirror of our habits and inclinations.'[2]

Ungers House III is an expression of a manifesto that places great importance on precision, craftsmanship and form. Yet at the same time, while embracing a library world of architectural history, the house does not suggest Ungers as a didactic Minimalist. Rather, it is a stunning response to, and reinterpretation of, a long and carefully considered architectural tradition.

1 Quoted in Mercedes Daguerre, *20 Houses by Twenty Architects*, Electa, 2002.
2 Ibid.

Biography

O. M. UNGERS (1926–2007)
Born in Kaisersesch, West Germany, Ungers studied architecture at Karlsruhe before founding his practice in 1950 in Cologne. A highly respected theorist, he taught at Cornell University from 1969 to 1975. He was as much fascinated by Classicism as by the Bauhaus and Modernism, designing a number of buildings with Neo-Classical influences. In later years he moved gradually towards increasing architectural abstraction and geometrical purity.

Key Buildings

Ungers House I Cologne, Germany, 1959
German Architecture Museum Frankfurt, Germany, 1984
Cube House Cologne, Germany, 1989
Baden Regional Library Karlsruhe, Germany, 1991
Wallraf-Richartz Museum Cologne, Germany, 2001

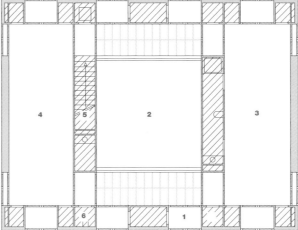

ground floor

1 main entrance
2 library/studio
3 living room
4 dining room
5 kitchen
6 w.c.

Fully bespoke furniture sits in sympathy with the cubist simplicity and sophisticated rhetoric of the house. This is a home reduced down to its essential elements, though with great richness of light, proportion and materials.

ground floor

1 entrance
2 living room
  and fireplace
3 kitchen
4 bathroom
5 bedroom

N >

The idea of submergence is increasingly fascinating in an age of growing ecological awareness. Green roofs are becoming commonplace, camouflaging buildings and bringing benefits in terms of insulation and creation of micro-habitats for plants and wildlife, while also recalling the traditional practice of turf roofing seen in northern parts of Scotland, Scandinavia and elsewhere. But other buildings go well beyond the simple green roof, excavating deep down into the soil to create bunkers folded into the landscape.

One thinks back to Carlo Scarpa's Villa Ottolenghi of 1978 (see p. 24), part of the undulating hillside landscape near Verona, with vegetation further concealing the structure. More recently, Barrie Marshall of Denton Corker Marshall (see p. 298) designed his own house to be largely concealed within the sand dunes and scrub of Phillip Island, near Melbourne. But perhaps the most familiar of this breed of discreet, ground-hugging houses is Future Systems' House in Wales.

Organically integrated into the contours of its clifftop location, the house is invisible from many angles. Roofed over with grass and without any visible garden boundaries, the building's boldest aspect is towards the sea, where it emerges from the vegetation and cliff-face as a glass eye.

The house was commissioned by a politician, Bob Marshall-Andrews, who had been coming to the area with his wife for many years, using a former army barracks building as a holiday home. As the area was situated within a national park, there were many restrictions on development, so Future Systems replaced the existing building with a new idea for a country house.

Their approach was the opposite of the traditional English country house – a visible statement of wealth and status, usually expressed in an imposing Neo-Classical building. Here the house effectively disappears, with just the slim metallic chimney of a wood-burning stove emerging from the roof line.

The house is built with thick concrete retaining walls and has a roof made of a special plywood skin, coated in turf, with additional steel supports. The layout inside is fluid and informal, with the house oriented towards the window lens, formed of aluminium-framed glazing dotted with portholes. The key elements of the interior were prefabricated off-site and

The new breed of country house disappears into the landscape, but still makes the most of it. The centrepiece of the House in Wales's open-plan living area is a large semi-circular sofa by Future Systems arranged around the wood-burning stove and facing the ocean.

292

consist of two pods containing the kitchen to one side and bathing to the other. These pods help to separate off the bedrooms at either side of the house.

The restraint of the design is impressive, especially for a practice such as Future Systems, which has built a reputation for hi-tech, futuristic, zoomorphic showcase buildings. Yet, at the same time it is still a recognizably Future Systems house, with a moon-base kind of feeling to it.

The building has been highly influential in suggesting another way forward for the contemporary country house, especially in places where planning restrictions on building in green-belt land and rural areas can be tight. In recent years, other houses have begun to extend this idea of submergence further, showing a great respect for landscapes that deserve our appreciation and discretion.

Biographies

JAN KAPLICKY (1937–2009)
Kaplicky was born in Prague and studied in the city and worked in private practice there before moving to the UK in 1968. He worked in the offices of Denys Lasdun, Richard Rogers and Norman Foster before founding Future Systems in 1979.

AMANDA LEVETE (b. 1955)
Born in Bridgend, Levete studied at the Architectural Association in London. She worked with Will Alsop at Alsop & Lyall and with Richard Rogers, and also in her own practice, Powis & Levete. In 1989 she became a partner at Future Systems.

Key Buildings

Hauer-King House Islington, London, England, 1994
Floating Bridge Canary Wharf, London, England, 1996
Media Centre, Lord's Cricket Ground St John's Wood, London, England, 1999
Selfridges Birmingham, England, 2003
Maserati Museum Modena, Italy, 2009

1997

HITOSHI ABE

YOMIURI GUEST HOUSE   ZAO, MIYAGI, JAPAN

Hitoshi Abe is not an architect who repeats himself. Each of his projects is very different and, even within his complex series of houses, it is not always easy to find the common ground. His has been described as an architecture without borders. 'My refusal to fall back on a template or any style,' he has said, 'constantly makes me seek new solutions and new models of expression for each new project I undertake.'[1]

If one can trace the thread, it might be that Abe's buildings challenge preconceived notions of space and function, and take this well beyond the idea of the 'universal room'. He does this within buildings that are abstract sculpted forms, often closely connected to the landscape.

One sees this in his Reihoku Community Hall of 2002 – a sinuous building coated in stained cedar and glass. The programme defined certain elements of the structure, such as the auditorium, but flexibility became an inherent part of the project, as Abe created a fluid, adaptable space that became somehow ambiguous.

Flexibility and ambiguity also define Abe's best known house, the Yomiuri Guest House, or YG House. In some ways, this does not feel like a house at all, more like an abstract shelter or a work of land art.

'The concept of this Guest House is a space contained within a 90 metre [295 ft] ribbon, which double-wraps this same space,' says Abe. 'The ribbon embraces the internal space while the exterior moulds itself to the landscape by picking up its topography in order to create a relationship with the surrounding nature.'

So the YG House, rather like UN Studio's Möbius House (see pp. 322–323), is largely defined by a geometrical idea which becomes its driving force, creating a dynamic circulation pattern – a centrifugal swirl that carries you in and up through the two-storey building.

Sitting within woodland and coated in dark cedar boards, the YG House folds around what are, essentially, two open spaces on each floor. On the ground floor, which is partially double-height, the space is mainly open-plan, with all service areas pushed to the sides and concealed in cupboards and alcoves. To one side, the room opens to a large veranda, which is itself partially protected by a wall of latticed timber, filtering the connection to the woodland beyond. Much of the upper floor is dominated by a tatami room, separated from the landing by a sliding shoji screen. These sleeping quarters can be subdivided with further screens.

The house is lent further ambiguity by the continued use of dark stained cedar within the house. Together with the presence of the veranda, this further undermines the distinction between outside and inside.

The YG House is one of those mysterious buildings that makes one reconstruct one's ideas about domestic space from scratch. In some respects – with its emphasis on detailing and craftsmanship, and its traditional sleeping quarters – the house is very Japanese. In other respects, it is so abstract as to be cross-cultural.

It is also a house that largely dissolves principles of separation and the idea of private space in the home, taking to extremes the traditional Japanese tendency towards open living. A totally communal space is created, rather like Abe's Community Hall but on a very different scale. This is reminiscent of the work of Shigeru Ban with his Naked House or Wall-Less House. But where Ban creates an architecture of translucency, Abe creates an architecture of rich enclosure.

1 Interview with online magazine *Designboom*, 11 October 2006.

Clad in dark cedar and sitting in the woods, the abstract and ambiguous Yomiuri Guest House questions all preconceptions of domestic space.

Biography

HITOSHI ABE (b. 1962)
Born in Sendai in Japan, Abe studied architecture there and at the Southern California Institute of Architecture. He worked with Coop Himmelb(l)au in Los Angeles from 1988 to 1992, then returned to Japan to found his own practice, beginning with the commission to design Sendai Stadium for the 2002 World Cup. He has taught architecture both in Japan and America, and his work is known for its structural originality and spatial innovation.

Key Buildings

Shirasagi Bridge Shiroishi, Japan, 1994
Miyagi Water Tower Rifu, Miyagi, Japan, 1994
Miyagi Stadium Sendai, Miyagi, Japan, 2000
K-House Sendai, Miyagi, Japan, 2003

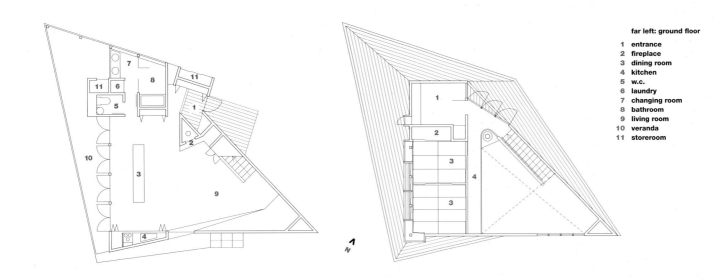

In the cool, cave-like interior, irregular window openings throw vibrant patterns of light, while the white staircase assumes particular importance, connecting visually with – and partially sheltering – the focal-point fireplace below.

1997

SHEEP FARM HOUSE AVINGTON, KYNETON, VICTORIA, AUSTRALIA

Denton Corker Marshall (DCM) usually take on house commissions only when they anticipate that something unusual will result. The Sheep Farm House is a typically powerful and complex experiment in domestic abstraction that – together with a handful of other DCM houses – forms a bold portfolio of buildings which both complement and challenge the landscapes in which they sit.

Within 750 acres (300 hectares) of farmland, pasture and granite outcrops in the gentle foothills of the Great Dividing Range in Victoria, DCM have reinvented the traditional Australian farmstead. In place of the usual compound of barns, outbuildings and farmhouse, the Sheep Farm House presents itself as an abstract sculpted wall 650 feet (200 m) long, sitting in the landscape. Both in terms of its scale within its countryside setting and its rejection of traditional vernacular influences – which continue to inspire many contemporary Australian architects – the house marks itself out as highly innovative.

'The initial idea was to make a line on the land with a windbreak that acted as a link element for all parts of the farmstead – owner's cottage, guest cottage, garages, sheep-shearing shed, yards, and so on,' says DCM partner John Denton. 'At the same time it acts

as the approach view, with everything protected behind the wall. The buildings themselves sit behind and attach to the wall, looking out across the open grass plains.'

The clients, Noel and Lyndsay Henderson, were not fond of traditional domestic architecture and wanted something unique and contemporary. Having bought Avington as open land, with the intention of running a superfine merino stud – which now totals 3,000 sheep – they were starting with a blank slate.

'They liked the idea of using the concrete slabs and were quite amenable to them forming the basis of the house,' says Barrie Marshall of DCM. 'It is quite abstract and doesn't look like a house at all as you approach it. It's only from the other side of the wall that it looks more like a house. In this landscape, like a Donald Judd or Richard Serra piece, the building becomes a kind of sculpture.'

The wall is recessed to the centre, forming a large courtyard with planted trees. A second, higher wall runs parallel to the first at the back point of the courtyard recess to frame an entrance, with a doorway formed by an oblique slash punched into the concrete. Behind these parallel lines sits the main cottage and also a breezeway that connects with the other structures attached to the windbreak.

The roof is a sloping steel blade punctured by steel supports. 'With the abstract wall,' says Marshall, 'the last thing you want to see when you come round the other side would be a standard, ordinary house. We decided that in essence it would be this sloping roof that's almost propped up against the wall and glazed in around the edges.'

The main cottage is a modestly sized pavilion with glass walls to three sides, opening the structure up to the rolling landscape beyond. Its sense of lightness – with the main living areas being open-plan, giving out onto terraces – sits in marked contrast to the weight of the great wall. Self-contained boxes at the back of the cottage hold two bedrooms, bathrooms, a farm office and other utilitarian spaces. The guest cottage, at the furthest remove from the machine- and shearing-sheds, was finished at a later date, and makes for a full complement of structures unified by the slab wall.

The Sheep Farm House maximizes function and addresses the elements, yet in its form it pushes out all the boundaries. It is a house which, executed on an extraordinary and dramatic canvas, challenges convention and expectation, and stretches the concept of a home into the realms of land art and sculpture.

DENTON CORKER MARSHALL (founded 1972)
Denton Corker Marshall (DCM) is one of Australia's best known and most original contemporary architectural practices, and now has a presence around the world. Founders John Denton, Bill Corker and Barrie Marshall undertake house commissions only rarely, yet it is these buildings that have arguably created the greatest impact.

Key Buildings

Phillip Island House near Melbourne, Victoria, Australia, 1992
Melbourne Exhibition Centre Melbourne, Victoria, Australia, 1996
Melbourne Museum Melbourne, Victoria, Australia, 1999
Manchester Civil Justice Centre Manchester, England, 2007

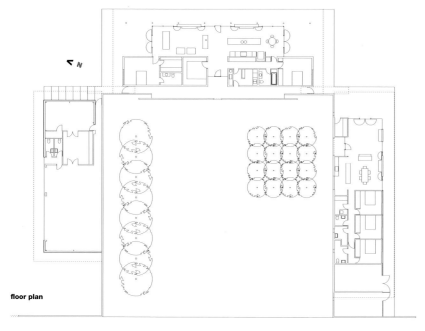

floor plan

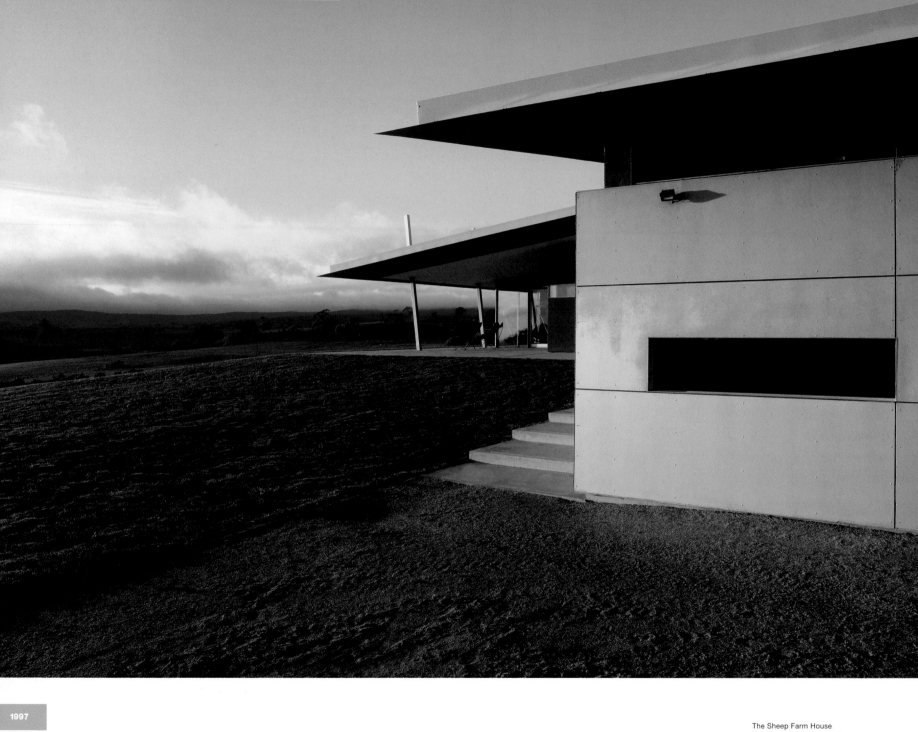

The Sheep Farm House has two very different and contrasting faces. The rear contains the main living space, expressed as a belvedere opening out towards the epic landscape. The way the supporting pins pierce the building continues the idea of sculptural abstraction that flows through the project.

The long slab wall helps to unify the disparate compound elements arranged behind it. The front entrance appears as an oblique slash, leading through to the main residence – a highly contemporary pavilion, whose openness is in stark contrast to the uniform closure of the front wall.

1997

HERZOG & DE MEURON

RUDIN HOUSE   LEYMEN, HAUT-RHIN, FRANCE

The heavy and uniform surfaces of the Rudin House give the impression of weight and mass, but this is challenged by the way the house seems to hover in the midst of open and rolling countryside. At night, the large windows turn the building into a lantern. By day, they open up to the landscape and draw it into the house.

'The strength of our buildings is the immediate, visceral impact they have on a visitor,' Jacques Herzog has said.[1] While his and Pierre de Meuron's early houses show a far greater sense of restraint and austerity than some of their later works, they also – in many cases – share this sense of visual impact. These early houses are not blank structures, but startling compositions. This is especially true of the Rudin House.

On one level, this is like a fairy-tale house – a form reduced down to its purest outline, with high pitched roof, single chimney and large windows. But, looking closer, one is surprised again by the layers of complexity that subvert the initial impression of abstract simplicity.

Now we see that the house is not actually sitting on the ground but, rather, appears to float. In fact it rests on a raised concrete platform, supported by modest pillars, with a stairway reaching up from the void under the platform into the lower level of the three storeys.

As the Pritzker Prize jury said, making their award to Herzog & de Meuron in 2001: 'Here, they set themselves the task of building a small house that would stand for the quintessential distillation of the word "house", a child's crayon drawing, irreducible to anything more simple, direct and honest … and they set it on a pedestal to emphasize its iconic qualities.'[2]

The house is made of raw concrete slabs, and rainwater is allowed to run down the surfaces, leaving patterns on the building. As with Herzog & de Meuron's Fröhlich House of 1995, there is barely any differentiation between the grey walls and the tar-board roof.

Inside, the three-bedroomed house again subverts the notion of simplicity with a highly imaginative arrangement of space. The central staircase linking the two lower levels carries on sweeping upwards to the height of the pitched roof above, while a separate access stairway links the second level to the attic.

As a work of sculptural abstraction and an enticing visual statement, the Rudin House has a deserved place within the Herzog & de Meuron canon. In many ways it is the antithesis of the practice's increasingly ambitious and large-scale projects, but it proves that powerful themes, ideas and images can be created in the most domestic and modest of contexts.

1 Quoted in online magazine *Great Buildings Online*.
2 Jury Award Announcement, The Pritzker Architecture Prize, The Hyatt Foundation, 2001.

Biographies

JACQUES HERZOG (b. 1950) & PIERRE DE MEURON (b. 1950)
Basel-born Herzog and De Meuron studied architecture at the Swiss Federal Institute of Technology (ETH) in Zurich and studied with Aldo Rossi. They founded their Basel-based practice in 1978. They have also taught in Switzerland and America. The austere minimalism of their early work has increasingly given way to innovative experiments with pattern, materials and textures woven into the façades and fabric of their buildings.

Key Buildings

Dominus Winery Napa Valley, California, USA, 1999
Tate Modern Bankside, London, England, 2000
Allianz Arena Football Stadium Munich, Germany, 2005
M. H. de Young Memorial Museum San Francisco, California, USA, 2005
Walker Art Center Expansion Minneapolis, Minnesota, USA, 2005
Beijing National Stadium Beijing, China, 2008

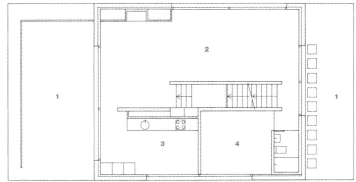

ground floor

1 terrace
2 sitting room/dining room
3 kitchen
4 bedroom/study

The work of Ken Shuttleworth is emblematic of a new spirit of dynamism that began to establish itself around the turn of the millennium. Liberated by advances in engineering, materials and computer-aided design, architects have increasingly turned to innovative forms in a wholesale reinvention of the standard ideas of form following function. Their new buildings are fluid, sinuous and decidedly futuristic in feel.

The Crescent House was one of Shuttleworth's first solo projects, and it became an example of the fresh direction of his own practice when he established this a few years later. He designed the house for himself and his family, but it was representative of the growing resurgence of a movement interested in creating a new type of English country house.

Shuttleworth was insistent in his refusal to impose a building on the site. 'We are suspicious of modern boxes dumped on unsuspecting landscapes,' he said. 'The building has to feel totally "of" its location. The simple form of the Crescent House reacts strongly with the location, reflecting the various contrasts of the site. The critical ingredients are a variety of spaces related to their function, a response to the changing quality of natural light, and sensory contact with nature and the changing seasons.'

Shuttleworth first bought the 5-acre (2 hectare) site, on the edge of the Marlborough Downs, in 1994. Much of the site was grazing pasture, incorporating a poorly built 1920s building, which was demolished to make way for the new house. The crescent design created a closed aspect to the street, driveway and neighbouring buildings to the rear and a fully open relationship with the meadows and unfolding landscape to the front.

Essentially, the house is composed of two vast, curving entities in concrete and glass. The enclosed convex rear section facing northwest – fully top-lit, with no standard windows – contains the five bedrooms and the bathrooms. The huge flowing concave room at the front of the house contains all the key communal living spaces – areas for cooking, dining, living and playing. The façade of low-emissivity glass looks out onto the gardens and planted woodland, helping to protect the house from the effects of the high sun in summer. Between the two crescents sits a double-height gallery, forming an entrance and artery for all parts of the house, and lit by high clerestory glazing.

Shuttleworth arranged the planting around the house, and was careful to make the building as environmentally friendly as possible. The concrete was sourced from a nearby factory, insulation standards are high, and the thoughtfully positioned building makes full use of solar gain and natural ventilation techniques.

Inside, Shuttleworth placed an emphasis on simplicity. Building on a relatively modest budget, he ensured that the design avoided the need for expensive detailing and fixtures. Instead, he created generous and welcoming living spaces, anchored by a monolithic fireplace which creates a focal point within the 80-foot-long (24 m) living zone. The enveloping arms of the crescent extend another 16 feet (5 m) on either side.

The Crescent House received a great deal of praise and press attention upon its completion, encouraging Shuttleworth to push on with the formation of his own practice. It also constituted one of the most eyecatching of the new country houses, suggesting that radical architecture, allied to a sensitive and sustainable approach, still has a role to play in the English countryside.

Biography

KEN SHUTTLEWORTH (b. 1952)

Born in Birmingham, Shuttleworth studied architecture at Leicester. He then joined Norman Foster's practice, where he became a partner in 1991, collaborating on the design of the Swiss Re headquarters ('the Gherkin'). He founded his own practice, Make, in 2004 and quickly developed a diverse portfolio of projects both in the UK and abroad, characterized by a dynamic and innovative approach to form and structure.

Key Buildings

Swiss Re Headquarters (with Foster & Partners) St Mary Axe, London, England, 2004
Dartford Dojo Dartford, Kent, England, 2006
St Paul's Information Centre St Paul's, London, England, 2007
55 Baker Street London, England, 2007
University of Nottingham Jubilee Campus Nottingham, England, 2008

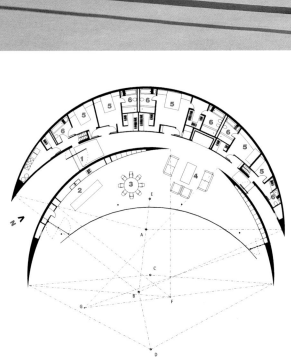

main floor

1 entrance
2 kitchen
3 dining area
4 sitting area
5 bedroom
6 bathroom/w.c.

The dramatic open-plan living area – or 'universal space' – within the crescent at the front of the house is only lightly delineated into different living zones by the positioning of furniture and elements contained within the sweeping rear wall, such as the galley kitchen, bookshelves and fireplace.

1998

REM KOOLHAAS

HOUSE NEAR BORDEAUX BORDEAUX, FRANCE

A theorist, writer and author of some of the most radical statements in contemporary architecture, Rem Koolhaas is widely regarded as a twenty-first-century figurehead. For some, his buildings embody the future itself, given that they push the boundaries of form, engineering and technology. Above all, there is his gravity-defying CCTV building in Beijing, created in association with Arup deputy chairman Cecil Balmond. This epic abstract tower, with a vast hole punched in its heart, seems to belong to another time and era altogether. Such statements give weight to the image of Koolhaas as a prophet of a new architecture.

His House Near Bordeaux, while built on a very different scale, is in a sense futuristic, but it is also grounded in an intimately considered response to the needs of his clients. The house was commissioned by a family with three children, after the husband had had a serious car accident that confined him to a wheelchair. Koolhaas was asked to design a bespoke home that might liberate the family from disability. 'Contrary to what you would expect, I do not want a simple house,' the client told Koolhaas. 'I want a complex house, because the house will define my world.'[1]

Koolhaas created a three-storey building pushed into a hillside site. The wonderful views across the town of Bordeaux and the River Garonne invited a belvedere, but Koolhaas – typically defying the obvious or conventional – placed a dramatic glass viewing platform between the solid rectangular forms of the upper and lower levels. The centre of the house, then, became a transparent, mainly open-plan living area, where the family came together.

Visually, as with so many Koolhaas buildings, the house seems impossible. Skilful engineering gives the impression of a great upper-storey slab floating in space, while sheltering the vulnerable glass zone below. The upper level, peppered with porthole windows, holds the bedrooms and a terrace. The lower level is largely a service area, with a kitchen, a wine cellar and the main entrance leading in from a large courtyard alongside the house. A separate caretaker's lodge and guest bedroom are situated to the other side of the courtyard.

Koolhaas's most sensitive and surprising move was to allow his client the freedom he wanted, not by placing dedicated spaces on one level, but by putting an open, elevating platform right at the heart of the building. This platform can easily access any of the three floors, and also doubles as an office and study. Until the client's death in 2001, it offered him

total mobility and access, while also placing him at the centre of the household and family life. For anyone who might feel alienated or intimidated by Koolhaas's work, such a humanistic – as well as practical – approach suggests another side to the practice.

The house – now a historic monument – was the focus of a film by Ila Beka and Louise Lemoine, *Koolhaas HouseLife* (2008). This quirky portrait of the daily life of the house reinforced its iconicity, while having some fun with the rituals of cleaning and maintaining such a place.

Named the best design of 1998 by *Time* magazine, the House Near Bordeaux is still regarded as one of the most important of Koolhaas's buildings, and one of the first to translate into reality the intense promise exhibited in the architect's theoretical essays.

1 Quoted in the Architect's Notes on House Near Bordeaux.

REM KOOLHAAS (b. 1944)

Born in Rotterdam, Koolhaas grew up in Holland and Indonesia. He initially became a journalist and writer, and his architectural writing is much respected. He studied architecture at the Architectural Association in London and at Cornell University, then in 1975 co-founded the Office for Metropolitan Architecture (OMA), based in Rotterdam. He has established himself as one of the most radical architects of his generation, constantly pushing the boundaries of form and engineering within increasingly futuristic structures. He teaches at Harvard and won the Pritzker Prize in 2000.

Prada Epicenter Store New York, New York, USA, 2001
Dutch Embassy Berlin, Germany, 2003
Seattle Central Library Seattle, Washington, USA, 2004
Casa da Música Porto, Portugal, 2004
China Central Television Building (CCTV) Beijing, China, 2009

1998

HOUSE NEAR BORDEAUX

As with a number of Koolhaas buildings, the Bordeaux house appears to be structurally impossible, with a seeming mass of weight bearing down on the slimmest of supports. The engineering drama of the house does not detract from its bespoke and practical nature, designed around the needs of the original client.

HOUSE NEAR BORDEAUX

ground floor

1 entrance
2 kitchen
3 elevator platform
4 wine cellar
5 laundry room
6 TV room
7 staff quarters
8 patio
9 guest room
10 driveway

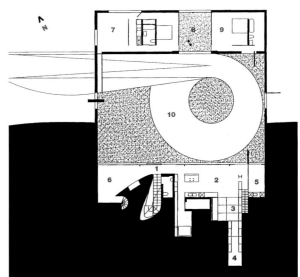

The central hub of the house
– an open, elevating platform –
is lined with bookcases from
top to bottom and doubles as
an office and study.

1998

EDUARDO SOUTO DE MOURA

MOLEDO HOUSE MOLEDO, CAMINHA, PORTUGAL

The work of Eduardo Souto de Moura has been described as 'mineral poetry'. It is an apt phrase for an architecture of sculpted monumentality that also ties in carefully to the landscape. The great walls of stone that have characterized Souto de Moura's buildings lend them a timeless quality, rich in texture and grandeur.

His house near Moledo began with a subtle re-landscaping of the site. The client, António Reis, had bought a hillside plot in northern Portugal for a weekend and holiday home. The plot consisted of a series of agricultural terraces, containing the ruins of a seventeenth-century building. 'On such rugged terrain,' says Souto de Moura, 'I could never have designed the house my client wanted, so I suggested completely refashioning the site, leaving the base and entrance area unchanged because these levels were essential to the topography. I doubled the surface area of the existing terraces and halved their number. It cost more to reshape the site than to build the house.'[1]

The rectangular, single-storey building sits within the terraces so discreetly as to become almost invisible from any distance. Its concrete walls are faced in the same granite stonework

that was used to construct the terraces, while the central section of the house becomes a transparent procession of recessed timber-framed windows and doors.

The structure sits upon its own modest plateau in such a way as to allow for a gap at the back of the building between the rockface and a wall of glass. This gap creates a lightwell, while also allowing the stonework to become a kind of wallpaper to the long access corridor that runs along much of the rear of the house.

Three equally proportioned bedrooms look out across the views from the front of the house, as does a large combined living room and dining room. Here, another stone-faced wall holds a fireplace and also acts as a divider between the living area and the kitchen beyond, with a small studio tucked away to one side.

Such is the organic subtlety of the house that its flat roof comes as a surprise; more of a found object in the landscape, when seen from the wooded hilltops above – 'as if fallen from the sky', as Souto de Moura puts it. But the overall impression is of a discreet belvedere, given texture and character by the stonework and natural timber finishes.

Certainly, one sees a kind of integration-architecture that has become a genre of its own. This is the kind of building that seeks not to shock or to shout, but to make only the most minor impact upon the landscape.

The Moledo House also marks a slow-burn approach that speaks of a gradual understanding of the needs of a client and a progressively considered response to a site. Overall, the landscaping and building works took seven years, with the design being gradually developed and modified.

One might draw parallels with the work of Frank Lloyd Wright, with Albert Frey perhaps, with Álvaro Siza, too, but ultimately Souto de Moura seems to operate in a highly individual way, while being firmly rooted in the Iberian context in which he works. The Moledo House offers an inspirational combination of old and new, past and present, mass and transparency. More than this, it is indicative of a fresh and enlightened approach to country house design and living.

1 Quoted in Antonio Esposito and Giovanni Leoni, *Eduardo Souto de Moura*, Electa, 2003.

The successful integration of the Moledo House into its ziggurat of agricultural terracing creates an individual and character-driven home, wedded totally to the site.

Biography

EDUARDO SOUTO DE MOURA (b. 1952)
Born in Porto, Portugal, Souta de Moura studied at the city's School of Fine Arts. In the 1970s he worked with Álvaro Siza before founding his own practice in 1980. He has taught in Porto and elsewhere, and has continued to base himself in his home city, where he has designed a number of buildings, though also working across Iberia and internationally. His work seamlessly combines traditional and vernacular influences with a contemporary and original approach to materials and form.

Key Buildings

Miramar House Vila Nova de Gaia, Portugal, 1991
Casa das Artes Cultural Centre Porto, Portugal, 1991
Santa María do Bouro Convent Hotel Amares, Portugal, 1997
Portuguese Pavilion, Expo '98 Lisbon, Portugal, 1998
Braga Stadium Braga, Portugal, 2000

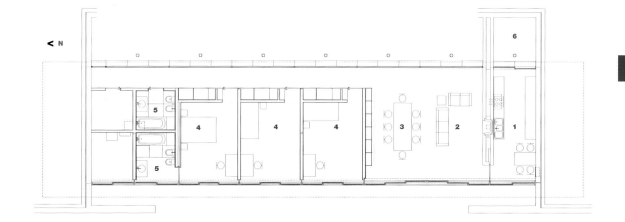

main floor

1 kitchen
2 sitting area
3 dining area
4 bedroom
5 bathroom
6 studio

1998

UN STUDIO

MÖBIUS HOUSE HET GOOI, NETHERLANDS

UN Studio is one of contemporary architecture's most dynamic and creative practices. In a range of buildings, mostly in Europe but increasingly further afield, Ben van Berkel and Caroline Bos have combined powerful imagination with geometrical precision and high engineering. At the same time – rather like Herzog & de Meuron and Caruso St John – they have shown themselves open to a range of influences, and have embraced the renaissance of interest in texture, materials and pared-down ornamentation within innovative, patterned façades, envelopes and screens. In this way, they have turned some rather ordinary building types into extraordinary structures.

Their electricity substations at Innsbruck and Amersfoort became vast sculpted artworks, clad in basalt plates and lava stone, and mysterious in purpose. So, too, their Bridge Master's House in Purmerend, an abstract concrete tower coated in metallic mesh. The Mercedes-Benz Museum in Stuttgart is widely regarded as one of their masterpieces, a rounded, triangular form coated in metal and glass, and containing a vibrant series of interconnecting ramps and walkways that carry the visitor through the building.

This sweeping and fluid interior architecture – developed in association with engineer Werner Sobek – owes an acknowledged debt to Frank Lloyd Wright's Guggenheim Museum, but also to the practice's own geometrical gymnastics, as explored in the Möbius House.

The Möbius strip – that twisted, double-looped band forming a figure of eight and named after the nineteenth-century mathematician – became a guiding idea for the circulation roots and, thence, the structure of the house.

The commission came from a professional couple with grown-up children. These progressive clients encouraged the creation of a new architectural language, but also emphasized the need for two studios, one at either end of the house, to be built on a generous plot in a residential area near Amsterdam.

'The Möbius House integrates programme, circulation and structure seamlessly,' say Van Berkel and Bos. 'Taking full advantage of its location, the house unfolds horizontally, allowing the occupants to take in the surroundings during their daily activities.'[1]

The two studios, three bedrooms, service spaces and a living room, complete with corner fireplace, were accommodated, along with a garage, veranda and roof garden.

As a unique home, the Möbius House fulfils the ambition of a new architectural form, while also meeting the needs and living patterns of the clients. As an experimental building, it has proved pivotal in the development of UN Studio, while being emblematic of a new wave of dynamic forms within contemporary architecture.

1 Ben van Berkel and Caroline Bos, writing in *UN Studio: Design Models*, Thames & Hudson, 2006.

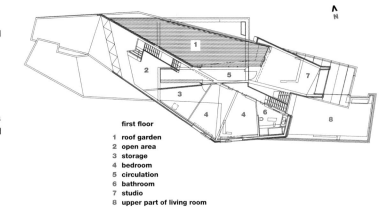

first floor

1 roof garden
2 open area
3 storage
4 bedroom
5 circulation
6 bathroom
7 studio
8 upper part of living room

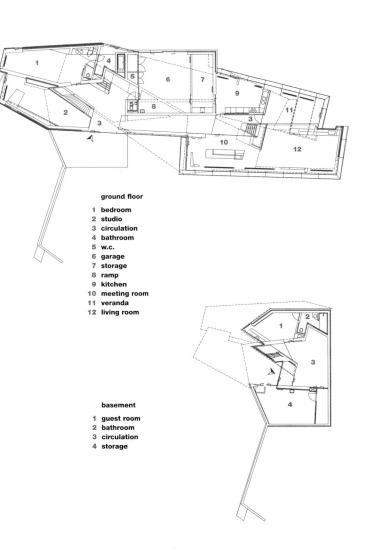

ground floor

1 bedroom
2 studio
3 circulation
4 bathroom
5 w.c.
6 garage
7 storage
8 ramp
9 kitchen
10 meeting room
11 veranda
12 living room

basement

1 guest room
2 bathroom
3 circulation
4 storage

The complex, intersecting floor plan of Möbius House allows its occupants to meet, cross over and interact as they move through the fluid, low-slung, concrete and glass building, which also makes connections with different aspects of the wooded landscape.

1998 / MÖBIUS HOUSE

Biographies

BEN VAN BERKEL (b. 1957)
Van Berkel studied architecture at the Rietveld Academy in Amsterdam, while also working as a graphic designer, and at the Architectural Association in London. In 1988 he co-founded Van Berkel & Bos Architectuur, which became UN Studio in 1999.

CAROLINE BOS (b. 1959)
After studying History of Art at Birkbeck, London, Bos worked as a journalist, editor and writer. She co-founded Van Berkel & Bos, becoming a partner as well as resident critic and analyst.

Key Buildings

Bascule Bridge & Harbour Master's House
Purmerend, Netherlands, 1998
Het Valkhof Museum Nijmegen, Netherlands, 1999
Electrical Substation Innsbruck, Austria, 2002
VilLA NM Bethel, New York, USA, 2006
Mercedes-Benz Museum Stuttgart, Germany, 2006

1998

MÖBIUS HOUSE

1999

Y HOUSE CATSKILL MOUNTAINS, NEW YORK, USA

For one of the simplest and most traditional of buildings, the barn has a powerful aesthetic presence and a strong emotional draw. The image of a barn sitting alone in an open landscape is mesmerizing. These most site-specific of buildings feel as though they truly *belong*, tied to the land not just by history but by materials, approach and construction.

With the Y House, stained a bold barn-red, Steven Holl takes the imagery of the barn in the landscape and both updates and subverts it to create an enticing and original home.

He conceived this hilltop, cedar-clad country house as two houses in one, modelling the form on a cleft stick, like a divining rod, that he stumbled upon during a visit to the 11-acre (4.5 hectare) site. Responding to this lyrical inspiration and to the topography of the site, he set out the Y-shaped formation in his sketchbook.

'The relation of all the site elements, the long, distant views to the southwest, the arc of the sun and the circle of approach from the bottom of the hill to the top, brought forth the thought of the house circling from the arrival point as a low one-storey structure, and then branching up and out into the Y shape,' says Holl.

The house seems to emerge from the ground at its lowest point and then begin to split into two, like a siamese twin. It was designed for clients who wanted to accommodate two generations of the same family in one building, so the split effectively creates two wings, each with its own bedrooms and living spaces, and each opening up to the countryside views, facilitated by balconies and porches.

'The house literally grows up and out of the landscape, branching into the south sun, so the porches help shade summer sun out and allow winter sun in,' says Holl. 'On one side of the house night-time functions [bedrooms] are below, and on the other side of the Y they are above, so you have this flipped action which allows privacy and windows inside the Y space.'

In some ways, the Y House links back to some of Holl's earlier projects, which also drew upon and re-examined vernacular influences. In particular, one thinks of the Berkowitz-Odgis House at Martha's Vineyard, Massachusetts, which reassembled the components of the traditional timber houses of the region. Similarly, the Round Lake Hut in Rhinebeck, New York, reinvented the idea of the simple, Walden-esque country cabin on the water's edge.

The landscaping of the eco-aware Y House, which also has facilities for rainwater harvesting, averts any need for a domesticated garden. The house can thus blend into the meadowlands without partition.

Part of the fascination with Holl is that his responses to particular contexts and sites take him in very different and surprising directions. In the case of the Y House, references back to the red-painted barn lead us to expect one thing, but our expectations are brilliantly subverted. Holl, in other words, shakes things up, but also creates houses intimately connected to the programme that his clients require.

Biography

STEVEN HOLL (b. 1947)
Born in Bremerton, Washington, Holl graduated from the University of Washington, then studied in Rome and London. He founded Steven Holl Architects in 1976 in New York, and has established himself as one of the most gifted architects of his generation with a wide range of commissions, from single houses to large-scale cultural projects. His work is diverse, but linked by a common sensitivity to context and a highly artistic, sculptural approach. Holl is also a painter and teaches architecture at Columbia University.

Key Buildings

Kiasma Museum of Contemporary Art Helsinki, Finland, 1998
Simmons Hall, Massachusetts Institute of Technology Cambridge, Massachusetts, 2002
Turbulence House Abiquiu, New Mexico, USA, 2005
Nelson-Atkins Museum of Art Expansion Kansas City, Missouri, USA, 2007

The two units of the Y-shaped format share a common access route, foyers and services, but can act virtually independently.

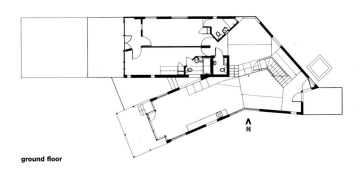

ground floor

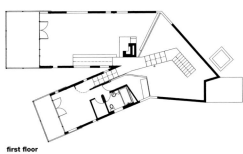

first floor

There is a mysterious ambiguity to the best of David Adjaye's houses. Buildings like the Dirty House, the Lost House and the Sunken House are almost abstract presences on the streetscape. Passers-by are unsure as to whether they are houses at all, or industrial spaces. They give little away until one steps inside and the process of discovery begins.

In some senses, Adjaye's houses can be seen as a reaction to urban centres, with the creation of closed façades that offer privacy and seclusion while making the buildings highly internalized and self-sufficient. In other ways, they are reminiscent of art installations and remind us that Adjaye has formed a close attachment to the art world, designing houses for a number of artists and often collaborating with sculptors and painters in the creation of public and cultural spaces.

'As cities grow, and as the experience of urbanism becomes overwhelming or intoxicating, I think the notion of the domestic retreat becomes more and more important,' says Adjaye. 'It's the respite, the refuge, the regenerator.... I also think that the idea of the modern house has been completely done.... The idea of excellent plumbing, or excellent services, is not really as interesting for me, as an architect, as the pursuit of the domestic realm. I want to explore what else that realm can be.'[1]

The first and perhaps the most notorious of these explorations came in 2000 with the Elektra House. The clients were an artist and a sculptor, with two children, who asked Adjaye to design and build a low-budget house on a site in the East End of London which previously held a single-storey workshop.

To the street, the new timber- and steel-framed two-storey house presents a completely closed and windowless façade, coated in sheets of plywood treated in a dark resin. A doorway to one side leads down an access alleyway to a side entrance.

At the front of the house, a double-height zone on the open-plan ground floor is top-lit from skylights high above, while to the rear the wealth of glazing – leading out to a small courtyard – adds to the generous and airy feel of the interiors. The white walls and concrete floors lend a minimalist quality to the house, which can double as a gallery-style space for exhibiting art. This enigmatic building is thus

an exercise in contrasts between light and dark, and openness and enclosure, but also offers that sense of refuge and retreat from the city.

Elektra is an unusual and controversial building, and one that earned Adjaye a good deal of attention. It forms part of a vibrant and original series of houses that made a strong foundation for the architect's career. Since then, he has made the transition to larger-scale public and cultural projects, both at home and abroad, building on the qualities and themes seen in his earlier work, while increasingly drawing inspiration from a broad range of references, including his upbringing in Africa and enduring fascination with the continent. But Elektra marked a beginning, suggesting a keen interest in ambiguity and in the unusual, eyecatching façades and coatings that have come to characterize Adjaye's buildings.

1 Interview with Geoff Manaugh, *Dwell*, March 2008.

Biography

DAVID ADJAYE (b. 1966)

Adjaye was born in Tanzania, the son of a Ghanaian diplomat. The family moved to London in 1979 and Adjaye studied at South Bank University and at the Royal College of Art. He worked with David Chipperfield and Eduardo Souto de Moura before co-founding a practice with William Russell in 1994 and then opening his own studio in 2000. Many of his projects have involved collaborations with artists, including Chris Ofili and Olafur Eliasson, and have become increasingly international in scope.

Key Buildings

Dirty House Shoreditch, London, England, 2002
Idea Store Whitechapel, London, England, 2005
Stephen Lawrence Centre Deptford, London, England, 2008
Museum of Contemporary Art Denver, Colorado, USA, 2008

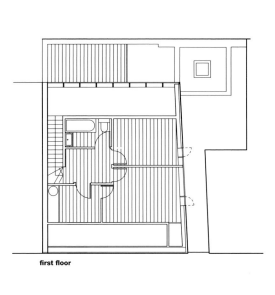

first floor

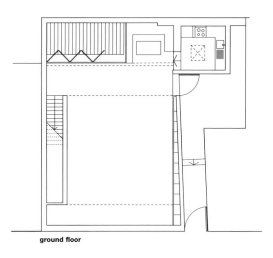

ground floor

Elektra House's interior is conceived as a kind of lightbox. Whereas the front façade is closed, skylights and a large bank of glazing introduce a high quality of light to the rear.

2000

CARTER/TUCKER HOUSE BREAMLEA, VICTORIA, AUSTRALIA

Australia sits at a cultural crossroads, fusing Western and Asian traditions. In many of his architectural projects, Sean Godsell has examined this fusion, creating buildings that splice the two traditions. This may be nothing new in itself, as one might gather from the Asian influences playing upon many of the Modernist pioneers, such as Frank Lloyd Wright and Rudolph Schindler, but what does seem fresh in Godsell's work is the way he combines this fusion with Australian vernacular and unusual, sustainable materials.

This approach is best exemplified in a sequence of houses that began with his own home – the Kew House – and continued with the Carter/Tucker and Peninsula Houses. All could be described as contemporary cabins that touch the earth lightly (to borrow Glenn Murcutt's maxim). To some extent they echo the agricultural buildings of the Australian landscape, but they also have a lightness of touch and possess something of the quality of an Asian timber pavilion.

The Carter/Tucker House was commissioned by photographer Earl Carter and his wife Wanda Tucker. They asked for a simple weekend home with flexible accommodation, particularly the ability to use the living room as a day-lit photography studio. They also supported Godsell's spirit of experimentation and his desire to build on themes explored in his own house some years earlier.

The Carter/Tucker House, embedded in sand dunes, is a highly adaptable and layered building – a box 39 feet (12 m) long and 19½ feet (6 m) wide. Its slatted cedar skin, which has the outward appearance of cabin-like simplicity, forms a complex and adaptable sun-shade system, filtering or diffusing natural light.

Inside, the three-storey house is also extremely flexible. The building is entered via an access bridge into the middle level, which consists of a largely open-plan master bedroom/sitting room. An open-plan kitchen, dining and living area is situated at the top of the house. Guest bedrooms are on the lower level, opening out onto a deck. The majority of each floor is one large single space, but this can be subdivided with sliding screens – again reminiscent of Japanese living – while slim rectangular side units hold elements like bathrooms, service spaces and a galley kitchen. Materials tend to be raw and simple, many of them recycled.

'The most potent aspect of the building,' says Godsell, 'is its apparent simplicity. In fact both the theory and plan are complex, and that these complexities could be successfully represented in such an apparently simple format was a relief.'

The themes of the Carter/Tucker House were explored further in the Peninsula House, with slats once again acting as filters. Together, these two projects point the way to a new and fresh kind of Australian home, drawing in ideas and themes from a number of directions. At the same time such fusion houses, with their sensitivity to nature and masterful understanding of light, offer a new model of flexibility and resourcefulness that has attracted attention around the world.

The steel-framed Carter/Tucker House is coated in a skin of louvered cedar panels, many of which form shutters that can be propped open to become awnings.

The cedar slats act as filters, throwing extraordinary patterns of light and shade across the interior.

334

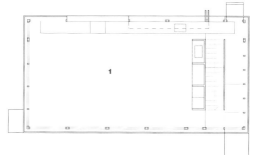

first floor

1 kitchen/dining/living room

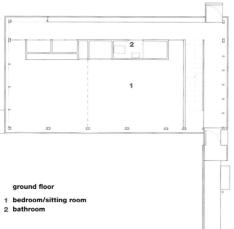

ground floor

1 bedroom/sitting room
2 bathroom

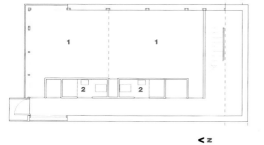

basement

1 guest room
2 bathroom

< z

2000

Within one groundbreaking twenty-first-century house, Werner Sobek combines two of the great fascinations of contemporary architecture: prefabrication and sustainability. As a structural engineer, he has collaborated on massive architectural schemes, from airports to office complexes, but, as an architect, he has increasingly been drawn to the development of a prefabricated, fully recyclable home.

With his own family home, sited on a hillside overlooking Stuttgart, Sobek was able to explore his ideas fully, turning the house into a richly experimental laboratory. What is surprising about the Sobek House – or House R128 – is that it is also a striking architectural statement, wrapped up in the form of a crisp four-storey glass box.

'The construction does not produce emissions of any kind and is self-sufficient from the viewpoint of energy supply,' says Sobek. 'The composition is based on a modular grid, and so the building ... was constructed in a short space of time and it will be possible to dismantle it equally rapidly and reutilize its components.'[1]

The steel frame for the house was erected in just four days and the building was then coated in triple-glazed, low-emissivity glass. Solar panels sit on the roof to power the house, while a heat-exchange system captures excess heat in summer within ceiling units containing water-filled elements. In the winter this process is reversed, so that the elements push out radiant warmth.

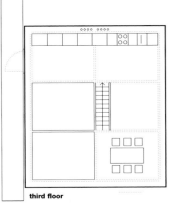

third floor

second floor

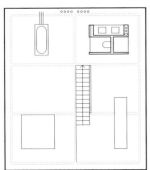

first floor

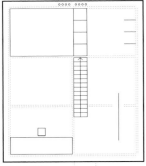

ground floor

Furnishing of the zero-energy, solar-powered Sobek House is minimalist, in order to maximize the sense of openness and connection to the outdoors, though a large red bookcase in the living room provides a splash of colour.

Sitting on a small plateau, which required no excavation works, the house is entered via a footbridge at the top level, which also holds the kitchen and dining room, benefiting from the most dramatic views out across the city. An impressive steel staircase winds down the centre of the building, and double-height voids in key areas increase the sense of transparency and drama across the largely open floor plans. The second level is dominated by the living room, while the bedrooms and an atelier are further down the house, and a terrace wraps around the base of the building.

There are no doors or switches in the house, and all service systems are hidden within easily accessible metal ducts. The spirit of experimentation is taken beyond energy efficiency and prefabrication to include a complex computer-controlled voice- or movement-activated lighting system.

The Sobek House, then, proves that energy efficiency and self-reliance need not come at the cost of technical and architectural brilliance or powerful design and aesthetics. This, of course, has great implications for the future of building design. There is no doubt that Sobek's work here – and with other houses, such as the H16 House of 2006 – will play a part in transforming the modern home in coming years. Within the parameters of such a new architecture, even a glass statement house becomes not just a dream building but a wholly acceptable eco home.

1 Quoted in Mercedes Daguerre, *20 Houses by Twenty Architects*, Electa, 2002.

Biography

WERNER SOBEK (b. 1953)
Structural engineer, architect and designer Werner Sobek was born in Aalen, Germany, and studied engineering and architecture at the University of Stuttgart. He worked with engineers Schlaich, Bergermann & Partner for four years before founding his own company in 1992, based in Stuttgart. His practice designs solo projects and collaborates with major practices such as UN Studio, contributing structural engineering expertise. Sobek's houses, in particular, have experimented with prefabrication techniques. He teaches at the University of Stuttgart.

Key Buildings

Sony Centre (with Murphy/Jahn Architects) Berlin, Germany, 2000
Interbank Lima (with Atelier Hollein) Lima, Peru, 2000
Mercedes-Benz Museum (with UN Studio) Stuttgart, Germany, 2006
Bangkok International Airport (with Murphy/Jahn Architects) Bangkok, Thailand, 2006

2005

MICRO-COMPACT HOME VARIOUS LOCATIONS

The mass-produced prefabricated home is something of an architectural holy grail. Since the early experiments of Richard Buckminster Fuller and Jean Prouvé, affordable and well-designed modular houses that can be factory-produced on a large scale have attracted the attention of architects, designers and futurists.

In recent years, the modular prefab has seen a great revival of interest, with a number of new designs put to the market to test the public appetite. Among them are The Retreat by UK architects Buckley Gray Yeoman and the weeHouse in the States by Alchemy Architects – projects that try to balance the possibilities of factory production with easy adaptability so that designs can be tailor-made for individual clients.

One of the most eyecatching of this new breed is the Micro-Compact Home. Architect Richard Horden had long been fascinated by the possibilities of prefabrication and in the 1990s developed the Ski Haus, a rugged-terrain living pod suited to the Alps. Other projects were influenced by his love of sailing and the broader application of production ideas associated with nautical design. Lydia Haack and John Höpfner, meanwhile, had a great deal of experience in energy-efficient and sustainable design, having been involved in the concept development of many innovative constructions, and having worked and taught internationally.

The Micro-Compact Home was initially developed in collaboration with students and colleagues at the Technical University in Munich, where Horden was a teaching professor. Other influences on the design included the automobile industry and its offshoots; the space industry (Horden contributed to the development of work-stations for the International Space Station in conjunction with NASA); and the simplicity of the Japanese tea house. The greatest impetus, however, was the world of aviation.

'Our inspiration,' says Horden, 'is from a detailed examination of current commercial aviation, and the compact high-quality living and sleeping spaces in business class on certain airlines. Architects tend to repeat the space standards of the past in prefabrication and that is a fundamental error, in my opinion. We need to review space standards and design homes like automobiles, i.e. the spaces must fit like a glove with integrated furniture and state-of-the-art technology.'

The Micro-Compact Home is a timber-framed cube of 8.5 feet (2.6 m), coated in a heavy-duty aluminium shell. It sleeps one or two people, with all elements – from beds to kitchenette to shower cubicle – fully integrated into the design.

Since 2005 Horden, Haack + Höpfner and the building's Austrian manufacturers have been marketing Micro-Compact Home and refining the concept. A small community of seven houses, known as the O2 Village, has been successfully established near Munich, with the structures proving suitable as affordable accommodation pods for students.

Micro-Compact Home has helped to promote the ideas of prefabrication, suggesting that the prefab home has a real part to play, both architecturally and socially, and can be a possible solution to a number of problems, from housing shortages to disaster relief to meeting the desire for an affordable country bolthole. Clearly there will not be one outright winner in the populist prefab race, but Micro-Compact Home is a fascinating and original contender.

Biographies

RICHARD HORDEN (b. 1944)
Born in Leominster, Horden studied at the Architectural Association and later worked with Norman Foster at Foster Associates, contributing to the Sainsbury Centre project in Norwich and to Stansted Airport. In 1986 he founded his own practice, which in 1999 became Horden Cherry Lee Architects, with a mix of commercial, cultural and residential projects.

LYDIA HAACK (b. 1965) & JOHN HÖPFNER (b. 1963)
Born in Germany, Lydia Haack studied in Munich and London before joining Michael Hopkins's office. German-born John Höpfner studied in Germany and the UK before working for Michael Hopkins and Richard Rogers. Haack + Höpfner, established in Munich in 1996, is known for its light, elegant, ecological buildings and its innovative designs.

Key Buildings

RICHARD HORDEN
Queen's Stand, Epsom Racecourse Epsom, Surrey, England, 1993
Millennium Tower Glasgow, Scotland, 1999
House on Evening Hill Poole, Dorset, England, 2002

HAACK + HÖPFNER
Petrol Station Building System various locations, Germany, 1999–2008
Parasite BO 01 Malmö Building Exhibition, Sweden, 2000
Glazed Car Wash Germering, Germany, 2005

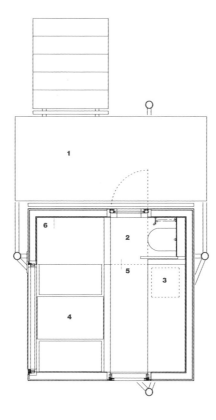

main floor

1 terrace
2 entrance/shower
3 kitchen
4 dining area
5 sliding door
6 overhead fold-up bed

Micro-Compact Home, with its
striking outline and aircraft-style
integrated 'cabin', has caught
the public imagination in a more
significant way than many
other prefab concepts.

Micro-Compact Homes can
easily be adapted: clients can
specify colour choices, or join
structures together to make
larger dwellings. The house can
be delivered fully assembled
on the back of a lorry, and can
even be delivered by helicopter
to remote locations.

BIBLIOGRAPHY

Author's note: where quotations have no references in the text, they are generally sourced from interviews or correspondence with the architect or clients of the house in question, or from materials supplied by them.

GENERAL

Andrews, Peter et al, *The House Book*, Phaidon, 2001
Arieff, Allison, & Bryan Burkhart, *Prefab*, Gibbs Smith, 2002
Barreneche, Raul A., *Modern House 3*, Phaidon, 2005
Betsky, Aaron, *Landscrapers: Building with the Land*, Thames & Hudson, 2002
Boissière, Olivier, *Twentieth-Century Houses*, Terrail, 1998
Bradbury, Dominic, *Mexico*, Conran Octopus, 2003
——, *New Country House*, Laurence King, 2005
——, *Mediterranean Modern*, Thames & Hudson, 2006
Coquelle, Aline, *Palm Springs Style*, Assouline, 2005
Cygelman, Adèle, *Palm Springs Modern*, Rizzoli, 1999
Daguerre, Mercedes, *20 Houses by Twenty Architects*, Electa, 2002
Davey, Peter, *Arts and Crafts Architecture*, Phaidon, 1995
Davies, Colin, *Key Houses of the Twentieth Century: Plans, Sections and Elevations*, Laurence King, 2006
Doordan, Dennis P., *Twentieth-Century Architecture*, Laurence King, 2001
Doubilet, Susan, & Daralice Boles, *European House Now*, Thames & Hudson, 1999
Droste, Magdalena, *Bauhaus: 1919–1933*, Taschen, 2006
Fiell, Charlotte & Peter, *Design of the 20th Century*, Taschen, 1999
Frampton, Kenneth, & David Larkin (eds), *The Twentieth-Century American House*, Thames & Hudson, 1995
Futagawa, Yukio (ed.), *GA Houses Special: Masterpieces, 1945–1970*, GA/Edita, 2001
——, *GA Houses Special: Masterpieces, 1971–2000*, GA/Edita, 2001
Glancey, Jonathan, *20th Century Architecture*, Carlton, 1998
——, *Modern*, Mitchell Beazley, 1999
Gordon, Alastair, *Weekend Utopia: Modern Living in the Hamptons*, Princeton Architectural Press, 2001
Gössel, Peter, & Gabriele Leuthäuser, *Architecture in the 20th Century*, Taschen, 2005
Jodidio, Philip, *Contemporary American Architects*, Vols I–IV, Taschen, 1993–1998
——, *Architecture Now! 3*, Taschen, 2004
——, *100 Contemporary Architects*, Taschen, 2008
Khan, Hasan-Uddin, *International Style: Modernist Architecture from 1925 to 1965*, Taschen, 1998
Melhuish, Clare, *Modern House 2*, Phaidon, 2000
Pearson, Clifford A. (ed.), *Modern American Houses*, Harry N. Abrams, 1996
Postiglione, Gennaro (ed.), *100 Houses for 100 Architects*, Taschen, 2004
Powers, Alan, *Modern: The Modern Movement in Britain*, Merrell, 2005
Rattenbury, Kester, Rob Bevan & Kieran Long, *Architects Today*, Laurence King, 2004
Rybczynski, Witold, *Home: A Short History of an Idea*, Penguin, 1987
Smith, Elizabeth A. T., *Case Study Houses*, Taschen, 2006
Soane, James, *New Home*, Conran Octopus, 2003
Street-Porter, Tim, *The Los Angeles House*, Thames & Hudson, 1995
Sudjic, Deyan, *Home: The Twentieth-Century House*, Laurence King, 1999
Thiel-Siling, Sabine (ed.), *Icons of Architecture: The 20th Century*, Prestel, 2005
Tinniswood, Adrian, *The Art Deco House*, Mitchell Beazley, 2002
Watkin, David, *A History of Western Architecture*, Laurence King, 1986
Webb, Michael, *Architects House Themselves*, Preservation Press, 1994
Welsh, John, *Modern House*, Phaidon, 1995
Weston, Richard, *The House in the Twentieth Century*, Laurence King, 2002
——, *Key Buildings of the Twentieth Century*, Laurence King, 2004

ALVAR AALTO

Pallasmaa, Juhani (ed.), *Alvar Aalto: Villa Mairea 1938–39*, Alvar Aalto Foundation, 1998
Pallasmaa, Juhani, & Tomoko Sato (eds), *Alvar Aalto Through the Eyes of Shigeru Ban*, Black Dog Publishing, 2007
Weston, Richard, *Villa Mairea: Alvar Aalto*, Phaidon, 2002

HITOSHI ABE

Abe, Hitoshi, *Hitoshi Abe*, Toto Shuppan, 2005

DAVID ADJAYE

Allison, Peter (ed.), *David Adjaye: Houses*, Thames & Hudson, 2005
——, *David Adjaye: Making Public Buildings*, Thames & Hudson, 2006

TADAO ANDO

Ando, Tadao, *Tadao Ando: Houses & Housing*, Toto Shuppan, 2007
Furuyama, Masao, *Tadao Ando*, Taschen, 2006
Pare, Richard, *Tadao Ando: The Colours of Light*, Phaidon, 1996

SHIGERU BAN

Ambasz, Emilio, & Shigeru Ban, *Shigeru Ban*, Laurence King, 2001
McQuaid, Matilda, *Shigeru Ban*, Phaidon, 2003

LUIS BARRAGÁN

Barragán, Luis, & René Burri, *Luis Barragán*, Phaidon, 2000
Zanco, Federica (ed.), *Luis Barragán: The Quiet Revolution*, Skira, 2001

GEOFFREY BAWA

Bon, Christoph, et al, *Lunuganga*, Marshall Cavendish Editions, 2007
Robson, David, *Geoffrey Bawa: The Complete Works*, Thames & Hudson, 2002
——, *Beyond Bawa: Modern Masterworks of Monsoon Asia*, Thames & Hudson, 2007
Taylor, Brian Brace, *Geoffrey Bawa*, Thames & Hudson, 1986

MARIO BOTTA

Pizzi, Emilio (ed.), *Mario Botta: The Complete Works Vol. 1: 1960–1985*, Artemis, 1993
Sakellaridou, Irena, *Mario Botta: Architectural Poetics*, Thames & Hudson, 2000

MARCEL BREUER

Cobbers, Arnt, *Marcel Breuer*, Taschen, 2007
Driller, Joachim, *Breuer Houses*, Phaidon, 2000

RICHARD BUCKMINSTER FULLER

Gorman, Michael John, *Buckminster Fuller: Designing for Mobility*, Skira, 2005
Hays, K. Michael, & Dana A. Miller, *Buckminster Fuller: Starting with the Universe*, Whitney Museum of Art, 2008

ALBERTO CAMPO BAEZA

Pizza, Antonio, *Alberto Campo Baeza: Works and Projects*, Gustavo Gili, 1999

PIERRE CHAREAU

Taylor, Brian Brace, *Pierre Chareau: Designer and Architect*, Taschen, 1992
Vellay, Dominique, *La Maison de Verre: Pierre Chareau's Modernist Masterwork*, Thames & Hudson, 2007

SERGE CHERMAYEFF

Powers, Alan, *Serge Chermayeff: Designer, Architect, Teacher*, RIBA, 2001

CHARLES CORREA

Correa, Charles, *Charles Correa*, Thames & Hudson, 1996
——, *Charles Correa: Housing and Urbanization*, Thames & Hudson, 2000

DENTON CORKER MARSHALL

Beck, Haig, et al, *Denton Corker Marshall: Rule Playing and the Ratbag Element*, Birkhäuser, 2000
Schaik, Leon van, *Denton Corker Marshall: Non-Fictional Narratives*, Birkhäuser, 2008

CHARLES & RAY EAMES

Koenig, Gloria, *Charles & Ray Eames*, Taschen, 2005
Neuhart, Marilyn & John, *Eames House*, Ernst & Sohn, 1994
Steele, James, *Eames House: Charles and Ray Eames*, Phaidon, 1994

PETER EISENMAN

Davidson, Cynthia (ed.), *Tracing Eisenman*, Thames & Hudson, 2006
Frank, Suzanne, *Peter Eisenman's House VI*, Whitney Library of Design, 1994

CRAIG ELLWOOD

Jackson, Neil, *Craig Ellwood*, Laurence King, 2002
McCoy, Esther, *Craig Ellwood: Architecture*, Alfier, 1968
Vacchini, Livio, et al, *Craig Ellwood: 15 Houses*, 2G/Gustavo Gili, 1999

JOSEPH ESHERICK

Lyndon, Donlyn, & Jim Alinder, *The Sea Ranch*, Princeton Architectural Press, 2004

ALBERT FREY

Golub, Jennifer, *Albert Frey: Houses 1 & 2*, Princeton Architectural Press, 1999

Koenig, Gloria, *Albert Frey*, Taschen, 2008

Rosa, Joseph, *Albert Frey: Architect*, Rizzoli, 1990

FUTURE SYSTEMS

Field, Marcus, *Future Systems*, Phaidon, 1999

Sudjic, Deyan, *Future Systems*, Phaidon, 2006

ANTONI GAUDÍ

Crippa, Maria Antonietta, *Antoni Gaudí*, Taschen, 2007

FRANK GEHRY

Co, Francesco Dal, & Kurt W. Foster, *Frank O. Gehry: The Complete Works*, Monacelli Press, 1998

Ragheb, J. Fiona, *Frank Gehry: Architect*, Guggenheim Museum, 2001

Steele, James, *Schnabel House: Frank Gehry*, Phaidon, 1993

SEAN GODSELL

Schaik, Leon van, *Sean Godsell*, Phaidon, 2005

EILEEN GRAY

Constant, Caroline, *Eileen Gray*, Phaidon, 2000

GREENE & GREENE

Arntzenius, Linda G., *The Gamble House*, University of Southern California School of Architecture, 2000

Bosley, Edward R., *Gamble House: Greene & Greene*, Phaidon, 1992

——, *Greene & Greene*, Phaidon, 2000

Smith, Bruce, & Alexander Vertikoff, *Greene & Greene: Master Builders of the American Arts & Crafts Movement*, Thames & Hudson, 1998

WALTER GROPIUS

Lupfer, Gilbert, & Paul Sigel, *Walter Gropius*, Taschen, 2006

CHARLES GWATHMEY

Breslow, Kay, *Charles Gwathmey & Robert Siegel: Residential Works, 1966–1977*, Architectural Book Publishing Company, 1977

AGUSTÍN HERNÁNDEZ

Mereles, Louise Noelle, *Agustín Hernández*, Gustavo Gili, 1995

HERZOG & DE MEURON

Mack, Gerhard, *Herzog & de Meuron: 1992–1996*, Birkhäuser, 2000

Wang, Wilfried, *Herzog & de Meuron*, Birkhäuser, 1992

JOSEF HOFFMANN

Sarnitz, August, *Josef Hoffmann*, Taschen, 2007

STEVEN HOLL

Frampton, Kenneth, *Steven Holl: Architect*, Electa, 2002

Garofalo, Francesco, *Steven Holl*, Thames & Hudson, 2003

MICHAEL HOPKINS

Davies, Colin, Patrick Hodgkinson & Kenneth Frampton, *Hopkins: The Work of Michael Hopkins & Partners*, Phaidon, 1995

Donati, Cristina, *Michael Hopkins*, Skira, 2006

RICHARD HORDEN

Horden, Richard, *Micro Architecture: Lightweight, Mobile and Ecological Buildings for the Future*, Thames & Hudson, 2008

ARNE JACOBSEN

Faber, Tobias, *Arne Jacobsen*, Alec Tiranti, 1964

Solaguren-Beascoa, Félix, *Arne Jacobsen: Works and Projects*, Gustavo Gili, 1989

——, *Arne Jacobsen: Approach to his Complete Works, 1926–1949*, Danish Architectural Press, 2002

PHILIP JOHNSON

Dunn, Dorothy, *The Glass House*, Assouline, 2008

Fox, Stephen, et al, *The Architecture of Philip Johnson*, Bulfinch, 2002

Whitney, David, & Jeffrey Kipnis (eds) *Philip Johnson: The Glass House*, Pantheon Books, 1993

LOUIS KAHN

McCarter, Robert, *Louis I. Kahn*, Phaidon, 2005

Rosa, Joseph, *Louis I. Kahn*, Taschen, 2006

MATHIAS KLOTZ

Adrià, Miquel, *Mathias Klotz: Architecture and Projects*, Electa, 2005

PIERRE KOENIG

Jackson, Neil, *Pierre Koenig*, Taschen, 2007

Steele, James, & David Jenkins, *Pierre Koenig*, Phaidon, 1998

REM KOOLHAAS

Koolhaas, Rem (ed.), *Content*, Taschen, 2004

Koolhaas, Rem, & Bruce Mau, *S, M, L, XL*, 010 Publishers, 1995

KENGO KUMA

Alini, Luigi, *Kengo Kuma: Works and Projects*, Electa, 2005

Casamonti, Marco (ed.), *Kengo Kuma*, Motta Architettura, 2007

CARL LARSSON

Segerstad, Ulf Hard af, *Carl Larsson's Home*, Addison-Wesley, 1978

Snodin, Michael, & Elisabet Stavenow-Hidemark (eds) *Carl and Karin Larsson: Creators of the Swedish Style*, V&A Publications, 1997

JOHN LAUTNER

Campbell-Lange, Barbara-Ann, *John Lautner*, Taschen, 2005

Escher, Frank (ed.), *John Lautner: Architect*, Artemis, 1994

Hess, Alan, *The Architecture of John Lautner*, Thames & Hudson, 1999

LE CORBUSIER

Cohen, Jean-Louis, *Le Corbusier*, Taschen, 2006

Jenger, Jean, *Le Corbusier: Architect of a New Age*, Thames & Hudson, 1996

Kries, Mateo, et al (eds), *Le Corbusier: The Art of Architecture*, Vitra Design Museum, 2007

Sbriglio, Jacques, *Le Corbusier: The Villa Savoye*, Birkhäuser, 2008

RICARDO LEGORRETA

Mutlow, John V., *Ricardo Legorreta Architects*, Rizzoli, 1997

BERTHOLD LUBETKIN

Allan, John, *Berthold Lubetkin*, Merrell, 2002

Reading, Malcolm, & Peter Coe, *Lubetkin and Tecton*, Triangle Architectural Publishing, 1992

COLIN LUCAS

Sharp, Dennis, & Sally Rendel, *Connell, Ward & Lucas: Modern Movement Architects in England 1929–1939*, Frances Lincoln, 2008

EDWIN LUTYENS

Edwards, Brian, *Goddards: Sir Edwin Lutyens*, Phaidon, 1996

CHARLES RENNIE MACKINTOSH

Macaulay, James, *Charles Rennie Mackintosh: Hill House*, Phaidon, 1994

CURZIO MALAPARTE

Talamona, Marida, *Casa Malaparte*, Princeton Architectural Press, 1992

ROBERT MALLET-STEVENS

Deshoulières, Dominique, et al (eds), *Rob Mallet-Stevens: Architecte*, Archives d'Architecture Moderne, 1981

Pinchon, Jean-François (ed.), *Rob Mallet-Stevens: Architecture, Furniture, Interior Design*, MIT Press, 1990

RICHARD MEIER

Goldberger, Paul, & Joseph Giovannini, *Richard Meier: Houses and Apartments*, Rizzoli, 2007

KONSTANTIN MELNIKOV

Fosso, Mario, et al (eds) *Konstantin S. Melnikov and the Construction of Moscow*, Skira, 2000

Starr, S. Frederick, *Melnikov: Solo Architect in a Mass Society*, Princeton University Press, 1978

PAOLO MENDES DA ROCHA

Artigas, Rosa (ed.), *Paulo Mendes da Rocha: Projects 1957–2007*, Rizzoli, 2007

Montaner, Josep, & Maria Isabel Villac, *Mendes da Rocha*, Gustavo Gili, 1996

LUDWIG MIES VAN DER ROHE

Vandenberg, Maritz, *Farnsworth House: Mies van der Rohe*, Phaidon, 2003

Zimmerman, Claire, *Mies van der Rohe*, Taschen, 2006

ERIC OWEN MOSS

Collins, Brad (ed.), *Eric Owen Moss: Buildings and Projects 2*, Rizzoli, 1996

Giaconia, Paola, *Eric Owen Moss: The Uncertainty of Doing*, Skira, 2006

Steele, James, *Eric Owen Moss: Lawson-Westen House*, Phaidon, 1993

GLENN MURCUTT

Beck, Haig, & Jackie Cooper, *Glenn Murcutt: A Singular Architectural Practice*, Images Publishing Group, 2002

Frampton, Kenneth, et al, *Glenn Murcutt, Architect*, 01 Editions, 2006

Fromonot, Françoise, *Glenn Murcutt: Buildings and Projects, 1962–2003*, Thames & Hudson, 2003

RICHARD NEUTRA

Hines, Thomas S., *Richard Neutra and the Search for Modern Architecture*, Rizzoli, 2005

Lamprecht, Barbara, *Richard Neutra*, Taschen, 2006

OSCAR NIEMEYER

Andreas, Paul, & Ingeborg Flagge, *Oscar Niemeyer: A Legend of Modernism*, Birkhäuser, 2003

Hess, Alan, & Alan Weintraub, *Oscar Niemeyer Houses*, Rizzoli, 2006

JOHN PAWSON & CLAUDIO SILVESTRIN

Pawson, John, *John Pawson*, Gustavo Gili, 1998

Silvestrin, Claudio, et al, *Claudio Silvestrin*, Birkhäuser, 1999

AUGUSTE PERRET

Britton, Karla, *Auguste Perret*, Phaidon, 2001

Cohen, Jean-Louis, et al (eds), *Encyclopédie Perret*, Monum, 2002

ANTOINE PREDOCK

Collins, Brad, & Juliette Robbins (eds), *Antoine Predock: Architect*, Rizzoli, 1994

Predock, Antoine, *Turtle Creek House*, Monacelli Press, 1998

JEAN PROUVÉ

Peters, Nils, *Jean Prouvé*, Taschen, 2006

Prouvé, Catherine, & Catherine Coley, *Jean Prouvé*, Galerie Patrick Seguin, 2008

Vegstack, Alexander von, *Jean Prouvé: The Poetics of Technical Objects*, Vitra Design Museum, 2004

GERRIT RIETVELD

Mulder, Bertus, & Ida van Zijl, *Rietveld Schröder House*, Princeton Architectural Press, 1999

Overy, Paul, et al, *The Rietveld Schröder House*, Butterworth, 1988

Zijl, Ida van, & Marijke Kuper, *Gerrit Rietveld: The Complete Works*, Centraal Museum Utrecht, 1993

RICHARD ROGERS

Powell, Kenneth, *Richard Rogers: Complete Works*, Vols 1–3, Phaidon, 1999–2006

PAUL RUDOLPH

Alba, Roberto de, *Paul Rudolph: The Late Work*, Princeton Architectural Press, 2003

Domin, Christopher, & Joseph King, *Paul Rudolph: The Florida Houses*, Princeton Architectural Press, 2002

Monk, Tony, *The Art and Architecture of Paul Rudolph*, Wiley-Academy, 1999

Rudolph, Paul, & Sibyl Moholy-Nagy, *The Architecture of Paul Rudolph*, Thames & Hudson, 1970

EERO SAARINEN

Merkel, Jayne, *Eero Saarinen*, Phaidon, 2005

Serraino, Pierluigi, *Eero Saarinen*, Taschen, 2006

HENRI SAUVAGE

Loyer, François, & Hélène Guéné, *Henri Sauvage: Set Back Buildings*, Mardaga, 1989

Minnaert, Jean-Baptiste, *Henri Sauvage*, Norma Editions, 2002

CARLO SCARPA

Beltramini, Guido, & Italo Zannier, *Carlo Scarpa: Architecture Atlas*, Centro Internazionale di Studi di Architettura Andrea Palladio, 2006

Co, Francesco Dal, *Villa Ottolenghi*, Monacelli Press, 1998

Los, Sergio, *Carlo Scarpa: An Architectural Guide*, Arsenale Editrice, 1995

RUDOLPH SCHINDLER

March, Lionel, & Judith Sheine (eds), *R. M. Schindler: Composition and Construction*, Academy Editions, 1993

Noever, Peter, *Schindler by MAK*, Prestel, 2005

Sheine, Judith, *R. M. Schindler*, Phaidon, 2001

Smith, Kathryn, *Schindler House*, Harry N. Abrams, 2001

Steele, James, *R. M. Schindler*, Taschen, 1999

SCOTT TALLON WALKER

O'Regan, John (ed.), *Scott Tallon Walker Architects: 100 Buildings and Projects, 1960–2005*, Gandon Editions, 2006

HARRY SEIDLER

Frampton, Kenneth, & Philip Drew, *Harry Seidler: Four Decades of Architecture*, Thames & Hudson, 1992

Seidler, Harry, *Harry Seidler, 1955–63: Houses, Buildings and Projects*, Horwitz Publications, 1964

Sharp, Dennis, *Harry Seidler: Selected and Current Works*, Images Publishing Group, 1997

ALISON & PETER SMITHSON

Heuvel, Dirk van den, & Max Risselada, *Alison and Peter Smithson: From the House of the Future to a House of Today*, 010 Publishers, 2004

EDUARDO SOUTO DE MOURA

Blaser, Werner, *Eduardo Souto de Moura: Stein Element Stone*, Birkhäuser, 2003

Esposito, Antonio, & Giovanni Leoni, *Eduardo Souto de Moura*, Electa, 2003

Wang, Wilfried, & Álvaro Siza, *Souto de Moura*, Gustavo Gili, 1990

BASIL SPENCE

Edwards, Brian, *Basil Spence: 1907–1976*, Rutland Press, 1995

Long, Philip, & Jane Thomas (eds), *Basil Spence: Architect*, National Galleries of Scotland, 2007

GIUSEPPE TERRAGNI

Schumacher, Thomas L., *Surface and Symbol: Giuseppe Terragni and the Architecture of Italian Rationalism*, Princeton Architectural Press, 1991

Terragni, Attilio, Daniel Libeskind & Paolo Rosselli, *The Terragni Atlas: Built Architecture*, Skira, 2004

Zevi, Bruno, *Giuseppe Terragni*, Triangle Architectural Publishing, 1989

UN STUDIO

Berkel, Ben van, & Caroline Bos, *UN Studio: Design Models*, Thames & Hudson, 2006

Betsky, Aaron, *UN Studio*, Taschen, 2007

O. M. UNGERS

Crespi, Giovanna (ed.), *Oswald Mathias Ungers: Works and Projects, 1991–1998*, Electa, 1998

Kieren, Martin, *Oswald Mathias Ungers*, Artemis, 1994

Lepik, Andres, *O. M. Ungers: Cosmos of Architecture*, Hatje Cantz, 2006

SIMON UNGERS

Urbach, Henry, *Simon Ungers*, 2G/GG Portfolio, 1998

USHIDA FINDLAY

Ostwald, Michael J., *Ushida Findlay*, 2G/GG Portfolio, 1997

JØRN UTZON

Møller, Henrik Sten, & Vibe Udsen, *Jørn Utzon Houses*, Living Architecture, 2007

Pardey, John, *Jørn Utzon Logbook Vol. III: Two Houses on Majorca*, Edition Bløndal, 2004

ROBERT VENTURI

Schwartz, Frederic (ed.), *Mother's House: The Evolution of Vanna Venturi's House in Chestnut Hill*, Rizzoli, 1992

CHARLES VOYSEY

Hitchmough, Wendy, *The Homestead: C. F. A. Voysey*, Phaidon, 1994

——, *C. F. A. Voysey*, Phaidon, 1995

OTTO WAGNER

Sarnitz, August, *Otto Wagner*, Taschen, 2005

FRANK LLOYD WRIGHT

McCarter, Robert, *Fallingwater: Frank Lloyd Wright*, Phaidon, 1994

Meehan, Patrick J. (ed.), *The Master Architect: Conversations with Frank Lloyd Wright*, Wiley, 1984

Pfeiffer, Bruce Brooks, *Frank Lloyd Wright*, Taschen, 2000

GAZETTEER

This listing contains addresses and contact details for houses open or accessible to visitors.

Note: access conditions to the properties below vary widely, so please make sure to contact the institution in question to make arrangements before visiting.

Any houses that are featured in this book but not listed below are strictly private and not open to the public.

ALVAR AALTO
VILLA MAIREA
RESTRICTED ACCESS BY APPOINTMENT
Noormarkku
Finland
Tel: + 358 10 888 4460
Email: info@villamairea.fi
www.alvaraalto.fi

MACKAY HUGH BAILLIE SCOTT
BLACKWELL
Bowness-on-Windermere
Cumbria LA23 3JT
UK
Tel: + 44 (0)15394 46139
Email: info@blackwell.org.uk
www.blackwell.org.uk

GEOFFREY BAWA
LUNUGANGA
Lunuganga Trust
Dedduwa Lake
Bentota
Sri Lanka
Tel: + 94 11 4337335 / + 94 34 4287056
www.geoffreybawa.com

RICHARD BUCKMINSTER FULLER
WICHITA HOUSE
The Henry Ford Museum
20900 Oakwood Boulevard
Dearborn, MI 48124
USA
Tel: + 1 313 982 6001
www.hfmgv.org

CHARLES & RAY EAMES
THE EAMES HOUSE/CASE STUDY #8
RESTRICTED ACCESS BY APPOINTMENT
Eames Foundation
203 Chautauqua Boulevard
Pacific Palisades
Los Angeles, CA 90272
USA
Tel: + 1 310 459 9663
Email: info@eamesfoundation.org
www.eamesfoundation.org

ALBERT FREY
FREY HOUSE II
RESTRICTED ACCESS BY APPOINTMENT
Palm Springs Art Museum
101 Museum Drive
Palm Springs, CA 92262
USA
Tel: + 1 760 322 4800
Email: info@psmuseum.org
www.psmuseum.org

GREENE & GREENE
THE GAMBLE HOUSE
4 Westmoreland Place
Pasadena, CA 91103
USA
Tel: + 1 626 793 3334
Email: gamblehs@usc.edu
www.gamblehouse.org

WALTER GROPIUS
GROPIUS HOUSE
National Historic Landmark
68 Baker Bridge Road
Lincoln, MA 01773
USA
Tel: + 1 781 259 8098
Email: GropiusHouse@HistoricNewEngland.org
www.historicnewengland.org

VICTOR HORTA
HOTEL SOLVAY
RESTRICTED ACCESS BY APPOINTMENT
224, avenue Louise
1050 Brussels
Belgium
Tel: + 32 2 640 56 45
Email: galeriewittamer@swing.be
www.hotelsolvay.be

PHILIP JOHNSON
THE GLASS HOUSE
National Trust for Historic Preservation
199 Elm Street
New Canaan, CT 06840
USA
Tel: + 1 866 811 4111
www.philipjohnsonglasshouse.org

CARL LARSSON
LILLA HYTTNÄS/LARSSON HOUSE
SE-790 15 Sundborn
Sweden
Tel: + 46 023 600 53
Email: info@clg.se
www.carllarsson.se

LE CORBUSIER
VILLA SAVOYE
Fondation Le Corbusier
82, rue de Villiers
78300 Poissy
France
Tel: + 33 (0)1 39 65 01 06
www.fondationlecorbusier.asso.fr
www.monuments-nationaux.fr

EDWIN LUTYENS
GODDARDS
RESTRICTED ACCESS BY APPOINTMENT
Lutyens Trust
Abinger Common
Surrey RH5 6JL
UK
Tel: + 44 (0)1306 730 871
www.lutyenstrust.org.uk
www.landmarktrust.org.uk

CHARLES RENNIE MACKINTOSH
HILL HOUSE
National Trust for Scotland
Upper Colquhoun Street
Helensburgh G84 9AJ
Scotland
Tel: + 44 (0)844 4932208
www.nts.org.uk

ROBERT MALLET-STEVENS
VILLA NOAILLES
Montée de Noailles
83400 Hyères
France
Tel: + 33 (0)4 98 08 01 98
Email: contact@villanoailles-hyeres.com
www.villanoailles-hyeres.com

LUDWIG MIES VAN DER ROHE
FARNSWORTH HOUSE
National Trust for Historic Preservation
14520 River Road
Plano, IL 60545
USA
Tel: + 1 630 552 0052
www.farnsworthhouse.org

JUAN O'GORMAN
RIVERA/KAHLO HOUSE & STUDIOS
Calle Diego Rivera 2, at Avenida Altavista
San Ángel
Mexico City
Mexico

EDWARD PRIOR
VOEWOOD
RESTRICTED ACCESS BY APPOINTMENT
Cromer Road
High Kelling
Norfolk NR25 6QS
UK
Tel: + 44 (0)1263 713029
Email: voewood@simonfinch.com
www.voewood.com

GERRIT RIETVELD
SCHRÖDER HOUSE
RESTRICTED ACCESS BY APPOINTMENT
Centraal Museum
Prins Hendriklaan 50
Utrecht
Netherlands
Tel: + 31 30 2362 310
Email: rhreserveringen@centraalmuseum.nl
www.rietveldschroderhuis.nl
www.centraalmuseum.nl

ELIEL SAARINEN
SAARINEN HOUSE
Cranbrook Art Museum
39221 Woodward Avenue
Bloomfield Hills, MI 48303
USA
Tel: + 1 248 645 3361
Email: ArtMuseum@cranbrook.edu
www.cranbrook.edu/

HENRI SAUVAGE & LOUIS MAJORELLE
VILLA MAJORELLE
1, rue Louis Majorelle
54000 Nancy
France
Tel: + 33 (0)3 83 40 14 86
Email: ecole-de-nancy@id-net.fr
www.mairie-nancy.fr/culturelle/musee/html/
majorelle.php

RUDOLPH SCHINDLER
SCHINDLER HOUSE
MAK Center
835 North Kings Road
West Hollywood, CA 90069
USA
Tel: + 1 323 651 1510
Email: office@makcenter.org
www.makcenter.org

SEELY & PAGET
ELTHAM PALACE
English Heritage
Court Yard
Eltham
Greenwich
London SE9 5QE
UK
Tel: + 44 (0)20 8294 2548
www.elthampalace.org.uk
www.englishheritage.org.uk

HARRY SEIDLER
ROSE SEIDLER HOUSE
Historic Houses Trust
71 Clissold Road
Wahroonga, NSW 2076
Australia
Tel: + 61 (0)2 9989 8020
www.hht.net.au/museums/rose_seidler_house

FRANK LLOYD WRIGHT
FALLINGWATER
Western Pennsylvania Conservancy
1491 Mill Run Road
Mill Run, PA 15464
USA
Tel: + 1 724 329 8501
www.fallingwater.org
www.paconserve.org

HOUSES BY TYPE

Hitoshi Abe, Yomiuri Guest House, Zao, Miyagi, Japan, 1997 **294**

Steven Holl, Y House, Catskill Mountains, New York, USA, 1999 **324**

ORGANIC
Antoni Gaudí, Villa Bellesguard, Barcelona, Spain, 1905 **11**

Arne Jacobsen, Rothenborg House, Klampenborg, Denmark, 1931 **70**

Frank Lloyd Wright, Fallingwater, Bear Run, Pennsylvania, USA, 1939 **100**

Geoffrey Bawa, Lunuganga, Dedduwa, Bentota, Sri Lanka, 1948 **116**

Carlo Scarpa, Villa Ottolenghi, Bardolino, Verona, Italy, 1978 **24**

Antti Lovag, Palais Bulles, Théoule-sur-Mer, Cannes, France, 1989 **246**

Ushida Findlay, Truss Wall House, Tokyo, Japan, 1993 **26**

Antoine Predock, Turtle Creek House, Dallas, Texas, USA, 1993 **268**

Future Systems, House in Wales, Milford Haven, Pembrokeshire, Wales, 1996 **292**

Eduardo Souto de Moura, Moledo House, Moledo, Caminha, Portugal, 1998 **318**

POST-MODERN
Robert Venturi, Vanna Venturi House, Chestnut Hill, Philadelphia, Pennsylvania, USA, 1964 **164**

Peter Eisenman, House VI, West Cornwall, Connecticut, USA, 1975 **218**

Eric Owen Moss, Lawson-Westen House, Brentwood, California, USA, 1993 **264**

Antoine Predock, Turtle Creek House, Dallas, Texas, USA, 1993 **268**

PREFABRICATION
Richard Buckminster Fuller, Wichita House, Kansas, USA, 1947 **20**

Charles & Ray Eames, The Eames House/Case Study #8, Pacific Palisades, Los Angeles, California, USA, 1949 **120**

Jean Prouvé, Maison Prouvé, Nancy, Lorraine, France, 1954 **146**

Matti Suuronen, Futuro House, various locations, 1968 **23**

Richard Rogers, Dr Rogers House, Wimbledon, London, England, 1969 **188**

Jan Benthem, Benthem House, Almere, Amsterdam, Netherlands, 1984 **230**

Shigeru Ban, Paper House, Lake Yamanaka, Yamanashi, Japan, 1995 **284**

Horden, Haack & Höpfner, Micro-Compact Home, various locations, 2005 **338**

SCULPTURAL
Oscar Niemeyer, Canoas House, Rio de Janeiro, Brazil, 1954 **142**

Charles Deaton, Sculptured House, Genesee Mountain, Golden, Denver, Colorado, USA, 1965 **168**

John Lautner, Elrod Residence, Palm Springs, California, USA, 1968 **182**

Simon Ungers, T-House, Wilton, Saratoga Springs, New York, USA, 1992 **260**

Ken Shuttleworth, Crescent House, Winterbrook, Wiltshire, England, 1997 **306**

UN Studio, Möbius House, Het Gooi, Netherlands, 1998 **322**

SUSTAINABLE
Rudolph Schindler, Schindler House, West Hollywood, Los Angeles, California, USA, 1922 **56**

Serge Chermayeff, Bentley Wood, Halland, East Sussex, England, 1938 **90**

Frank Lloyd Wright, Fallingwater, Bear Run, Pennsylvania, USA, 1939 **100**

Alvar Aalto, Villa Mairea, Noormarkku, Finland, 1939 **106**

Richard Neutra, Kaufmann House, Palm Springs, California, USA, 1947 **110**

Geoffrey Bawa, Lunuganga, Dedduwa, Bentota, Sri Lanka, 1948 **116**

Albert Frey, Frey House II, Palm Springs, California, USA, 1964 **166**

Pierre Koenig, Koenig House #2, Brantwood, Los Angeles, California, USA, 1985 **234**

Charles Correa, House at Koramangala, Bangalore, India, 1988 **238**

Glenn Murcutt, Simpson-Lee House, Mount Wilson, New South Wales, Australia, 1994 **280**

Shigeru Ban, Paper House, Lake Yamanaka, Yamanashi, Japan, 1995 **284**

Sean Godsell, Carter/Tucker House, Breamlea, Victoria, Australia, 2000 **332**

Werner Sobek, Sobek House/House R128, Stuttgart, Germany, 2000 **336**

TRANSPARENT
Pierre Chareau, Maison de Verre, Paris, France, 1932 **19**

Richard Neutra, Kaufmann House, Palm Springs, California, USA, 1947 **110**

Philip Johnson, The Glass House, New Canaan, Connecticut, USA, 1949 **126**

Kengo Kuma, Water/Glass House, Atami, Shizuoka, Japan, 1995 **27**

Shigeru Ban, Paper House, Lake Yamanaka, Yamanashi, Japan, 1995 **284**

Werner Sobek, Sobek House/House R128, Stuttgart, Germany, 2000 **336**

HOUSES BY TYPE

All colour photography by Richard Powers unless otherwise stated.

a: above; b: below; l: left; r: right

11 José Fuste Raga/AGE Fotostock/Photolibrary; 13 János Kalmár/akg-images; 14 Carl Larsson Gården, Sundborn; 15 VIEW Pictures Ltd/Alamy. © DACS 2009; 16 Fritz von der Schulenburg/ The Interior Archive. © DACS 2009; 17l Juri Tscharyiski/Bulgarian Cultural Institute 'House Wittgenstein'; 17r RIBA Library Photographs Collection; 18 Lightworks Media/Alamy. © DACS 2009; 19 Mark Lyon; 20l Lou Embo/Eredi Malaparte; All rights reserved; 20r © The Estate of R. Buckminster Fuller, Santa Barbara; 22 Bill Maris/Esto/VIEW Pictures Ltd; 23l Bettmann/Corbis; 23r Scanpix Sweden/PA Photos; 24 Vaclav Sedy © CISA A. Palladio; 25 Arcaid/Alamy; 26 Ushida Findlay Architects; 27 Mitsumasa Fujitsuka; 31b plans courtesy Lakeland Arts Trust/Blackwell; 34b plans courtesy The Landmark Trust; 39b plans courtesy Villa Majorelle/Musée de l'Ecole de Nancy; 41b plans courtesy The Hill House; 47b plans courtesy Simon Finch/Voewood; 51b plan artwork by David Hoxley, with thanks to Michael Max; 55b plan artwork by David Hoxley, drawn with kind permission of Gamble House; 57b plan artwork by David Hoxley, drawn with kind permission of Architecture & Design Collection, University Art Museum, University of California, Santa Barbara; 59b plan artwork by David Hoxley; original plan courtesy Chana Orloff Association; 61b plan artwork by David Hoxley; original plan courtesy Collection of Cranbrook Art Museum, Bloomfield Hills, Michigan. Gift of Loja Saarinen (CAM 1951.67); 64 plan artwork by David Hoxley, drawn with kind permission of Fondation Le Corbusier; 65–69 © FLC/ADAGP, Paris and DACS, London 2009; 75b plan artwork by David Hoxley, with thanks to Pernille Iben Linde; 76–79 © ADAGP, Paris and DACS, London 2009; 78b plan courtesy Villa Noailles; 83a plan courtesy John Allan; 86a architectural plan by Seely & Paget, courtesy English Heritage; 89b plan artwork by Thames & Hudson; 92a plans courtesy abq studio; 94–95 © DACS 2009; 95b plans courtesy Historic New England; 98a plans courtesy Avanti Architects; 100–105 photos courtesy Western Pennsylvania Conservancy. © ARS, NY and DACS, London 2009; 103b plans courtesy

Astorino/Western Pennsylvania Conservancy; 109b plans courtesy The Alvar Aalto Museum, Jyväskylä, Finland; 112b plan courtesy Marmol Radziner Architects; 114 plan artwork by David Hoxley; 115 David Sundberg/Esto/VIEW Pictures Ltd; 118b plan Bawa Archive; 121b plan artwork by David Hoxley, © Eames Office; 128 plan courtesy Philip Johnson Glass House/National Trust for Historic Preservation; 135b plan courtesy Rose Seidler House/Historic Houses Trust; 137b plan courtesy Farnsworth House; 142–145 photos Leonardo Finotti; 144b plan artwork by David Hoxley; 146–149 © ADAGP, Paris and DACS, London 2009; 149l plan artwork by David Hoxley, with kind permission of Catherine Prouvé; 150–153 photos Tad Fruits, courtesy Indianapolis Museum of Art; 153b plan courtesy Irwin Management Company, Inc.; 154–155 photos Roberto Schezen/Esto/VIEW Pictures Ltd; 155b plans courtesy Wright; 158b plans courtesy John Pardey; 163b plan courtesy Sergison Bates Architects, London; 165b plans courtesy Venturi, Scott Brown and Associates, Inc.; 166b plan courtesy Palm Springs Art Museum; 174al plan courtesy Gwathmey Siegel & Associates Architects llc; 177bl plan artwork by David Hoxley; 180–181 Armando Salas Portugal/Luis Barragán © Barragan Foundation, Birsfelden, Switzerland/ ProLitteris, Zürich, Switzerland/DACS; 184al plans by Benjamin Larkin Richards, courtesy of Karine Gornes; 191b plan courtesy Richard Rogers/Rogers Stirk Harbour + Partners; 195b plan artwork by Thames & Hudson; 196–197 photos Mark Luscombe-Whyte/The Interior Archive; 197b plans courtesy Agustín Hernández; 201b plan courtesy Paulo Mendes da Rocha; 204br plan courtesy Scott Tallon Walker Architects; 208b plan courtesy John Pardey; 210r, 211b plans courtesy Architect Mario Botta; 216a plans courtesy Richard Meier & Partners; 221b plans courtesy Eisenman Architects; 224b plans courtesy Hopkins Architects Ltd; 226al Leslie Brenner/Esto/VIEW Pictures Ltd; 226br, 227 Tim Street-Porter/Esto/VIEW Pictures Ltd; 228, 229a Shinkenchiku-sha/The Japan Architect Co., Ltd; 229b plans courtesy Tadao Ando; 233br plan © Benthem Crouwel Architekten BV bna; 237b plans with permission of Gloria Koenig; 238–239 photos Claire Arni/Charles Correa Associates; 239a plan courtesy Charles Correa Associates; 245b plans courtesy Claudio Silvestrin; 246bl Antti Lovag, Espace Cardin, Théoule-sur-Mer, 1992, drawing, 60 x 83.5 cm, inv. 000 04 26.

Photo François Lauginie. Collection FRAC Centre, Orléans, France; 251b plans courtesy Legorreta + Legorreta; 257b plan courtesy Estudio Arquitectura Campo Baeza S.L., Madrid; 258–259 Hisao Suzuki, courtesy Estudio Arquitectura Campo Baeza S.L., Madrid; 263b plans courtesy Roettger Architektur; 267b plans courtesy Eric Owen Moss Architects; 272b plans courtesy Antoine Predock; 275b plans courtesy Anthony Hudson; 282al plan artwork © Françoise Fromonot; 284–285 photos Hiroyuki Hirai/Shigeru Ban Architects; 284br plan courtesy Shigeru Ban Architects; 290b plan courtesy O. M. Ungers, Cologne; 292–293 photos Richard Davies; 292b plan courtesy Future Systems; 294–297 photos Shinichi Atsumi/Studio Shun's; 296a plans courtesy Atelier Hitoshi Abe; 298 plan courtesy Denton Corker Marshall; 304–305 photos Christian Richters; 305b plan © Herzog & de Meuron; 310b plan © make architects, courtesy Ken Shuttleworth; 312–317 photos Ila Bêka & Louise Lemoîne, "Koolhaas HouseLife", 2008. © Bêka/Lemoîne www.koolhaashouselife.com. © DACS 2009; 316b plan © OMA; 321b plan courtesy Souto de Moura; 322–323 photos Möbius House, Het Gooi 1993–1998/U.N. Studio; 322r plans courtesy U.N. Studio; 324–327 photos © Paul Warchol; 326b plans courtesy Steven Holl Architects; 328–331 photos Lyndon Douglas Photography; 329l plans courtesy Adjaye/ Associates Ltd; 332–335 photos Earl Carter/ Sean Godsell Architects; 335b plans courtesy Sean Godsell Architects; 336–337 photos Roland Halbe Fotografie; 336r plans courtesy Werner Sobek Stuttgart GmbH & Co.; 338 plan courtesy Richard Horden, Horden Cherry Lee, London, and Lydia Haack & John Höpfner, Haack + Höpfner, Munich; 339 Sascha Kietzsch; 340–341 Dennis Gilbert/ VIEW Pictures Ltd.

TO FAITH AND DANIELLE

ACKNOWLEDGMENTS

Dominic Bradbury and Richard Powers would like to express their sincere thanks to the many owners, architects, guardians and custodians of the houses featured on these pages for their generous help and support. Without their assistance this book would not have been possible. We are grateful to the many architectural practices mentioned in the book and to their staff, who have helped us again and again during the production of this publication.

In addition, particular thanks are due to John Allan & Avanti Architects, Catherine Coley, Claire Curtice, Albert Hill & Matt Gibberd, Sarah Kaye, Coralie Langston-Jones, Davide Macullo, Marmol Radziner Architects, Lyz Nagan, John Pardey, Catherine Prouvé, Sergison Bates Architects, Theresa Simon, Paul Stelmaszczyk & Rogers Stirk & Harbour, Shannon Stoddart at TKCM, Ariane Tamir, Sara Tonolini & Mornatti Consonni Architects, Anna Utzon, Richard Whitaker at Sea Ranch, Sidney Williams at the Palm Springs Art Museum, and the staff of the RIBA Library. Special thanks and gratitude are due to Jonny Pegg, Gordon Wise and Shaheeda Sabir at Curtis Brown, to Louise Thomas, and to Lucas Dietrich, Cat Glover, Sarah Praill, Jenny Wilson, Jane Cutter and Sam Ruston at Thames & Hudson.

First published in 2009 in hardcover in the United States of America by Thames & Hudson Inc., 500 Fifth Avenue, New York, New York 10110

thamesandhudsonusa.com

Library of Congress Catalog Card Number 2009902032

ISBN 978-0-500-34255-8

Printed and bound in China by C&C Offset Printing Co Ltd